Laura Bradshaw

STUCK IN A MOMENT

STUCK IN A MOMENT
~
THE BALLAD OF
PAUL VAESSEN

By

STEWART TAYLOR

GCR BOOKS LIMITED
www.gcrbooks.co.uk

First Edition - 2014

Published by GCR Books Ltd.
Registered in England & Wales. Reg No. 6949535
www.gcrbooks.co.uk
ISBN 978-1-9090500-6-8

Cover design by Steve Wade
stevewade.artwork@hotmail.co.uk

Front cover image © PAImages

Printed and bound by CPI Group (UK) Ltd, Croydon, CR0 4YY

For the late David Russell.
Sorry you missed Anfield, Rusty.

"You've got to get yourself together
You've got stuck in a moment
And now you can't get out of it
Don't say that later will be better
Now you're stuck in a moment
And you can't get out of it"

'Stuck In A Moment You Can't Get Out Of', U2 (2000)

Contents

Foreword

"There are all kinds of addicts, I guess. We all have pain. And we all look for ways to make the pain go away."

Sherman Alexie in 'The Absolutely True Diary of a Part-Time Indian' (2007)

Paul played for Arsenal but was forced to retire due to injury and fell into a life of crime and drug addiction before dying at the age of 39. Some people get it but most people don't. I am one of the lucky ones. I have lived 17 years now, a day at a time, alcohol free but more importantly clear of mind and most of the time emotionally well: No prison for me in the last 17 years and no A&E.

Football-wise I just missed Vas. He was just leaving the Arsenal after having had his day and I was just starting my football career as a 16-year-old kid who had not yet had his. I think our paths crossed one pre-season training year as I was invited along as a 15-year-old school boy to take part with the pros and Vas was one of those young pros. Paul made his league debut against Chelsea on 14 May 1979 and I signed school-boy forms for the Arsenal in October 1979. Paul turned professional in July the same year, scoring five goals in 18 appearances in 1979–80. The most famous of these goals was the one he scored against Juventus at the *Stadio Comunale*. I remember Arsenal manager Terry Neill sending Vas on as a substitute after 75 minutes and Paul heading home at the back post from a Graham Rix cross in the 88th minute to make the aggregate score 2–1 to Arsenal and put The Arse into the final. I can still see the sheer euphoria on his face after scoring….

I watched Vas's story and his career unfold, first through my beer spectacles then sober ones. The denial of addiction is so strong that all the time I was drinking my judgment of Vas after his enforced retirement was that he was a druggy and a no-hoper - probably so I didn't have to look at my own problems: Here was I married to a crack addict and so deep in my own alcohol addiction that I just could not see the similarities between us. My thinking was genuinely "at least I am not as bad as him." As soon as I got sober I could see this illness for what it was and I could identify with Vas's problems, thoughts and feelings. This disease wants you dead and sadly for Vas and his family it took him to his grave. I don't know why I have been freed from the bondage of self-destruction but I am truly, deeply grateful that I have been and that I have been given a second chance. I wish the Sporting Chance Clinic had been there to help Vas, I wish I could have helped Vas, I wish Vas had found recovery, I wish he could have had some peace of mind here on earth and I wish we could have shared some sober/clean days together. Unfortunately all I can do is, by writing this foreword, support Vas's story and pray that someone out there may read this book and identify with Paul's story and seek help.

This is a family illness - as we, the addict, affect everyone around us. So now my prayers are for Paul's family and friends - that they may find acceptance and peace around Paul's situation. Paul was a sick man who never found his medicine.

Finally I have a smile on my face remembering Vas's goal against Juventus but a tear in my eye and sadness in my heart for a fellow footballer and addict who didn't make it.

Tony Adams
October 2013

Preface

"Life is never easy for those who dream."

Robert James Waller

This is the story of a human tragedy and a football tragedy.

Paul Vaessen, born in Gillingham to a footballing family, joined Arsenal as an associated schoolboy in March 1977. By the summer of 1983 injury had ended his career. By the summer of 2001 drugs had ended his life.

Paul Vaessen packed a lot into his relatively short life, some of it good, some of it bad, all of it unforgettable. This book tells the story of the lows as well as the highs.

The case of Paul Vaessen is one of the reasons why football and the Professional Footballers' Association (PFA) has focused its attention much more on lifestyles for footballers, noting that a support system is essential for those hours away from the club when things can go wrong, particularly if a player doesn't make the grade or has to retire early due to injury.

Mental health, welfare, rehabilitation are all key words now in the football family. The Sporting Chance Clinic set up by Tony Adams is used extensively by the PFA and there is a whole network of trained therapists now available to help players through difficult times when so many are in danger of repeating the tragic story of Paul Vaessen.

Whilst today's professionals can become multi-millionaires in just a short time, this book is a timely reminder that the game also has an overriding obligation to look after those youngsters who, for one reason or another, do not make it and then find it impossible to cope with the feeling of let down.

I hope this book can be used as a lesson to be learnt by all youngsters entering the game and helps make sure that Paul's life was not lost in vain.

Gordon Taylor, Chief Executive, PFA
February 2013

Introduction

"I learned…that no one is perfect but most people are good; that people can't be judged only by their worst or weakest moments; that harsh judgements can make hypocrites of us all; that a lot of life is just showing up and hanging on…Perhaps most important, I learned that everyone has a story - of dreams and nightmares, hope and heartache, love and loss, courage and fear, sacrifice and selfishness."

Bill Clinton, 'My Life' (2004)

"F--king hell!"

I was getting pretty used to this by now, this sort of reaction.

To be perfectly honest, it was something I hadn't anticipated when I'd first started out. I just assumed that people would know, that word would have gotten round, like bad news usually does.

So I hadn't expected to hear, "How is he?" or "What's he up to these days?" I didn't imagine I'd be the one breaking the news ten years down the line. And, similarly, I don't think those on the other end of the phone were expecting the answers they got in return.

But it sort of said it all though really and just acted to reinforce my motivation for writing Paul's story. Not that, I should say, it was their fault. Some of these people had once been close to Paul in some capacity but you just move on, don't you? Sometimes you just drift apart. No. If anything, it was more a reflection of something somebody once described as "a very absent-minded community."[1]

The truth is Paul Vaessen had been forgotten and discarded by the sport he devoted his young life to long before his passing in August 2001. I'm not going to pretend Paul Vaessen was my football hero. He was not by any stretch of the imagination one of the great players of his generation, let alone at his club. And like thousands of other success-starved Arsenal fans I was far too distracted by Arsenal's struggles on the pitch during the early eighties to follow the trials and tribulations of Paul Vaessen's life.

There was one exception, though, and I was reminded of this a short while back when researching for an article I was writing for

xiii

the official Arsenal magazine. I came across my old scrapbooks, and the immaculately kept volume covering the 1984-1985 season in particular made for pretty grim reading. Things were going okay up until about mid-October, Arsenal topping the old First Division table. But after that things began to fall apart as I documented my dismay at Charlie Nicholas being dropped by Gunners boss Don Howe (along with legendary goalkeeper Pat Jennings) for the visit of Luton Town at the beginning of December, a horror exacerbated by the fact that his replacement, the decidedly straight-laced and un-glamorous Ian Allinson, scored one of the goals in a 3-1 win.

By March 1985 the Gunners had been knocked out of the League Cup by lowly Oxford United, had required a second game to get past even lowlier Hereford United in the third round of the F.A. Cup (even Charlie managed to score in the 7-2 replay victory at Highbury) and then suffered the ignominy of defeat at even lowlier still Fourth Division York City in the following round. On top of all that I reported how once again we'd missed out on a raft of supposed transfer targets, including French ace Jean Tigana.

And then, on the very last page, was the most shocking item of all under the headline, 'VAESSEN STABBED'. This page was devoted entirely to the news that the former Arsenal star was critically ill in hospital after being stabbed off of London's Old Kent Road.

I had clearly already by my early teens acquired a predilection for the morose, a contemplative tendency which had been nurtured through years of avoiding parties, discos, snooker halls and all other usual forms of pubescent social interaction, in favour of staying in, doing homework, watching (rather, studying) old black and white films with my dad and by generally being Very Serious and Mature way before my time. They were inclinations which I successfully developed into full blown depressive and anxiety disorders by the time I'd reached twenty and which set me off in search of the company of fellow tortured souls.

And football - indeed, sport in general - is not a bad place to look for them. For so many involved in the game, it is quite simply an addiction, the only thing they know how to do and the only thing they want to know how to do. It is an obsession fuelled by promises of glory and fame but which in so many cases delivers only heartache, anonymity and institutionalisation, leaving its casualties ill-equipped for what often turns out to be the infinitely more

INTRODUCTION

difficult challenge of living the rest of their lives.

Paul Gascoigne, Jimmy Greaves, George Best. They are all stories with which - due to their honesty but in large part to their celebrity - we are familiar. But what of those for whom the whistle blew a lot earlier than expected, those who fell for the allure of the football dream and then faded into obscurity when injury robbed them of their only purpose in life? Those who weren't around long enough to write many chapters in footballing history, let alone their own life stories. Those such as Paul Vaessen who died a lonely death at the age of thirty nine, practically disabled by the sport in which he had invested his dreams.

The idea of writing a book about Paul was, quite understandably, an uncomfortable proposition for some. Polite as people were initially being, I could sense a distinct scepticism and nervousness about the whole thing. It wasn't just that the market was apparently already awash with similar hard luck stories. It seemed more that Paul Vaessen just wasn't deemed famous enough nor his story cheery enough. I lost count of the number of times I was asked, "Who's going to want to read a book about Paul Vaessen?"

It is true that Paul's story is not one of back-slapping bravado and bonhomie and I warn you now that if that's the sort of thing you're looking for, this book is probably not for you. There were good times but they were over all too soon. No. This is a sombre tale about the fragility and fickleness of sport, a story without a happy, uplifting ending, at least as far as Paul and his loved ones are concerned.

And, yes, it is true that Paul was not well known outside of London N5 or his SE16 home. Paul's time in the spotlight was fleeting and it came well before the hyperbole, razzmatazz and fiscal vulgarity of the Premiership. It was a time before sponsorship and product endorsement, before *Sky*, a time before *Hello!* and *OK!* and exclusively featured weddings, sports supplements and WAGs. It was a time when you could almost go unnoticed if your face didn't appear in the late*st Panini* sticker album and even now Paul's name is rarely mentioned until fate throws together Arsenal and Juventus, the club against whom he enjoyed his crowning moment in that April 1980 European Cup-Winners' Cup semi-final tie. Indeed, these were the days before the advent of the lucrative Champions League, an era when the Cup-Winners' Cup not only still existed but was actually considered something quite important.

No. Paul was not one of the most significant footballers of all time. He doesn't even make it onto the list of 'Untimely Deaths' in the *Official Arsenal Miscellany,* nor is there mention of him under 'RIP - Gunners Who Died Young' in the *Official Arsenal Encyclopedia.* But his tale is, nonetheless, one of the most significant and heartrending you'll come across. And his is by no means the only one.

I do admit, however, that I let this general uneasiness about the project get the better of me at the start and that I consequently packed it all in after little more than a few weeks. I found, though, that in the ensuing weeks, Paul Vaessen nagged at me relentlessly. I didn't realise how deeply, in such a short amount of time, I'd got involved. Once put off, I am usually put off for good. But Paul had got under my skin and I began to feel that I'd let him, his family and the countless others like him, down, that I'd been dissuaded too easily.

This most uncustomary doggedness was, however, soon rewarded as gradually more and more people came forward in support. Word was seemingly getting round and Paul Vaessen started becoming of more interest than I could have hoped for. Fans and friends responded to appeals in local newspapers, ex-playing colleagues were more than happy to help and I was delighted when Gordon Taylor of the PFA and then Tony Adams gave the project their personal endorsement.

I was a little unsure as to what reaction, though, I'd get from Arsenal. Certainly there were those who felt that, "once he got injured, (Arsenal) just chucked him on the streets, he had nothing." I was not confident the club would be willing to talk about what one contributor called their "dirty little secret" but my fears were soon allayed in the form of Director and gentleman Ken Friar who in turn put me on to Terry Neill and the ball started rolling. The club was also happy to place appeals for assistance in both the match day programme and on their website for which I am very grateful.

Indeed, just as there were those still pointing an accusing finger towards London N5, so too were there those who had found themselves in circumstances similar to Paul's - professionally, at least - who were sincere in their admiration for the club and the support it provided them. Just about everybody connected with the club were adamant that Arsenal, when it comes to looking after their own, are (still) quite simply a cut above the rest. Arsenal *are* in a

INTRODUCTION

different class. It's the main reason so many of us support them and why, on the evening of 23rd April 1980, so many of us were elated by the events unfolding in Turin, Northern Italy.

For let us not forget it was Arsenal who provided Paul with the platform from which he sprung that evening to head in Arsenal's historic winner at the home of the mighty Juventus. Indeed, for that fleeting moment, Paul was on top of the world. But one way or another it was a moment in which he would become entrapped, a moment which effectively became the point of reference against which he and others would measure and assess the rest of his life, a moment he would later revisit and relive with anybody willing to listen.

It was a hell of a height from which to fall. Could Arsenal, or anybody else for that matter, have done more to cushion the impact? He was, after all, injured in the line of duty. Did his club, his sport, the system, fail in their duty of care to a former employee struggling to cope with life without them? Where does that duty of care end? Where do you draw the line? "Am I," as Paul's former manager Terry Neill proffered, "my brother's keeper?"

In Arsenal's defence, there is no reason to believe Paul was treated any differently to anyone else at the club at the time. Arsenal had made an investment in Paul and persevered until it was clear he could no longer go on. After that, what more could or should they have done? Paul's path into drug addiction was probably pre-destined and therefore inevitable irrespective of whether he'd played first class football or not. As one of Paul's school friends told me, "The thing with Paul was he was quite addictive in anything he did, you know? It was all or nothing. Even the bad things. He was the same in that. I don't know how his life would have panned out if he hadn't had football because I think he was always going to be faced with situations where he was going to do things he shouldn't. The football kept him on the straight and narrow for a long time." His brother Lee agrees that, "He was a proper manic compulsive. Whatever he did, he had to do it full on or not at all. That's why he's dead now, in a way."

And the chances are that, having got to 'know' Paul as I have, all the help in the world wouldn't have made a blind bit of difference because nothing could bring back the one thing he craved: football. The pain in his left leg which he carried around with him for the remainder of his days was a constant reminder of that.

In any case, it is not the purpose of this book to apportion blame or to judge. Too many raw nerves have been touched already for that. This is, after all, not an investigation, a post mortem or a cold case review. My objective has been merely to have Paul's story told and listened to and that perhaps its significant lessons be learnt.

In order to do all this I had to get as close to Paul as someone who never personally knew him possibly could. I wanted to get inside his head, think his thoughts, feel his feelings and find out what exactly it was like to be Paul Vaessen.

He walked me through the streets he'd once walked, we hung around the same estates he'd once hung around, we listened to the music he used to listen to. There were tears on occasion. One of those came when, sitting in the basement of the British Film Institute's archive, I watched what is apparently the only tape in existence of the Juve game. As the final few minutes approached I was shaking with the sort of sickly tension, expectation and emotion that is only ever matched when watching re-runs of Michael Thomas at Anfield in May 1989.

There were many other occasions on which we fell out. There were also a lot of times when Paul went missing and was difficult to pin down and I should therefore apologise in advance for any omissions.

Of course there were many, many people who joined us along the way, many of whom are speaking publicly about Paul for the first time. I conducted over sixty interviews with those with whom Paul grew up, with those he went to school with, those he played with, those he used with. I spoke to former managers, coaches and physiotherapists, playing colleagues from Arsenal, journalists and fans. And, of course, there was Paul's family: his mother Maureen, his father Leon ('Big Lee') and brother Leon ('Little Lee') whom I am now proud to count amongst my friends.

The Vaessen family have gone through an incredible amount, drawing upon inner strengths which are difficult to comprehend and some of which Paul could probably have done with himself. Paul's mum, in particular, is an amazing human being and considering what she has had to face, it is quite simply astonishing to find her still standing. And standing proud.

They all let me - a stranger – into their lives and made me welcome where often I felt I was trespassing. In doing so they have candidly shared with me their inner-most thoughts and feelings, as well as many, many memories, both good and bad.

I wish to state that it has never been my intention at any point - as one or two seemed to assume - to go around "digging up shit." There was definitely shit there for the digging and a lot has been omitted from this book. Admittedly there were a lot of times when I felt I should perhaps back off, that I should maybe let sleeping dogs lie. Indeed, Paul was approached on at least a couple of occasions during his lifetime to do a book but had turned the opportunities down, ashamed by his addiction. Paul's family were of the mind, however, that it was time for his story to be told and remained adamant throughout that we continue and that we tell it how it was. "I'm not going to paint him as an angel," Maureen told me at the outset. "He wasn't an angel. Let people see the good side and the bad side and make their own judgements." It was one of her hopes that such candour may prevent just one other family from being decimated by drugs. I cannot thank them all enough for their honesty and for allowing me to write this book.

There are many others to whom I owe a debt of gratitude: Liam Brady; Steve Brignall; Terry Burton; Clifford Cant; Gus Ceasar; Gary Chivers; David Cork; Paul Davis; Dermot Drummy; Ken Friar; Steve Gatting; Perry Groves; John Hollins; Don Howe; Pat Jennings; Robert Johnson; Gary Lewin; Brian McDermott; Raphael Meade; Terry Neill; Sammy Nelson; Richie Powling; Kenny Sansom; Brian Sparrow; Frank Stapleton; Fred Street; Nicky Sullivan; Alan Sunderland; Brian Talbot; Dean Tonkin and Steve Walford.

I would also like to say a huge thank you to: John Adams; Gerry Avery; Mark Brindle; Barry Cameron; Barry, Iris and John Clubb; David Collins; Magnus Falk; Michael Farmer; Kevin Foord; Dean Goodman; Peggy Goulding; Gary Humphrey; Anthony Jones; Laraine Kempster; Peter Kirkwood; John Morgan; Tom O'Brien; David Palmer; Barnaby Phillips; Mark Richardson; Paul Rulton; Adam Rutherwood; Simon Scott-Daniels; John Spurling; Steve Underwood; Tom Watt; Kevin Welling; Jamie Winterton; Emilio Zorlakki and to Charlie, Nelly, Sue and Viv.

Also to: Richard Clarke, Andy Exley, Joanne Harney and Vic Wright at Arsenal; Rob Hughes at the *New York Times* and the *International Herald Tribune*; Jamie Jackson and Amy Lawrence at the *Observer*; Pat Mooney at the *Hampstead & Highgate Express*; Gav Hollinder and Jon Surtees at *Southwark News*; ace commentator,

Martin Tyler, and Kevin Whitcher at *The Gooner*.

I must also pass on my gratitude to the authors and publishers of the various newspapers, books and publications from which I have quoted, and to Arsenal statistician Fred Ollier for the details contained in Appendix 2. Sorry you had to do it twice, Fred.

A special mention must go to: Bobby Barnes, Christian Smith, Gordon Taylor and Jemma at the PFA; Colin Bland at Sporting Chance; John Devine whose cheerfulness withstood the constant phone calls; Steve Gorham, who managed to get hold of many of Paul's former school mates; Nicky Law up in Alfreton; Roger Thompson for his friendship; Warwick Bean and Graham Rix for their hospitality, and to Peter Browes - despite the repeated attempts to Chelsea-ise my children!

Arsenal colossus, Tony Adams, took the time to write the foreword for this book. They say you should never meet your heroes but Tony blew that old adage out of the window for me. Thank you, Tony.

Jem Maidment's enthusiasm often reinvigorated me and helped convince me to keep going when self-doubt came knocking. Jem also opened up some important doors, one of which led to Greg Adams at GCR Books to whom I am eternally grateful for giving a fellow Gooner a chance. Greg worked incredibly hard on this project and has also become a good friend.

Jem and Fred Atkins – author of the excellent book, *The French Connection: How The Arsenal Became L'Arsenal* – are also due thanks for reading the draft manuscript and suggesting improvements. Steve Wade is also to be commended for getting the front cover spot on.

I would also like to acknowledge the role Ronald Reng played in the writing of this book. His magnificent, touching biography of the tragic Robert Enke, *A Life Too Short*, inspired me to complete this project at a time when I had very nearly let Paul Vaessen slip away from me.

There were indeed times over the past five years when I let things get on top of me. But I admit rather selfishly that writing this book has also been somewhat cathartic ("I write some shit but it's good for me/Pick up a pen and paper and you will see."[2]). In fact, when I finally finished the book I felt somewhat deflated, empty and lost because it had been such a huge part of my life. It also proved a more than useful diversion away from my own problems and in redirecting our therapy sessions away from OCD and depression and towards progress on the book (yes, I did notice!), Nick at the Bethlem Royal Hospital helped as much as any during the crucial early stages. We also found we had a shared love for *El Diego*, perhaps stemming from the fact that we are supporters of the two English clubs for whom Diego Maradona so very nearly signed - Sheffield United and Arsenal. Bearing in mind what Diego did to England back in Mexico in 1986, our conversations and opinions if overheard would probably have amounted to high treason.

I want to say thank you to my long-suffering wife, Amanda, for not just allowing me to do this but for the encouragement she gave, which she has given me from the first day we met. I'm sorry I've not always been there for you and I'm sorry I've been so distracted these past five years. Thank you for our three wonderful boys to whom I wish to say sorry for the intrusion and the grumpiness. It's out of my system now, boys.

Finally to Debbie, Ernie, Sally, Jackie, Charlie, Nelson and Eddie, Red and Archie, and, of course, Leon, Lee and Maureen. I hope this brings you some closure.

It was only in speaking to so many people that I felt I could justify writing this book. In fact, they painted such a vivid picture of Paul that I decided the best way to tell his story was primarily through their words. They knew him best and there was simply no reason for much elaboration or literary intervention from me. I have therefore kept my interference to a minimum and can't really therefore take credit for anything more than being an editor.

From a personal perspective, undertaking this project has brought me into contact with a lot of good, honest people, something which has gone some way to restoring the faith in humanity which I, like Paul, found I was losing.

I was on the trail of Paul Vaessen for quite a while. He has been in my head every day for the past five years. He became something of an obsession and it's not surprising, therefore, that he featured in many of my dreams during that time. One in particular sticks in my mind. I dreamt one night – it was in January 2013 - that Paul's spirit paid me a visit. He was standing outside my window, looking in, watching over me, keeping an eye on what I was doing, what I was writing. He was silent and I like to think that had he been uncomfortable about what I was doing, he would have said something. But he seemed content. I tried calling out to him a couple

of times but barely made a sound.
      Then he was gone.
      And that's the closest I ever got to Paul.
      Time to move on now.
      Rest in peace, Paul.

Prologue
The Moment

"Heroing is one of the shortest-lived professions there is."

Will Rogers in 'The Will Rogers Book' by Paula McSpadden Love (1961)

La Vecchia Signora was well into her preparations for the evening. It was to be a big night and a special reception had been prepared for her guests. She enjoyed nothing more than the spectacle of a public execution and, after all the acrimony of the past two weeks, this was one she was going to savour.

The brutality of her legions during the first encounter in London had stunned their hosts and ignited a fuse which had been smouldering away ever since. It had been a war of attrition. Gladiators had fallen, casualties accrued and an antagonism born which had continued long after the end of the confrontation as the two sides cast aspersions upon each other from afar. The Italians had been "violent", "disgraceful", "savages." In return, they had called for English heads to roll. The diplomats had tried to intervene in the ensuing days to calm tempers but could do little to persuade the *bianconeri* from venting their anger. The Old Lady was not used to being spoken to like this and as the day of the return meeting approached, she had little intention of acquiescing.

Through the ancient streets of Turin, the condemned were embarking upon what was meant to be their final journey, accompanied by a furious black and white procession of taunting *tifosi,* out in force to defend the honour of their Lady, impatient for the formality of victory and baying for the blood of the English invaders.

Inside the intimidating fortress, in a small enclave up high on the slopes, a small travelling army had tentatively gathered, torn now between their desire to voice their loyalty and their instinct to remain as inconspicuous as possible. Sure enough their presence in the amphitheatre would later prove intolerable to their Latin counterparts.

They were used to things going their way here. There was a certain order to things. Sentence had been passed and would now be carried out in the customary manner; slow and painful death by suffocation courtesy of the *catanaccio* noose, a fate which no British force had ever before had the luck or audacity to cheat. And the Old Lady was not in the mood for her authority to be challenged now.

Eventually, the two factions emerged into the arena to a cacophony of noise, ritualistic chanting, drumming and whistling. Explosions lit the sky, forewarning the English trespassers of the fireworks which would soon follow. The foundations of the ancient city would indeed be rocked tonight and the reverberations felt all the way to the basilica on the Superga hills overlooking the city.

Back in the arena, hostilities were about to be renewed.

Dressed in black, the executioner started the proceedings.

There would, of course, be an initial struggle. That was only to be expected. But nothing could delay the inevitable. Soon enough the pretenders would realise the futility of resistance and would yield. And, indeed, as the evening wore on and everything fell into place, the hoards lit fires and sang in celebration of their imminent triumph.

Lost in the moment, perhaps the Old Lady had forgotten that the last time these crusaders had visited Italy, the likes of Kennedy, Radford, George, Kelly, McLintock et al had fought toe-to-toe with the *Aquilotti* on the streets of the capital; that forty years prior to that a lone combatant by the name of Copping had almost single-handedly decapitated Mussolini's *Azzurri* during what legend would recall as the 'Battle of Highbury.'

Perhaps she should have known that this opponent would not concede quite so easily nor go so quietly. This was a stubborn foe who had already recently marched undefeated through a tempestuous Istanbul and communist East Germany. Maybe she should have known that despite the exertions of the past nine months they would find an inner strength and the fresh resources to produce one final effort to slip the noose.

And sure enough, driven by the unbreakable spirits of the likes of Rice, O'Leary, and Brady and with time fast running out, it was Rix who managed it, in a blur, catching the home rear-guard by surprise and bursting down the left flank to supply the ammunition for the killer blow, delivered unforgivingly by an unknown soldier.

In a matter of a few seconds, the tables had been turned,

leaving the Old Lady and her legions - Zoff, Gentile, Cabrini, Bettega, Scirea - gasping for breath, on their knees amidst the deafening silence which had now enveloped their citadel.

Stunned by the impudence of the imposters and the abruptness of events, the indignation of the Italian masses would momentarily turn to a venomous rage. And it would be unleashed upon the small pocket of gate-crashers whose wild celebrations up high on the battlements had all of a sudden blown their cover.

The home forces charged as one like the bull on their city's municipal coat of arms. Running battles ensued as their missiles reigned down upon the *Inglese* retreating in the stands. But once again, although unarmed and hopelessly outnumbered, they would not surrender and fought back as the melee spilled out onto the streets where they were joined by reinforcements in the form of local insurgents loyal to the Old Lady's sworn enemy, *I Granata*. Bones were broken, blood spilled and weapons bared as the visitors fought their way through the skirmishes to their battered transport and made haste from the city.

Turin had not seen such scenes for years. It had been razed to the ground by Hannibal on his descent from the Alps in 218bc; it had been occupied by Napoleonic armies in the early nineteenth century and it had been ransacked by the retreating Nazi army only a few decades ago.

And now, as the *conquistatore* sped with his comrades from the scene of the carnage towards the relative security and serenity of their rustic Asti retreat, the smoke billowing out into the Turin sky informed the city that she had fallen once more, this time to a young Saxon warrior with Dutch blood coursing through his veins who'd foreseen his glory in a dream just the night before and whose name was not yet even well known in his own land...

STUCK IN A MOMENT

1
In the Beginning

"The deepest definition of youth is life as yet untouched by tragedy."

Alfred North Whitehead

A million miles away from the baroque palaces, piazzas and botanical gardens of Turin are the concrete tenements, paved backyards and parks of Bermondsey, South East London.

With the former boasting its colonnaded walkways, museums and grandiose royal apartments and the latter its shopping parades and council flats, it is true that there are few similarities between the two. Both do have their ruins. Turin's - in the form of the impressive Roman Palatine Towers - are, however, somewhat more admired.

In the former Italian capital you'll find the headquarters of industrial giants such as Fiat and Lancia. The business of Bermondsey is conducted by the small enterprises and local traders operating from its warehouses, industrial estates and market places.

Turin gave the world *Martini*.

Bermondsey offered up the chocolate biscuit.

Turin produced sophisticated singer and model, Carla Bruni.

Bermondsey produced the late Jade Goody.

And for the *Stadio Comunale*, read The New Den.

The former is of course the home of Juventus, two-times champions of Europe and one of the most prestigious football clubs in the world. In contrast, Millwall Football Club's fame struggles to extend beyond these shores and owes more to the notoriety of its followers than it does to any footballing prowess. It is true that not many people like Millwall and it is also true that they just don't care.

From an away fans perspective a visit to Zampa Road, SE16 is not quite as daunting as running the gauntlet down Cold Blow

1

Lane. But the New Den has managed to retain the intimacy and - when full - ferocity of its grim predecessor a quarter of a mile away in New Cross, closed a record five times by the Football Association and finally shut for good in 1993. However, if you've got any sense at all, you still don't wear your colours down this way on a match day and you still get in and out as quickly as your legs will carry you. Fortunately, to facilitate this, there is a walkway which runs directly from the North Stand to South Bermondsey Station which should get you to the relative neutrality and safety of London Bridge within minutes via Southern Rail.

Running as it does along a viaduct, you can't miss the New Den from up here on the station platform, poking up through the cranes and incinerators. It's not that welcoming, it has to be said, and it's already looking its age, like it has been left out in the rain for too long.

With the contrasting affluence of the silver city skyline shimmering in the background - as much an altogether different world as Turin - I walk down the steps and along the slope, past the aforementioned chicken run. It's closed off today. There's no police presence today. This is not a match day and I'm not here for the football.

I'm here to see Paul.

So I continue on, six-yard skips piled up high in the Welcocks yard to the right, the residential boxes and caravans of a permanent travellers' site to the left. It was built by the council some twenty years ago to stop the travellers from pitching-up illegally. At Christmas the site was lit up like Vegas, the result of a bit of nifty hot-wiring involving the nearby street-lamps.

You reach ground level and there at the bottom of the steps is - quite unmistakably - Paul's mum, Maureen.

It is amazing, knowing what Maureen has been through, that she looks so well. We've spoken on the phone a few times before but this is the first time we've met in person. She is not the downtrodden, broken figure you might expect. We greet like old friends. It's nice to meet you at last.

How are you?

How's Ernie, the birds, the dogs?

They're all fine.

2

IN THE BEGINNING

We come out onto Ilderton Road, turn right and there's the parade of shops, a bakers, a post office, a general store and the Vaessen's former home, the flat above the bookies at number 5. It's not pretty and it's not a great deal different to how it was back then, except the bookies was a launderette.

Across the road is Maureen and Ernie's current home in Delaford Road. The intercom's not working. A solid shove with the shoulder against the communal front door and we're in. Maureen's place is first on the right.

You get quite a welcome here.

"F--k you," squawks Nelson as you pass him in his cage in the hallway.

He and Eddie are apparently having some sort of argument.

It's a modest little place. Maureen is proud of it. She has come full circle having been brought up in a house which used to stand not fifty yards away in the same street. That was when they were all Victorian places.

There are surprisingly few pictures around. There's one of Paul and his brother Lee, a few of the grand-children. None of Paul in his playing days. Nothing to hint at his choice of profession, his former illustrious employers or the high profile company he once kept. But after a little while of getting to know each other out come the few remaining photos and newspaper cuttings. Here's one of Paul receiving a junior Player of the Year award; here's the associate schoolboy beaming away for the camera during an early photo shoot at Highbury; here's the young professional basking in the glory of that moment in Turin, his whole career, his whole life ahead of him.

There aren't that many pictures at all, not as many as you might have imagined. A lot of stuff got slung out by mistake by Maureen's mum when they moved from Lucey Way. It was all in black sacks. Easy enough mistake to make, I guess.

By then the family had gone its four separate ways.

I begin to worry that talking about certain things is going to be a problem. It isn't. Maureen's going to tell me, she says, how it was, how it is now. Warts and all. And to prove it she produces disturbing images of Paul's knee after that last operation, some ghastly *Meccano*-like contraption protruding from his leg to fuse it straight. We watch a DVD of Paul talking about his addiction and faith at the rehabilitation centre at which he, albeit only temporarily,

3

achieved recovery. We flick through the bibles and self-help books with Paul's hand-written notes in the margins. We read through the final letter home and consider the prayer that was found on him at the end.

We have tea and after a while set off again.

"Deal or no deal," says Eddie in the hallway.

"F--k you," Nelson replies.

We drive up Galleywall Road, along 'The Blue', the market place once frequented by shoppers who now head instead for the impersonal shopping experience offered by the huge complex at Canada Water.

We pass Paul's old primary school, then turn into a huge, grey estate.

Lucey Way.

Like Paul, like the Vaessens, it's had its problems and maintains something of a reputation.

We pass the caged playground area and park by the shops.

We negotiate the long slope which will take us up to the landing.

There are ghosts here.

"I can see him now coming down that slope on his way to the shops," Maureen reflects.

She points out the place on the left where Debbie, who would become Paul's partner and mother to Jamie, used to gaze longingly at the handsome famous footballer living opposite.

"Oh, my goodness," Maureen says as she catches sight of her old family home. "What a mess. It didn't used to look like that when I was here."

It's a compact three level unit, front room and kitchen in the middle, two bedrooms upstairs and a dinette downstairs. There are loads of them, all stacked together in huge blocks, one on top of the other, small boxes in which people try to live their private lives.

Paul dragged most into his. He had to, to survive.

Neighbour Sue got caught up more than most. She still lives along the landing, the only house I can see with flowers out front.

"This is a lovely little place", I say as we settle down.

"You wouldn't say that if you were here weekends," Sue replies. Maureen hasn't seen her since the funeral. I don't think we were expected.

4

"We had our ups and downs," Sue sighs, "but a lot of it was to do with Paul. I found it difficult not to be involved with Paul. I knew of him. I'd often heard about this young man. And then I came here and this man introduced himself and he was such a dynamic person, you know, you just had to sort of listen. That's how Paul was. He could be very strong, demanding, very manipulative. There were times when I could quite cheerfully have killed him because he came between me and my own family. But at the same time you never wanted to say 'no' because he had such charisma and charm. He flattered you and you wanted to help."

Shadowy figures pass close-by outside.

"He had the most horrendous addiction that you could possibly imagine," Sue continues. "And I always managed to see beyond that. I truly believed I was the one to save him. You thought you were helping but all I did really was make things ten times worse. I just wanted to help. You just wanted him back the way he was. I just could not say 'no.'"

Neither, unfortunately, could Paul.

Sue needs to get to work. We've probably set her back half an hour or so. More likely a few years. She probably neither wanted nor expected to be talking about Paul this morning, most likely put him out of her mind years ago.

Lucey Way is not quite the ornate apartments and squares over which the Savoys of Turin once ruled but it is, nonetheless, part of the patch over which the Vaessens once reigned and to which, on the morning of 24th April 1980, Paul's subjects - irrespective of their allegiances - flocked to salute a returning local hero.

"They were all over, all down here, chanting his name. He had to have a police escort. He got as far as here," Maureen says indicating the end of the landing, "and they tried to mob him." That was the day all the journalists turned up and autograph hunters started knocking at the door. A few years later and the neighbours were crossing the road to avoid him and much more sinister characters were at the door for altogether different reasons, reasons which eventually drove Maureen out.

There aren't many people about today. It's pretty quiet, as it is in the memorial garden along Culling Road SE16 which, despite it's proximity to the busy A2000, manages to retain an aura of tranquillity.

5

F. A. Albin & Sons look after Paul now.

You may have heard of them, 'Albins'. In 2003 they were the subject of an ITV documentary series, *Don't Drop the Coffin*, and Barry Albin-Dyer who runs the outfit is an author, writing about his experiences as an undertaker and about business management. They are probably one of the best known funeral directors in the country, a family business going back over two hundred years. They even have their own museum (viewings by appointment), opened in 2009 by Princess Anne. And they have buried just about everyone, from war heroes to rock legends and, of course, an ex-Arsenal footballer who was famous for a day back in April 1980.

They look after Paul and they look after Maureen too, greeting her as we enter their offices like a close friend which I guess she is by now.

It's been eleven and a half years.

As you enter the gardens, you can light an electronic candle with your loose change and not too far in you'll find plot 39, where I finally get to meet 'Vas'.

Maureen says, "Hello love," introduces me, tends to the flowers we brought along with us and places kisses with her hand on his small oval portrait.

Paul is beaming away.

He features twice at Albins. There is also a gallery inside which pays tribute to some of its more famous clients. Paul is up there next to James Marshall 'Jimi' Hendrix.

Every year there is a service of remembrance.

"I didn't want him going up into a cemetery. He was a Bermondsey Boy. I thought I'd love him overlooking the park, you know, where he used to go and play. And he's near to me for me to go up and see him whenever I like. He's in a lovely place."

It's a nice day. The sun's out and Southwark Park, with its floral displays, galleries and band-stand does look welcoming.

Maureen knows Bermondsey inside out. She is after all a Bermondsey Girl, albeit belatedly.

"My mum and dad were both from Bermondsey but I was actually born in Maidenhead. It was 1942 and we'd been evacuated from London. Dad was in the Air Force. He drove for Lord Beaverbrook. He was his personal chauffeur." Beaverbrook, aka William Maxwell Aitken, was a powerful press baron who turned the

Daily Express into one of the best selling newspapers in the world. He was also great pals with Winston Churchill who gave him several top jobs in his wartime coalition cabinet.

Maureen's father, John, managed to get leave to drive down to Maidenhead for the birth but missed it. He got lost in thick fog.

After the war they moved back to Bermondsey, to Delaford Road, and Maureen went to Galleywall Road School, where Paul would later go. Maureen's mother, Nelly, was a housewife but worked part-time jobs for a little bit of extra money whilst John worked as a supervisor in a factory for twenty seven years and then as a driver for Whitbreads.

Leon Vaessen was born in Market Harborough in Leicestershire in November 1940. His mother, Dolly, was English, his father, also Leon, was Dutch.

"They met during the war. You can probably imagine what went on during the war," says Leon. "They met and then they just parted. My father did come over and see us one time and gave my mum some money. He was a jewellery rep, a very smart man. I did meet him a couple of times later, just after Paul was born. I was twenty one and his sister, who lived over here in Haringey, obviously saw the family name in the paper or something and got in touch with me, sent me a telegram with his phone number. He came over on a four day visa visit and we met up and had a talk and this and that. We met one other time and then we lost contact. I sent him photos of Paul as a baby but they all came back. He never got to see Paul."

When the war ended Leon and his mother came back to London and went to live with Leon's grandmother, Gertrude, off the Old Kent Road. When Leon was nine, Dolly met and married William and they moved to Peckham.

Maureen left school as soon as she could.

"When I left school - I didn't like school at all, except for art and swimming - I worked in a chemist, then at *C&A's* but I didn't like it. Then I started at a local hairdressers and they sent me over to classes over the West End to become a hairdresser. But I really wanted to travel. I wanted to go to lots of places but I never got to. I stuck with the hairdressing for nine months but the money wasn't good enough so I packed it in."

No matter. She didn't really need to work any longer.

Maureen had by now caught the eye of a local footballer who was earning what was good money back in those days.

"I met Leon through a mutual friend. I went round to meet him at his mate's house not far away. He was messing about with his motorbike and he was as black as anything. I didn't even recognise him when he came over Sunday to take me to the pictures!"

"I loved playing the game," says Leon. "Obviously I had some ability to play. It was basically all I could think about at the time. I got picked for the under-16 trials for the South and played against the North. They then selected the best from the two to go into the England side. That was my one and only cap. We lost 2-1 to Scotland at Wembley. It was partly down to me really because I committed the foul which gave them the free kick from which they scored one of their goals. I feel guilty to this day."

There were, however, already one or two clubs showing an interest.

"Just prior to getting into the England under-16 side we were playing a London youth game at Tottenham and a lot of the scouts were there. It was at the time of the Busby Babes and somebody came into the dressing room after and said, 'How would you like to come to Manchester?' But I was too young, too naïve. I didn't care who I played for. Football was football to me. I would have gone and played for Southend."

Arsenal also showed a bit of interest but then Ted Drake's Chelsea came in. Not really having any preference but with Chelsea being a London club, Leon signed up as an apprentice.

"It was called ground staff then and I got £9 a week, £1 for expenses and luncheon vouchers which were three shillings and thrupence. I was so proud the first time I got paid. It was in cash and I went home to Mother and gave her £3. My parents never had a lot of money. My stepfather was only earning about £5 a week as a foreman. Anyway, my mother just took it, never asked a question. The second time it was the same and then the next time she finally said, 'Where do you get this money?' I said, 'I play football, Mum.' She's thinking of football round the park with the boys. She didn't realise you could make money from playing football. She wasn't that worldly, my mum. She just said, 'Get yourself a proper job!'

"Anyway, we used to have these behind closed doors full-

8

scale practice games if things weren't going quite right and on this particular day, as the game is going on, I heard one of the players say, 'Look at that woman standing on the terraces, have a look.' So I looked round and it was Mother! She'd got through the back gate and she had her full regalia on, handbag, the lot, just standing there watching the game, making sure, you know, that I was telling the truth!"

Leon played in the South East Counties League where Chelsea came up against other London youth sides from the likes of Arsenal, Tottenham, West Ham and Fulham. "It was quite a good standard," says Leon. A raw but already highly accomplished Jimmy Greaves was about a year ahead of Leon who talks with reverence when it comes to the young prodigy.

"He was one of 'Drake's Ducklings', part of an outstanding Chelsea youth side which included the likes of Barry Bridges, David Cliss, Ken Shellito and Mel Scott," says Leon. In his first season in the youth side, 1955-56, Greaves struck an impressive fifty one goals. In his second he scored an astonishing and record breaking 122 times.

"Then he got into the reserves, had just a couple of games, scored some goals and they put him into the first team. I don't think he was eighteen, Jim, but he was that good. And we all know what he went on to achieve."

Leon didn't hang about that long, staying at Chelsea for just eighteen months. "Millwall was just round the corner from me and said, 'Would you like to come and play for us,' you know, 'we'll buy your mum a new coat, a nice new fridge,' all that sort of stuff which clubs just turned a blind eye to. Ted Drake knew what was going on and called me into his office and gave me a real roasting, asked me why I wanted to leave a top division club like Chelsea for Millwall (who were then in the Third Division South). But like I say, I was young, coming up to seventeen, and naïve. It was a little bit more money, something for my pocket which meant something to you at that age. So I signed on pro for Millwall on my seventeenth birthday and made my debut against Walsall away towards the end of the 1957-1958 season."

That was the year that the top teams from the Third Division South and Third Division North went on to form the new Third

Division. Millwall missed out and started the following season in the new Fourth Division.

"I was there with Pat and Ray Brady, elder brothers of Liam who of course played a bit with Paul."

Leon's first contract was for a year which was standard.

"I got £18 per week, £16 per week off-season. Then I went and saw the board and it went up to £20 per week throughout the year plus a £4 win bonus, £2 the draw. Then I had the audacity to ask for appearance money, a fiver an appearance, but they gave it to me!

"I started off playing my first three or four games on the left wing then I took a fancy to the middle and that was brilliant. I used to love playing in the middle. Not many people realize that that's where Paul started off."

Leon and Maureen got married on April Fool's Day 1961 at St Crispin's Church in Southwark Park Road. The reception was in a pub along Milton Road. It was South Bermondsey society's 'do' of the year.

"Quite a big wedding, I had," Maureen reflects. It was also quite eventful. "My bridesmaids - my younger sister Diane, two cousins and my two little nieces - were in a car crash coming back from the church. It was my Uncle Alec that was driving the car and he swerved to avoid a dog and hit a tree. They were shaken up, taken to hospital but they were okay. The two little ones had broken teeth but we'd already had our photos taken at the church. Of course, I didn't know anything about it for a while and was sitting at the top table wondering where they were."

Leon had also gone off by then too.

"It was a Saturday and he couldn't get the day off from playing football for his own wedding! He was going to be heavily fined so we just had time to cut the cake, say a speech and then he was off."

"That's right, I forgot that. They wouldn't give me the day off. They said they wanted me to captain the reserves in the afternoon. I had to go straight off to the game and came back to the reception after. I would have got fined because you had a professional contract. You did what they said, basically."

Maureen recalls, "He came back about half past five after the game and he had a load of blisters on his feet. He couldn't dance, he

10

couldn't do nothing. So we just had a good drink and it went off lovely. My family were a real Bermondsey family so out came the piano and we had a right old fashioned knees-up. Half of Bermondsey was there."

Within the space of a few months the newly-weds were on the move.

"The season I left Millwall a couple of clubs had come in for me but Millwall wanted to bring in Pat Terry, a good centre forward who was at Gillingham so I went in exchange. Gillingham gave me the money I wanted plus the bonuses so it gave me a reasonable living."

"We lived in one of the football houses. They were all together opposite the club," Maureen recalls. "They were lovely times we had down there. The social life was absolutely brilliant. They used to finish training and we'd all meet up at the bowling alley, have something to drink and eat. There was even a creche there for the kids."

Paul Leon Vaessen had arrived on 16th October 1961. Maureen went in at five thirty in the afternoon and had had Paul by ten past eight that evening. Leon spent the two and a half hours sitting outside the delivery suite. It was different back in those days. The men didn't go in.

"He was born in a private nursing home because one of the directors of Gillingham was a gynaecologist," says Maureen.

Dr Clifford Grossmark joined Gillingham in 1954 as the club doctor. Invited onto the board of directors three years later, he was elected chairman in 1961. He is one of the longest serving chairman in English football history and only relinquished his post after suffering a fatal heart attack on the way to an away fixture at Walsall in November 1983.

"He was the one who actually delivered Paul," says Leon. "He was later one of the three members of the FA Disciplinary Committee - the naughty boys' council - at Lancaster Gate. He was a nice man, a good man."

Maureen is as chuffed today as she was back then.

"I had my own room, my own nurse. It was lovely. He was a very good baby. I couldn't stop looking at him. It was the proudest day of my life. "

STUCK IN A MOMENT

****

"The very next season (1961-1962) Millwall went zooming up and won the league!" Leon laughs. "I missed out on some bonuses there! They hadn't been doing too badly anyway, finishing sixth the season before and fifth the one before that. But we didn't have a bad side at Gillingham. We were good contenders. Millwall came down to us and we beat them 3-0 and we got the 0-0 draw in the return at The Den when they were supposed to mash us up but they went on and won promotion. So same again, really. I should have stayed where I was. I should have stayed at Chelsea basically but like I say, out of naivety you sometimes make mistakes."

The Vaessens stayed in Gillingham for two years and then moved to Dover.

"The quality of Leon's football had gone down a bit because of his knee injury so he decided to go to another club. Leon played part-time for Dover FC and worked part-time on the railways."

"When I was at Millwall I'd had my cartilages done - both taken out of my left leg and one out of my right - but I got over that. I got the bad injury at the end of my first season at Gillingham. That's what put me out of the game. It was an identical injury to the one which Paul got years later, strangely enough. Anyway, it was against Darlington, just a normal tackle but I did my cruciate ligament. Back then, it was quite a big thing. I was told to rest for a year but after a few months I started to feel better, feel good. So I reported back, you know, and said, 'I wanna start playing again.' It was great in training but the very first game back I played, I took off for a ball off of the left foot, coming down on the left and the pain was tremendous."

Leon stayed on another season but it was a struggle after that.

"The injury was a life changer really. I slipped into depression. But after a while you just have to get on with it, don't you? I had to go to work but I carried on playing."

The Gillingham Manager, Freddie Cox, an ex-Arsenal winger, felt that Leon was still good enough to play part-time so he accepted an offer from amateur side Dover in the Southern League.

12

Funnily enough, as with Millwall, the season after he left Gillingham they went on to win promotion to the Third Division as champions.

"The reason I went to Dover, it was the same money as when I was playing full-time. At the same time, I worked down the rail yards driving a crane. It wasn't a lot of money but I quite enjoyed it."

That all lasted for a couple of seasons but then it started to catch up on him. Besides, Maureen wanted to get back to London.

"To be perfectly honest, I didn't blame her. It was okay for me but she was forever going back and forth to see her mum and dad. She was only young and was missing her family, so we moved back to Bermondsey."

Paul was nearly four years old.

Maureen took up the position of manager of a laundrette in Ilderton Road with the middle and top floors above it coming with the job, rent free. As a consequence Maureen received only a small wage but they would end up staying there for the next thirteen years.

"It was terrible there really," says Leon, "but it suited Maureen because her parents lived just round the corner." Leon got a job on a building site at first and then went to work as a driver for the Post Office where he would stay until he retired.

"I was glad I did that really. It was a steady job. It involved a lot of hours but you could earn a reasonable living out of it."

Paul was enrolled in the nursery at Galleywall Road for six months before graduating up to the primary school where he forged his first friendships, such as with Paul Rulton.

"I was with Vas from when I was four or five. We were at Galleywall Road together. I lived down 'The Blue' in a place called Stafford End Street, off of St. James Road there, not far from Paul. He used to live above a laundrette."

When Paul was six, a brother – Lee – came along, born in Guys Hospital and looking just like his dad. Paul took after his mum. As they grew up together the brothers were as thick as thieves.

"Lee idolised Paul," Maureen recollects with a smile. "He put him on a pedestal. He was his idol."

It didn't stop Paul getting up to mischief, though.

"He could be a right c--t," recalls Lee. "Him and his mates used to use me for target practice. They used to take me down the railway arches just by where we lived in Ilderton Road, make me run up and down the wall and throw stones at me. Like a duck! Just for the fun of it! They were only throwing them at my legs, mind. They weren't throwing them at my head. To him and his mates it was funny. I can laugh about it now but it weren't funny at the time, getting clattered with stones."

There were fun and games on holiday too according to family friend Iris Clubb. "I remember one holiday, I don't remember what Paul had done, but Maureen had had enough. It was a sight! She got this broom and went after him. She was chasing him around and he was bouncing from bed to bed!" The holidays, spent in the chalets of Devon and Cornwall, were, though, on the whole idyllic.

"Paul and Lee had a lovely upbringing," Maureen reflects. "They were very well known round here. They had lovely dispositions, you know? They weren't like out in gangs or anything like that."

"I always remember Paul as being so polite to people," says childhood friend Barry Cameron. "Everything had a 'thank you' at the end of it and a 'please.' I never heard a bad word about him. He'd avoid trouble, walk away from it. It makes it all the more shocking what happened."

"We didn't really ever have any real trouble with Paul at school," says Maureen. Leon recalls having to go up there a couple of times but for nothing serious.

"It wasn't that he was abusive or anything like that," says Maureen. In her eyes he was simply misunderstood.

"The thing about Paul was that he was very grown up for his age, very mature. He wouldn't speak to you unless you spoke to him like an adult. If he felt the teacher was talking down to him, he'd be destructive. Talk to him on an adult level and he'd do anything for you. One particular day, they were having a discussion at school about something and after a while he apparently stood up and said, 'If you can't talk to me like an adult, then don't talk to me at all!' That sort of summed him up. He was very, very forward. You didn't go round the houses with Paul. He didn't like that. You told him how it was and he was the same. He was only ten, eleven but he acted like fourteen, fifteen."

They were traits that Paul would carry with him into

14

secondary school, the South East London School in Deptford SE8.

"He was very sure of himself," according to Paul Rulton. "His dad's like that too. They're quietly confident people. They were like three peas in a pod, him, his brother and their dad, you know? They were all very much alike. Paul absolutely worshipped his dad."

When Paul was fourteen, Leon played the unwitting accomplice when Paul got himself into a spot of bother with the law.

"We were still living in the flat at Ilderton Road," recalls Maureen. "He came running in one night, said, 'I'm going to bed,' and went straight up the stairs which was a bit unusual because it was quite early. About eleven o'clock there was a knock at the door so my husband went down and it was the police. They asked to come in and asked for Paul. We told them he was in bed. They asked us to get him up because they wanted to speak to him. Well, he came down and they asked him where he'd been that evening. 'I've been in bed,' he said. They wanted to know where he'd been before that but he just stood there. 'You're very fit, aren't you?' they said to him. Apparently, him and a mate had nicked a car and he'd legged it so fast they couldn't catch him. He'd run and run, over hedges, fences, rail tracks, everything. His friend obviously hadn't been quick enough and had got caught and given Paul's name."

Leon continues, "There were two of them but he was the only one who was a decent driver. He was only fourteen but I'd taught him a few things about cars, how things work, this and that, and he obviously managed to work the rest out for himself."

They all went down to Deptford Police Station.

"The police were good, really," Leon continues. "They were lenient. They got away with just a chastising by the Chief Constable, you know, 'Don't do it again', that sort of thing."

One friend recalls, "They came and knocked him up and carted him off. I think he got a caution for it. He did it a couple of times but put it this way, the times that I know about the car was put back where it was taken from. It was all very, well, above board!"

"He got caught just as he was starting to get into it and that frightened him off and he never done it again," recalls brother Lee.

Maureen laughs. "He could be a little git! I was worried about letting him out with his mates for a while after that. This one night I was cleaning everyone's shoes and he wanted to go out but I

15

said 'no'. He gave me some backchat and I took up my broom and said, 'How dare you talk to me like that. If you speak to me like that again I'll whack you with this broom.' Well, he did and I was so mad I went wallop! Well, that broom - I'll never forget - snapped in half across his back! He didn't even flinch! So what did he do? He picked up one of my shoe brushes and threw it clean through my window! He could be a little git!"

Back at school Paul wasn't exactly setting the world on fire. His school reports for 1975 and 1976 do contain some positive remarks, 'B' grades and references to his potential but they are interspersed with comments such as, "Paul has some ability but has tended to waste it by chatting and messing around in class…Coasts along on the bare minimum…Paul is content to do as little work as possible…Lazy boy wasting his ability…Too easily involved in behavioural lapses…Paul has charm - which he uses - and ability - which he wastes in some subjects…I expect very much better than this from a boy of Paul's potential…Late: 17 (disgraceful!)."

There was a very simple reason, documented by the Head of Year: "Not a very successful term, more interested in football than work…"

****

Although football was in Paul's genes, his interest and ability still came as something of a surprise to Leon.

"To me, swimming was going to be his sport. I used to take him swimming and by the time he was three years of age, he could swim to a very good standard."

"We would always," recalls Barry Cameron, "come rain or shine, go swimming together. In fact, he taught me how to swim."

"He got better and better," Leon continues, "and by the time he was seven he was going in off the boards and everything."

Maureen recalls one particular day when she and her father – "Paul was very close to his grandfather" - went to see Paul swim in a gala.

"He was seven or eight years of age. When they finished all

16

the races - Paul won all of his - they let them just have a swim about. We were sitting up in the stands and after a short time I looked over to say something to my dad and the look on his face! He said to me, 'Do NOT look down there! Do NOT look!' You know why? Paul was up on the high board. You see, whereas Paul's friends would maybe go off the bottom or middle boards, Paul would go off the high one. My dad started shouting, 'Get down boy! Get down boy! Don't do it!' Well, Paul didn't take a blind bit of notice. He was up and in. My dad! He was so relieved. Then Paul got out and did it again!

"Another time I was working in the laundrette when all of a sudden one of his mates came running in. They said that Paul had been involved in an accident, that he'd dived off of the high board and hit his head on the side of the pool on the way down. Well, I ran up to the butchers to use the phone but a panda car was coming along and a friend of mine flagged it down.

"By the time they got me to hospital my legs were shaking. I didn't know how badly he'd been hurt, if he was alive even. They had a system at the hospital. You were told to go and sit either by the green light or the red light. Well, they told me to go and sit by the red light. I got called in and there were two boys in there - Paul and another. All I could tell was that Paul was obviously still alive. He had a great big gauze on his head and the other boy had one across his chin. The doctor asked me if I was aware what had happened and I said that I was, that he'd been diving and had hit his head on the side of the pool. They said, 'Well, yes he did dive in but this other boy had been surfacing at the same time Paul was entering the pool and they collided.' They said they could have killed each other!

"Paul was shaking and asked me how bad it was so I lifted the gauze and had a look and just said, 'Oh, it's okay. A couple of stitches and you'll be alright.' I was feeling sick. I could actually see his skull. His dad had to hold his hand while they stitched him up. He - both of those boys -were very lucky."

Leon adds, "Paul actually had the savvy to pull the other boy from the water. He got a commendation for that."

Paul showed such promise as a swimmer that he was asked to consider pursuing the sport as a career. He turned down the offers, much like Leon before him.

"He just had a natural ability in the water and, of course, he

17

was tall and slender. Ladywell Baths, they asked if they could take him on and some other club I can't remember now. They said they wanted to train him up, that he could make international level."

"He was the best at school," says Lee. "He could swim like a fish. They took him to the London trials. He got picked for the district first, then for London. He could have gone on to swim professionally. He could have gone on to do anything he wanted. Anything he put his mind to he'd become the best at it."

Paul's mind was not, however, on swimming.

"All he was interested in was his football," Maureen reflects. "All he wanted to do was play football."

"He had shown no real, serious interest in football up to that point whatsoever," remarks Leon. "I used to kick the ball around with him, you know, but he didn't follow a team of anything like that. So when he came home one evening - he was coming up to eleven - and said, 'Dad, I'm going to play football', well, it was a bit of a shock."

Paul's friends were, however, already in on the secret.

Gerry Avery laughs and shakes his head.

"He was always football, football, football."

Barry Cameron nods in agreement.

"He was football mad. Sometimes you used to think, 'Oh, change the subject!' Just football mad, all the time. It was all about football, everything was about football. If a problem was being resolved, football would come in to it somewhere."

"His whole life was football," adds David Palmer. "I mean, nothing else really mattered."

John Morgan remembers the camaraderie amongst the group. "We were so wrapped up in our football we didn't really know a lot else, you know? Outside football, we were probably lost to the world, really. We were so wrapped up in it, we didn't really care about anything else."

"Where Maureen's house is now, there used to be Victorian houses and a park," Barry Cameron continues. "Paul used to be the only one in there early morning. I can't remember him playing any other sports. He sometimes played cricket but that wasn't for him."

"We used to go round the flats in Camilla Road, round there," reflects Paul Rulton. "They had a little grass pitch there, it

18

was about sixty metres long and that's where we learnt to play our football really, you know? Every day after school we were round there. They also used to have a cinders pitch round the back of where Millwall's new ground is and we used to go there after school as well."

John Morgan remembers the fun that was had over in Southwark Park during the summer.

"There used to be a five-a-side tournament there. It was born out of a kids club run out of Rotherhithe School. In the winter we played table tennis and badminton in the school and in the summer they took it all over to the park and we'd have this huge football tournament. It was quite a big thing for the area, really. There were quite a lot of teams over there, probably about eight teams in about six leagues. It was the be-all-and-end-all. You know, you got home from school and you got yourself over the park."

"It was every night of the week," recalls Gerry Avery. "Everyone got to know one another from the different estates, including the so-called notorious ones. They were all there playing five-a-side. We all helped to set it up, we all helped to put it away. It's crying out for something like that today to be honest with you, to get the kids to know each other. That's where I got to know Paul."

According to Barry Cameron, "When the teams were picked, no matter who was picking the teams, they would always want Paul on their side because, believe it or not, he could do things with a ball we'd only seen on telly, even at that age. He was so skilful and the older boys, they were jealous of what he could do with the ball at his feet, you know? He could go around anyone with it. And he used to get kicked all over the place because they took their frustration out on him."

As well as playing for his school – "I never met a guy more devoted to his football," says games teacher Steve Underwood – Paul played Sunday league.

"He played for a side run by a fella who had a scaffolding firm in Bermondsey," recalls Leon. "I can't remember the name now but I went down to have a look and spoke to this man. He must have seen Paul somewhere, kicking the ball about and he'd invited him to play for his side. He told me, 'He's got some ability, this boy.' I thought to myself I didn't even know he had an interest, let alone any ability! It just went on from there.

"Another day he came to me and said, 'I'm going to play for a team up the road in Eltham.' So, like last time, I made a few enquiries and found out the team was Villacourt Rovers, which was actually quite a good grade of football for that age, it really was."

"Villacourt were a big club in the area at the time," confirms John Morgan.

Dean Tonkin would later be a colleague of Paul's at Arsenal.

"I probably first came across him when he was about thirteen and playing for Villacourt Rovers. I played for a side called Davidson and I also came up against him at district level. He represented Blackheath and I was with South London.

"Paul was outstanding for his age, very confident. He was awesome. He already had a reputation as a kid. You knew who were the ones you had to look out for, the teams you had to raise your game against. At the time he was so much more talented than anyone else. He had pretty much everything you needed. He was good in the air, good with both feet. The only thing he didn't have was great pace but he had a decent touch."

And it wasn't only his footballing prowess that singled him out.

"And his size!" continues Tonkin. "He was taller than everyone in his age group. And so strong. At thirteen he was probably already eleven stone. He was built like a man."

Maureen agrees.

"As well as thinking older than he was, my Paul looked it as well."

"He was bigger than everybody else, you know?" There is reverence in Paul Rulton's voice. "He was one of those kids who was two foot taller than everybody! And he was quite a strong kid as well. It was predominantly black, our school at South East London. I think most of the blacks were scared of Paul, you know. He was a big lump. There were fights with West Greenwich School but we never got in to any bother, you know what I mean? He was just like my idol, really."

"A sort of larger than life character," agrees Gerry Avery. "He was a big lad, which with school football is always an important factor."

"This meant," says Steve Underwood, "he could play up a year in schools football if needed. He played for the school's senior team when he was just 16."

"But," Gerry Avery points out, "It wasn't just the fact that he was big. He was a good footballer with it as well. He had great skill for such a big lad."

Mark Richardson was another who played alongside Paul.

"He was so good sometimes that he would go down the wing and he'd really annoy the full-back, shouting, 'Chase me! Chase me!' trying to wind them up. A goalkeeper would just kick it out up to the half-way line and he'd just volley it straight back into the goal. I mean he was that good."

"He actually started off in midfield," reveals Leon, "which may come as something of a surprise to those Arsenal fans accustomed to seeing him play as a striker."

Steve Underwood confirms, "His position was as a central midfield player where his strength and outstanding passing ability plus good technical skills helped him dominate play. He was two footed and had a wonderful shot on him."

"He played in midfield, central midfield," says Jamie Winterton. "I used to play in goal and as soon as I got the ball, I'd be looking for Vas, I just gave it to Vas and we were away."

Paul Rulton in particular benefitted from having Paul as a teammate.

"Vas was midfield, a box-to-box sort of player and I played up front. I got seventy seven goals one season for Villacourt Rovers. It's a record. But he must have made ninety percent of them. He would beat seven or eight players and roll it to me on the goal line, you know? That was the thing with him. His assists were unbelievable."

David Palmer was another who was grateful to be playing alongside Paul.

"He may have played in midfield but to be honest he could play anywhere. He was so far in advance of the game that we played. I remember him going out on his own and standing on the centre spot before games and just keeping the ball up, flicking it on his shoulders, just to sort of put the frighteners on the other team.

21

Sometimes he used to play teams on his own. He was that good, you know? He just found the game very, very easy. He played in the district team, the school team. He just sort of walked into those types of teams. He was just different class to most people."

Paul left a lasting impression on his opponents too.

"I remember one game we played against Blackheath," says Dean Tonkin. "I remember my dad after the game pointing out something he'd done. He'd cleared the ball off of his own goal-line and a few seconds later had scored at the other end, finishing off a move he'd started in his own penalty area. My dad said, 'Did you see what that kid did?!' I remember that. Like I said, he was the sort of player you never forgot. I haven't got the best memory but I can recall the three or four times I played against him."

Paul was, according to the others, the obvious choice for captain.

"He was the leader on the pitch. He was very vocal," recalls Steve Gorham. "He was captain of the school team up until he left to do his apprenticeship at Arsenal. We had quite a successful side. We had some exceptional footballers in the side. I think it was the 1976-77 season we won the Blackheath Under-16s Cup. We beat Sedgehill School in the final. Paul was captain. He lifted the cup that day. Paul was very much the stand out player in a side of very, very good players. For most of the time he probably picked the team as well if truth be told.

"We also played for a local boys' club in Bermondsey called St. Joseph's. We'd play for the school in the morning and then go and play for the boys' club in the afternoon."

Gerry Avery agrees. "He'd be the one on the pitch who was doing this, doing that, telling you what to do, telling you where to go."

"He was quite outspoken, quite up front, quite loud," says John Morgan. "Not in a nasty way. When you play football I think you should be loud and you should be talking a lot. They're the better players, that's how I see things. If you don't talk on a football pitch then you'll get lost and you'll get pushed into a corner somewhere. He was quite loud. You couldn't run him over. He was always coming forward, always outspoken."

Gerry Avery smiles. "He was definitely, definitely, definitely

22

not the shy, retiring type!"

"He was enormously confident," explains Steve Gorham, "very talented. He had good balance, good strength. Everything you'd want in a player really."

David Palmer agrees. "He was the most naturally two-footed player that I ever saw, that I ever played with."

"He could play with both feet," says brother Lee. "He could spread thirty, forty yard passes with pin-point accuracy with either foot." He laughs to himself at one particular memory.

"One day we were in Hyde Park just knocking the ball about and there were these birds with bikinis on laid out sunbathing. He told me, 'Lee, go and stand over there, about ten yards away from them.' So off I went and next thing he's pinged the ball over from forty yards away and it's come down and hit one of the girls smack in the stomach. Well, I've never heard a scream like it! She's jumped up and the first face she's seen is mine and I'm trying to tell her, 'It weren't me! It was me brother!' Of course, I look over and Paul's gone. He's hiding in some bushes somewhere. She was chasing me all over the place.

"He just dominated games, it was so easy for him. I remember he'd come off and say to our old man that he needed a better challenge than this."

"He had absolute faith in his own ability," reflects Steve Gorham. "Football was his life. He knew from an early age he was going to be a professional footballer and that was that."

****

Word was getting around.

Leon takes up the story.

"One day - it was less than a season after he'd started playing for Villacourt - he came home and said, 'I'm going to play for a team called Chelsea. Where is it based?!' It was all so naïve. He said, 'Two blokes called Jimmy and Kenny want to speak to you, Dad.'

"Jimmy Thompson had played for a few clubs in his day

23

including Chelsea and was quite well known as a top scout around this time. He was the one who first spotted Greavsie. Kenny Shellito, I knew quite well. I'd been on the ground staff with him at Chelsea. He spent his entire career at Stamford Bridge and like me he'd had to pack up because of a knee injury. He had been looking after the youth side at Chelsea for some years.

"So we went over to their training ground on a Saturday and the youth side were playing in a South East Counties game. We met Kenny as we went through the gates. He said to me, 'Do you want to give him a go?' I wasn't sure he'd be up to it yet physically but they decided to put him on and see how it went. They were playing Portsmouth and they gave him half an hour. Well, he amazed me really. He sort of ambled along for a little while and then all of sudden, wallop! Goal! The ball came to him, he turned and he went bang! A little bit of magic. Kenny turned to me and said, 'That's just what we're looking for!'

"So then they asked if they could try him out in a few full games. He must have played three or four times for Chelsea in the South East Counties but he was only fourteen, coming up to fifteen then, so they kept it a bit quiet, you know. It was the done thing then, although it was obviously frowned upon. I think they even arranged a game against Paul's local team."

Friend Jamie Winterton was also singled out by Chelsea.

"Me and Vas were there in the days when Eddie McCreadie was manager and our coaches at the time were Ken Shellito and Dario Gradi. We were spotted whilst playing for Villacourt Rovers. We played some games for Chelsea's youth team. We had a good laugh there. We used to go after school. We used to have to get to Elephant & Castle and then catch the Northern Line all the way down to Morden and then we'd get out there and we'd get a bus from Morden station to the training ground which was then in Mitchum. Fortunately, we'd all get a lift home in the van. The Chief Scout - he was called Eddie Heath - he used to give us all a lift home."

"Anyway," Leon continues, "Kenny was going on at me, trying to get me to say 'yes' to Paul signing up. He was determined that Paul didn't go to another club. He said that, knowing that he would get even bigger and stronger, they'd guarantee him a first team place by the time he was sixteen. The thing is, other clubs were now coming in for him."

"On the Tuesday we went to Fulham," recalls Jamie Winterton. "One of our teachers, Mr Nash, was an ex-pro and he got us involved with Fulham. When we went there, though, we got kicked to bits by the other players there. We weren't liked very much there for some reason! On the Wednesday we trained at Millwall and then on the Thursday we were at Chelsea. And we were also both invited up to West Brom for a week, although we decided not to go. I can't remember why. I think Paul was quite happy with Chelsea at the time."

"All the clubs were after him by then," confirms Dean Tonkin. "I'm sure Manchester United wanted him. There was a London trial held once where he was apparently surrounded by scouts."

"Paul was hitting his peak," explains Jamie Winterton. "He was going from strength to strength and obviously a lot of clubs were interested."

One of those clubs was Arsenal.

"Ernie Collett was our full-time chief scout for the London area and it would have been him who would have spotted Paul first," says former youth team manager Roger Thompson. Like all sixteen Arsenal scouts working across the country, Ernie was looking out for boys with two key ingredients – skill and enthusiasm. He saw an abundance of both in Paul.

"Paul was then invited to a big trial game one Sunday at Highbury Fields," Roger continues, "and he stuck out like a sore thumb. We knew we wanted him there and then."

Arsenal pulled out all the stops, prizing Paul away from Chelsea.

"I don't know what word you'd use," says Steve Gorham, "if they poached him or what. I don't know how it worked in those days but he definitely went from Chelsea to Arsenal."

"Yes, they poached him," agrees Jamie Winterton. "I know because he was still at Chelsea at the time. Arsenal hounded him like you wouldn't believe. They never left him alone. I'm sure they were phoning him and also writing him letters, inviting him to the ground and stuff. And eventually, obviously, he went. Arsenal did that to quite a few of them. They really did snap up most of the best players

25

that I can recall playing against in London at the time. They got Nicky Law, Brian Sparrow, Chris Whyte…"

"I went to Chelsea for a little while as a schoolboy," says Nicky Law, "then I went to the Arsenal and Paul did as well. At that time there were a few clubs who were willing to pay, you know, to attract young lads to go to their club. I know that's not allowed but there's ways of doing it, you know, expenses, that sort of thing. But whatever would have happened I would have gone to Arsenal anyway, it was such a great place, it had good people."

Arsenal's interest didn't come as any surprise to his friends.

"When Arsenal took him on I don't think too many of us were shocked because I think it was just a matter of time before he took that first step," remarks Barry Cameron.

"He probably knew from the time we went to secondary school," says Paul Rulton. "You could see Paul was going to make a living from it."

Leon reveals that before Paul signed his associated schoolboy forms for Arsenal, there was one potential stumbling block.

"When Arsenal came in for him, for me they offered the best grounding for any young professional. I don't know what it was but Arsenal had that way about them. That's why they call them 'The Arsenal'. I had a look around and they were a different world entirely. But he didn't initially want to go to Arsenal because of their colours! He said to me, 'I'm not going to play for this side. I don't like their colours.' So I said to him, 'What do you want? Bright blue, dark green, yellow?!' I explained that there was a bit more to it than that! Really, I coerced him into it and eventually he said, 'Okay then. I'll give it a try.'"

Islington Gazette, Friday 4th March 1977:

Kids sign up

ARSENAL have signed…Blackheath striker Paul Vaessen on associated schoolboy forms.

26

"I didn't dare go anywhere near Kenny Shellito after Paul signed for Arsenal," says Leon. "He could be quite feisty could Ken!"

****

"Sometimes maybe you need an experience. The experience can be a person or it can be a drug. The experience opens a door that was there all the time but you never saw it."[3]

Having got to know Paul reasonably well during the course of my research, I would imagine Paul would probably have taken signing for Arsenal completely in his stride. He may have been vocal but I don't think Paul was one to boast about his football. He had his feet on the ground. There would, therefore, have been no fanfare. Maybe he would have just joined his mates for a kickabout over the local park. Maybe he would have gone down to the local *Wimpy* bar for a burger and chips or listened to the latest sounds from *Pink Floyd*, *Thin Lizzy* and *Yes*. And just maybe he would have popped a tablet or two or perhaps enjoyed a bit of puff. After all, everyone was at it, Paul included.

"Unknown to us," Maureen reveals, "Paul was apparently experimenting with stuff – tablets, I was told - back when he was at school, when he was thirteen, fourteen years of age."

One former friend confirms, "As far as the drugs in those days were concerned, I think that we just took what we called 'black'. It's just like a little block of tar and you broke it up and you put it in the tobacco. That's what we used to do at school. Paul I assumed was into that which everyone was really in that area at that time, even at a young age."

Another corroborates the story. "He used to smoke a bit of dope and stuff. Back then it wasn't like skunk or hard stuff, it was just mild weed and block cannabis that he would smoke."

"I'm not being funny but Bermondsey and that way was renowned for being a bit rough, you know," says another.

Dad Leon had his hunches. "I didn't know for sure something was going on but I was very suspicious, put it that way."

27

One friend recalls the first time he and Paul tried some puff. "We went back to Paul's place and his dad was there. We were just giggling. We couldn't stop giggling."

"I couldn't put my finger on it," Leon continues, "so I made further enquiries, put my head together with some of the other parents and eventually put two and two together. But we couldn't really do anything about it."

Paul had taken up drugs. He had signed for Arsenal. He had, by the age of fifteen, made the two decisions which would shape the rest of his life.

2
Teenage Kicks

"I never let schooling interfere with my education."

Mark Twain

I very nearly didn't recognize Roger.

That's not being unkind.

It's just that we'd never met before and all I had to go on were some photos taken almost thirty years ago. They appear in an article in the official Arsenal Annual from 1980, 'Roger's lads who made it to the top.' There is one picture of him working youth team goalkeeper Rhys Wilmot and then another of him parading the F.A. Cup on an open-top bus after Arsenal's 1979 final victory over Manchester United. Roger Thompson had every right to be part of those celebrations, having done more than most to nurture the likes of Frank Stapleton, Graham Rix and David O'Leary through the youth ranks and into the first team. They were all part of that 1974 youth team out of which John Devine, Trevor Ross and Wilf Rostron also graduated and for which Roger refuses to take much credit.

Because Roger is modest. He understates the influence he has had on the lives of his numerous young charges, and is genuinely surprised and humbled by the praise that comes his way.

"Roger Thompson was a life saver," effuses Devine. "He was brilliant, absolutely brilliant. He was a real people person, he was a good man. You see, what many people don't understand is how hard it is to come over as a young fourteen year-old boy from Ireland to a huge city like London and an institution like Arsenal. It was very difficult. To come away from home, on my own, was the hardest thing I've ever done in my life. But to know I could go to Roger, that he was there for me, well, he was an absolute life saver. He was fundamental in keeping a lot of us homesick kids there at Arsenal. And what also helped was his training. I looked forward to the training. He was such a good coach, a top coach."

What quickly becomes clear about Roger is that he is one of life's nice people. He greets me like a long-lost friend when we meet for the first time in the plush lobby of the Hilton Hotel in Islington. He puts you instantly at ease and after only three-quarters of an hour I find that it is me who is opening up, telling Roger about my battles with anxiety and depression.

Roger is more than happy to reciprocate with some disclosures of his own, primarily in the hope that his honesty may help somebody else. Roger has been through the mire too.

"Alcoholism took me to a dark place," he says. "I just couldn't stop drinking. Alcohol stripped me bare mentally, physically, financially and professionally. I ended up living like a tramp in a battered old caravan somewhere on the outskirts of Las Vegas where I had once had a lovely home.

"But, thankfully, I had what I can only call a spiritual awakening. I poured all the drink away one day and slept that night like I was on a cloud. In the morning when I woke up, the DTs, the sweats, the cravings were all gone. I felt like a new person."

Roger has been that person for the past twenty two years during which he hasn't touched a drop. He is a Christian which has helped him stay strong, sober and happy all that time.

"Alcoholics Anonymous encourages you to put your faith in a power greater than yourself."

Roger tells me he has just come away from running a soccer camp for children with special needs.

"I feel God has given them something to help them cope with their disabilities. They've got something special about them. They are such a joy to work with."

That's Roger for you. He is selfless, more interested in others, in you. He exudes a sincerity which leaves you in no doubt that, yes, he does want to listen to you and yes, he really does care.

"He was like a father figure to me," says Graham Rix. "He *really* cared. He was a caring coach. He looked after us boys as if each one of us were his son, especially those of us who were living away from home."

"They were my kids," Roger tells me, "that's what I called them. You see, I had their best interests in my heart because, not having made it myself, I didn't want any of them to fall short."

Most of all, Roger wanted to make it at his beloved Aston

Villa.

"It was 1956 and I convinced my parents to let me leave school at fifteen so I could join the ground staff at Villa. I promised I'd carry on with my studies two nights a week to get some qualifications but I never went."

Life for one learning their trade was a far cry from today. As well as training, Roger and all the other ground staff boys were expected to do work around Villa Park including cleaning the toilets, painting and decorating, and sweeping the terraces. Doing the same, a year behind Roger, was one George Graham.

Roger spent four and a half years at Villa but never made the breakthrough into the senior side.

"I worked my way up through the youth side and got into the reserves but I started getting a lot of injuries, hamstring injuries and it affected my confidence. I couldn't get back into the reserve team. I went to see the manager, the legendary Joe Mercer, and he suggested that I should go out on loan and that Nuneaton Borough in the Southern League Premier were really interested.

"I was absolutely gutted to leave Villa. I'd been stood on the terraces at Villa Park with my dad as a boy. I was a supporter from the age of five. All I wanted to do was play football for the Villa. But now I had to get on with my life."

That life was spent in the lower leagues, Roger spending six successful years at Nuneaton, the last four of which were part-time as he opened up a paint and wallpaper shop. He was also awarded a benefit game against Jimmy Hill's newly-promoted Coventry City, a local derby which attracted a crowd of 25,000 and earned Roger the princely sum of £1,000.

After a couple of years at Barnet, where Roger first took an interest in coaching, he spent three fruitful seasons at Metropolitan London League side Epping Town as player-manager where he did the league and cup 'double' twice.

It was then, in 1973, that Roger's friend, Bob Wilson, recommended him to Arsenal Manager Bertie Mee for a coaching role. Seven happy years followed during which Roger was responsible for the youth and then reserve team set-ups.

"I loved going in to work at Arsenal, every day," says Roger. "There was a lovely atmosphere about the place. A lot of positives. It was a fun place to be."

After six months as first team coach at Fulham with Malcolm Macdonald, Roger went stateside, working with the likes of the Edmonton Drillers, Golden Bay Earthquakes and the Cape Cod Crusaders. In between there was an unsuccessful spell as manager of the late Stan Flashman's Barnet but it was back in America at his Florida beach concession where he would hire out his deckchairs, snorkeling equipment and sailing boats, that Roger would enjoy his longest stint in charge in the US.

Back in the UK, Roger took on the post of commercial manager at Leek Town and then Congleton Town in Cheshire where he is today. For a while he also carried out the same role for Conference side Alfreton Town which is managed by one of Roger's former young Arsenal charges, Nicky Law.

Nicky, who played in central defence, never made it into Arsenal's first-team. The nearest he came was one Monday morning when he was called up into the senior squad.

"They got in touch with college which is where I should have been and they said I wasn't there. I was up Oxford Street or somewhere like that. Anyway, I missed out because I wasn't at college and they found out."

Instead, Nicky became something of a journeyman, amassing over five hundred league appearances at a host of lower league clubs.

So many don't make it that far.

I open up that Arsenal Annual again and the warnings are there in another article entitled, 'Tough Climb to the Top'. It is something of a cautionary tale, outlining just how difficult it is to make it to the top like Rixy, Stapleton and O'Leary, how the 'near-misses' as they are called, "face a hell of a rude awakening if they have to find themselves another job of work."

To avoid that, Paul Vaessen would first have to ensure that he was amongst that small percentage of associate schoolboys to be taken on by Arsenal as apprentices.

"The Football League allowed clubs to sign schoolboys on what they called 'B' forms after their fourteenth birthday," explains Roger. "Vas was fifteen years old when he signed on as an associate schoolboy. That entitled the club to invite him to training and coaching sessions during evenings and school holidays. I used to have them in at Highbury on Tuesday and Thursday nights.

"Vas was a good trainer, a very good listener. He always wanted to learn. Even though he was just a schoolboy, he was in many ways a model professional."

As for playing time, that was largely down to Paul's South East London School.

"The school had first dibs on him," says Roger, "but if he wasn't playing for his school or his district, or it was during the summer holidays, then he was free to play for us in the South East Counties League."

Paul's Arsenal debut came in a 2-1 pre-season friendly win away to Hitchin Town at their Top Field stadium on Saturday 6th August 1977. He was still just fifteen. Lining up alongside him was a mishmash of players including reserves Steve Gatting, Steve Walford and Trevor Ross, rookie goalkeeper Nicky Sullivan, and 1971 'double' hero Peter Simpson who, at more than twice Paul's age, was in the twilight of his eighteen year Arsenal career. Also included was young first teamer Graham Rix who, three years down the line, would combine with Paul to produce one of the most dramatic moments in Arsenal's illustrious history.

At Hitchin there were no goals for Paul, no headlines, just a steady performance curtailed by substitution and just four days later he played the entire ninety minutes in another friendly, a 1-1 draw at Worthing.

It was another month before Paul turned out for the first time for the youth team at London Colney against Watford and another week before he registered his first strike. That came in a 3-2 defeat at Millwall, the other goal coming from Brian McDermott.

"I got to know Paul really well," says Brian. "He was younger than me by a couple of years, I don't know how old he was. But he was a big strong lad and obviously had masses of potential. I remember he had a decent touch and he did have an eye for goal."

By the following month Paul had already started attracting attention from the local press after scoring an outstanding goal for the youth team in front of Gunners boss, Terry Neill:

Islington Gazette, Friday 30th September 1977:

Crystal Palace Youth 1 Arsenal Youth 2
(Southern Junior Floodlit Cup, 1st Round)

Revenge was sweet for Arsenal's youngsters when they knocked powerful Crystal Palace out of the Southern Junior Floodlit Cup at Selhurst Park on Tuesday.

FA Youth Cup holders Palace KO'd the Gunners last season but this time it was a different story.

According to manager Terry Neill his kids showed true grit to come back fighting after trailing 1-0 at the interval. "They really showed a lot of character," he said.

Clifford Cant made no mistake from the penalty spot to level and substitute Paul Vaessen came on in the 70th minute and with his first touch grabbed the match-winner after bursting past three defenders.

Paul had arrived and word was already beginning to spread across the red and white half of North London:

Islington Gazette, Friday 14th October 1977:

Giant Paul is one for future

TEENAGE GIANT Paul Vaessen is one of the aces in the pack of promising youngsters who are guarding Arsenal's playing future.

Six-footer Vaessen, who is aged 16 on Sunday, scored a magical matchwinner when he came on as a substitute in the Southern Junior Floodlit Cup against formidable Crystal Palace recently.

His explosive burst past three defenders showed that the 12-stone Bermondsey youngster is capable of great things.

It is a feeling that is echoed amongst the backroom boys at Highbury but coach Roger Thompson while praising Vaessen warns that he has a lot of hard work ahead of him if he intends to make the grade.

34

"Paul is a tremendous prospect with all the attributes required to make it to the top - the touch with his feet, good vision and lots of natural composure. If there is a deficiency in his game at present it is that he does not work hard enough in action."

"He is very versatile and can play in all positions but he feels more relaxed and confident when running at defences from midfield."

Paul had made a good start to his Arsenal career and just about everyone who knew him, or knew of him, were expecting international recognition with England schoolboys when the trials came around. Paul was, however, overlooked, a decision that was greeted with disappointment, surprise and suspicion.

Dean Tonkin was amongst those astonished by Paul's omission.

"How he never played for England, I'll never know. Don't get me wrong, all those who got through were also talented players, but Paul was at that time outstanding."

Leon agrees. "It's funny, really, that he never got picked for the England schoolboys' side. It was a real shame. I don't know fully what went on there but I was shocked because it was acknowledged that he was the best in the country in his position."

"I remember," says Mark Richardson, "he had terrible trouble with the England schoolboy set-up. He was convinced - and I know he was sometimes a bit cock-sure - but he was convinced that being in the schoolboy England side came down to favouritism and even - I know it sounds silly - even to the power of the dads. That upset him a lot, that he wasn't picked for England schoolboys because he was much better than those who were but it was the influence of the dads and other people that apparently got you into that England side. I know he was really upset about that."

Paul's teacher, Steve Underwood, has an alternative explanation.

"It was recognised that Paul was one of the outstanding players in his age group in the country. He played for Inner London County and went to the national trials for the England Schools team. He did well but when the team was announced his name was missing. When enquires were made the ESFA (the English Schools' Football Association) told him that only one player per district could

35

be chosen. As Nicky Law from his district team had been chosen, he couldn't play."

Paul may have been slighted but he didn't let it put him off his stride. The 1977-78 Arsenal youth team was not the most successful - they would eventually go on to finish fifth from bottom of the South East Counties League that season – but Paul continued to make good progress and by 7th February, still just a schoolboy, he was considered ready for a substitute's appearance for the reserves in their Football Combination 2-0 loss at Swindon Town.

Arsenal, though, had already seen enough and knowing there was still interest from other clubs, were eager to sign Paul up as a full-time apprentice professional as quickly as they could.

"Arsenal obviously liked what they saw," says Leon, "and wanted him to sign apprentice forms early, so we had to get permission from the school to release him early."

Maureen remembers the delegation from Arsenal which visited them in Lucey Way. "They came round, Terry Neill I think it was and some others, to the house and said they thought Paul had great ability and that they wanted him to join them. We said we'd think about it but Paul was thrilled. We all were, really."

"The school was flattered too," says Steve Underwood, "and let Paul leave before he took any exams. This was unusual. But to be honest, it was seen as an honour. The school was flattered that Arsenal wanted Paul and they wanted him badly. That's why they sent one of the top men down to the school to get him released early."

Even though the school felt privileged that one of their boys was attracting such attention, they did put up something of a fight.

"We had a hell of a time getting Paul's release from school to go and play for Arsenal," recalls Maureen. "They didn't want to let him go. They said he had great potential, that he could have gone on to college, university."

"I have to say that Paul was a bright able pupil who was in some of the top classes," agrees Steve Underwood.

"But all he wanted to do was play football for the Arsenal," Maureen continues. "So we went up to the school, I'll never forget it. He stood there in the headmaster's office with his coat over his arms - he wouldn't sit down - and he caused havoc! You should have seen the face on him! They said, 'Well, it'd be best if you stay on another year.' He stood there and he started. 'You can't make me come to school! You can't make me work! If you make me stay I won't do any work. I won't come to school. You'll have to drag me in.' He was ranting and raving and I was sat there thinking, 'Oh my God!' This was all in front of the headmaster, the school directors. 'I won't go to college. I won't do this, I won't do that. I only wanna play for the Arsenal. I don't wanna do anything else!' And then he stormed out and waited in the corridor. He was head strong, very head strong. He knew what he wanted and they could see that he was adamant about it and eventually the heamaster just said, 'I'm wasting my time, aren't I?' and just signed the papers. So Paul got his way."

"I was quite upset," Steve Underwood reflects. "I was like his school football manager and nobody bothered to tell me. Worst of all Paul failed to get the exams that would have given him alternatives when injury ended his top line professional career."

"When he signed that first apprentice contract," says Leon, "his Mum got £20 a week for housekeeping, Paul got £20 for himself and the rest was made up in expenses."

"He signed apprentice for Arsenal around Easter time," recalls Steve Gorham, "because they wouldn't let him play in the latter stages of the All London Schools and Blackheath Senior cups. We got knocked out of both."

"It was all done official-like," Leon tells me. "We had to go up to the stadium at Highbury and we went into the manager's office. There was Terry Neill there and his top coach, Don Howe. I had to sign the forms, being Paul's guardian."

Islington Gazette, Thursday 23rd March 1978:

Kids sign

ARSENAL this week signed former England defender Nicky Law and midfielder Paul Vaessen as apprentice professionals.

"Arsenal basically told him he was going to go a long way in football, that this was just the beginning," says brother Lee.

"I don't know whether it was a good thing him going to Arsenal now or not," reflects Maureen today.

Leon has already made up his mind.

"I wish he'd carried on with the swimming now."

****

On Tuesdays Paul and his fellow apprentices would train at Highbury or at the training ground at London Colney in rural Hertfordshire. Wednesdays were taken up by ball work in the mornings and weight training and country runs in the afternoon. Thursdays were spent at London Colney working on ball skills, team work and set pieces and the afternoon was free. There was another afternoon off on Fridays after five-a-sides in the morning followed by a South East Counties match on Saturdays.

Paul could now concentrate totally on football.

Well almost.

Mondays were spent at college.

Supposedly.

"We used to send the apprentices to college - North London Polytechnic in Holloway Road - one day a week," says Roger Thompson. "They used to go on Mondays, for the whole day. I think it was Bertie Mee who started it because he was into education. I thought it was a good thing. Some of the players liked it but some didn't. The thinking behind it was that, bearing in mind the stats and the percentage that don't make it in football, at least they might have some schooling to pursue another career."

"We never went to be fair," admits Nicky Law. "We used to go and do other stuff, you know?"

"We didn't used to go a lot," confirms fellow trainee Robert Johnson. "We used to play golf. We used to play at South Herts Golf Club in Totteridge. All of us at Arsenal had automatic membership down there. To be fair, we'd go in to college - I think me and Lawsey were doing carpentry, the others were doing something else - we'd go in and say to each other, 'See you in ten minutes.'"

Brian Sparrow was part of the gang.

"I did cookery, for the obvious reason. I thought they'd be more women in that class! Turns out I was right. Problem was most of them looked like they'd been eating their cakes! Anyway, I'd bake a cake, then one of the others would pop in and say we've got to go in to training. I'd ask one of the girls if she'd take my cake out of the oven when it was done and we'd go off and play eighteen holes!"

"As far as Arsenal were concerned, we'd signed in," says Johnson.

"I don't know whether we ever checked up on them," concedes Roger Thompson. "A lot of it was done on trust."

"The fact was," continues Johnson, "that at half past ten we were out on the first at South Herts. That's not being clever. That's how it was. We were footballers. Our thoughts were on football, not on going to college. The last thing I wanted to do was make a table! It was the same when I was at school and I was playing for England Schoolboys. I didn't think about anything else."

Brian McDermott acknowledges there is still something of a problem today.

"Every club paid lip service to college and stuff but when you're sixteen, seventeen you've got no interest in going to college. You just want to play football. Even now all the young kids want is football. They can't believe that they're not going to make it as footballers but the majority of them don't."

Thirty five years later, Robert Johnson, now a cabbie in London, admits to having some regrets.

"In hindsight we should have taken college more seriously. Looking back we should have done business studies or something like that or perhaps we should have been told what to do. It was our own choice really, what we chose to do at college. We had to do it, it was part of the apprenticeship to do it so you picked something you enjoyed doing really, not what was most useful. I did carpentry. In hindsight maybe I could have been a carpenter after football but there was every chance I wouldn't, do you know what I mean? I thought I'd be a professional footballer all my life. Then I thought when I come out of playing football, I'll be a coach. We all thought that, you know?"

****

To his credit, Paul didn't bunk off all the time.

"I can tell you that for a fact," says Lee, "because he made his mum a coffee table! It had a glass top and he gave it to her as a Christmas present. She was absolutely thrilled to bits and kept it for about twenty years."

When he did skive off, though, it was invariably with his great mate Nicky Law. The pair already had something of a reputation in the dressing rooms of Highbury and London Colney.

"They were like a double-act, like Laurel and Hardy," according to Roger Thompson. "They were like two loveable rogues, both so full of life, both larger than life. They were a couple of the biggest piss-takers going, they were. Paul and Nicky were always up to pranks and they were very good at it because they hardly ever got caught. They were probably up to all sorts behind my back but I didn't notice. They were also very sharp, very quick-witted. They had the quickest minds in the dressing room when it came to witticisms but they were a delight to be with."

"They were thick as thieves them two," recalls Nicky Sullivan. "They were jack-the-lads, they ducked and dived. If there was ever anything going down it was them two, you know? Up to no good. After training they'd always be shooting off somewhere because Nicky was the first one amongst us who had a car. I think he had a Capri. So him and Vas were always off somewhere, always up to no good.

"It was the antics, you know? He was a practical joker. If there was anything going down he'd be involved somewhere. Fire hydrants going off, people's gear going missing out of their rooms, things like that. If there was a fire alarm going off in the hotel it would be him. You know, it was the typical stupid things really but he didn't have a malicious bone in his body. He was jack-the-lad but he wasn't a horrible jack-the-lad. He was a joker. A South London wide kid. But it was all harmless really."

Paul wasn't, however, everybody's cup of tea.

"I got on alright with Vas," recalls Robbie Johnson. "He wasn't a great bloke and he wasn't a horrible bloke. But the non-London boys, if you like, didn't take to him because he was brash. He would tell them how it was, what he thought of them, whereas the boys from the valleys and the boys from Ireland, a long way from home, were more reserved. He wouldn't, for example, acknowledge the fact that they were homesick. He would embarrass you. There was a little bit of that on the pitch too. He would be quite brash. That's what Vas was like, a little bit. To want to be a pro you had to have confidence and he had it in abundance. He was very confident, bordering on arrogant."

"Paul wasn't shy," says Brian McDermott. "He was a London boy, obviously, so he was a confident boy, confident in his own ability as well, but fun. He liked a laugh. He and Lawsey, they used to be quite vocal, you know? Good lads really, as they all were."

Nicky Law has fond memories of these times.

"We'd have been about fourteen when we first met, I reckon. We played for the district together and became mates and knocked about together, you know?

"On a Friday we used to go training in the cinder gym and we had this thing where the last one to score had to clean the boot room out. Tony Donnelly was the kit man and what Tony used to do when he was polishing the boots was he used to use a brush and the old polish, flick it all over the f--king floor. I remember that down there at the Arsenal, there used to be black and yellow twelve inch tiles on the floor in the boot room. Well, me and Vas were in there one day - one of us was last to score so we had to clean it up - and Tony was saying, 'Oh, sorry lads, I'll sweep it up.' Well, you can imagine when he swept all the boot polish up, it was f--king everywhere. So me and Vas, we thought we were being clever and we went into the medical room and got this great big bottle of *Zoff* which is used to get plaster adhesive off and we put it all over the floor and we're scrubbing it up and we came out of there high as f--king kites! We were wobbling about all over the place!

"They also had the little gym down at Highbury, upstairs above the first team dressing room. Me and Vas were up there one day, the physio had sent us up there for rehabilitation. Of course, me and Vas were meant to be doing something and we obviously weren't doing it. We had a newspaper and Vas had ten minutes reading it and I just sat there with this f--king skipping rope, not using it but just whipping it around and hitting the floor, so downstairs it sounded like we were doing it. Anyway, so I said to him, 'Come on, give me the paper now,' so he had a go. We must have been there about an hour and this skipping rope, honestly, never stopped. And I think it was Fred Street who twigged on then. He's probably thought to

41

himself, 'F--king 'ell. They're going something, them too! They haven't stopped!' And Vas is sat there swinging the rope about, hitting the floor and I'm reading the f--king paper!

"Sometimes if you messed about when you were cleaning up or whatever, Tony used to have you in on a Sunday. There used to a be a stock-room there so me and Vas always used to make sure we got caught so that we would have to go in and we'd nick all the f--king boots and trainers out of the stock room! There were hundreds of them, all top stuff, top brands. We'd flog them, flog them to anybody who'd have them!

"Later on when I had the car, in the afternoons we used to go around Bermondsey and do the sort of things that probably normal people did but footballers shouldn't have done, you know, like we used to go to the pub. It was obvious we were going to become players so we had good contracts, you know, so you have the car, the clothes and go out but to be fair to Paul when we went out all he wanted to do was go to the pub.

"And I used to give Vas lifts back from training and games. We'd go over the bridge and I'd drop him off in Bermondsey. When we were driving along in traffic and there was a woman walking along he'd reach his arm out the car and slap their arse! One day he did it and the woman was shouting and took her shoe off and was whacking it on the top of my car!

"Another time we went to Augsburg in Germany, we were in a tournament there, and me and Vas were rooming together upstairs. We were about five or six floors up. We started filling carrier bags up with water from the bathroom and chucking them out of the window! We hit this bloke and there was f--king uproar! I think it was the mayor of f--king Augsburg we'd chucked it all over!

"And Roger, Roger was like our Fagan and we were his little Oliver Twist boys! We all used to get tickets for the first team games and on a Friday, Roger used to get all the tickets off everyone and me and Vas would run up to Kings Cross where we used to take them to Stan Flashman. We used to take all the tickets up round the back of Kings Cross station - he had some offices there - and we used to go and pick the money up from him for the goods, if you like, bring it back and Roger would divy it out. We used to get to keep the money. We got over face value.

"We had some f--king laughs to be fair, we really did."

TEENAGE KICKS

****

Back at the Islington Hilton it is time to leave.

As we get up, I notice for the first time what a snappy dresser Roger is. It brings to mind another photograph I have of him. In it Roger is standing with his triumphant Arsenal squad having just won the 1976 Pontins national six-a-side tournament at Wembley, the final having been played out prior to the Charity Shield match between Liverpool and Southampton. Roger is there on the end of the back row, resplendent in his dark shirt and tie and white suit. He looks as if he's just stopping off before a night out at Tramp.

As we part there is a big warm hug.

I'm not very good at hugging.

I come from an undemonstrative family.

I wonder whether Roger can sense the awkwardness.

What with all the personal insights we have shared over the past couple of hours, I feel like I've made an important friend today. I'm not sure, though, when I'll see Roger again. He lives in Macclesfield and doesn't tend to get down this way that often. He's in London at the moment because he attended a function at Emirates Stadium last night in aid of Bob Wilson's *Willow Foundation*. He was delighted to go. He saw so many old faces, most of them from the 'double' era like Wilson himself and Charlie George, coach Don Howe. Some of them, such as Pat Rice and Sammy Nelson, were former colleagues of Paul Vaessen.

There was no reason for any of them to have thought of Paul last night but I wonder, as I exit the hotel's foyer and head down Upper Street towards Angel tube station, if maybe a glass was raised to absent friends.

STUCK IN A MOMENT

3

Learning to Fly

"A flight of fancy on a windswept field
Standing alone my senses reeled
A fatal attraction is holding me fast
How can I escape this irresistible grasp?"

'Learning to Fly' by Pink Floyd (1987)

Maureen and Leon didn't last the distance.

Hardly surprising considering what they went through with Paul and then Lee.

Lee won't mind me mentioning that he's had his fair share of problems.

What with Paul as well, the family couldn't take the strain.

That's why Maureen's in SE16 and I'm here in SE12 to see Leon.

We've spoken a lot on the phone but I must admit that I'm a little apprehensive about meeting 'Big Lee' in person.

He sounds quite a character.

A tough cookie.

A man's sort of man.

As he walks me from Lee station to the nearby home he shares with partner, Viv, he is charm personified.

Turns out I needn't have worried.

There is coffee waiting and we start chatting, Leon's low, gravelly voice grinding away like a well-used cement mixer.

We talk about his own career, about Paul's, about the parallels and I'm curious as to what sort of soccer dad Leon made. I wonder, was he the sort you'd find barking away from the touchline, attempting to live his life, realize the career he should have had, through his son? Or was he a less conspicuous figure, in the background, adopting the laissez-faire approach which would allow

45

Paul the freedom to express himself, to find his own feet?

Certainly Leon seems very laid back if this meeting is anything to go by.

What is clear is that Leon became more hands-on as Paul's potential became apparent.

"I went to watch Paul play a few times obviously and thought, yeah, he's got a certain amount of ability. I didn't realise how much ability because it all sort of came on him quite quick, so I started taking him round the park." It was there, I've heard, that a father "very ambitious" for his son to make it as a professional footballer put that son through his paces. "Me, him and his dad used to go over the park," recalls Jamie Winterton, "and his dad used to stand on the corner putting the ball over so Paul could get the timing right for his headers."

Surely, though, this was nothing more than Leon passing on to Paul a few tricks of the trade, to help him along a bit?

"It was just things I taught him, you know," explains Leon, "like, if you watch any centre-forward and centre-back. They're usually big lads and when there's a long ball coming down the middle, they'll both go for it. Alright, one of them might get a decent header on it but nine times out of ten it's not going anywhere. So it was just one thing I said to Paul, that when there's a long ball coming down, move right away. Inevitably the centre-half will be watching the ball and as he's standing there waiting for the ball to come down you then move straight in, right across him and win the ball, get your header in. He perfected that.

"Another thing was to again move away and then come in late behind the centre-back as the ball's coming down. We'd practice it. He'd be the centre-half and I'd come in behind him, little shove on his shoulders and he'd say, 'That's a foul!' But it wasn't. It was just a little touch to help you get that bit higher, not enough for a foul. And he perfected that too.

"He was great at using his height, getting up high. He'd get so high at times he could pull the ball down on his chest."

And there was a good reason Leon was drilling Paul in the ways of the target man.

That was where Arsenal now wanted him to play.

"He came to me as a midfielder who liked to get forward but

46

I used to play him up front," confirms Roger Thompson. "I thought he was a bit like a young Ray Kennedy who scored so many goals for Arsenal during the 'double' season. We could play the ball up to Vas because he had a terrific ability to hold the ball up. His first touch with both feet was fantastic."

There is some irony in the comparison with Kennedy. Top scorer during Arsenal's triumphant 1970-71 season, the burly Kennedy was pushed back into midfield by Bob Paisley soon after his transfer to Liverpool in 1974. Arsenal boss Bertie Mee declared to Roger minutes after the deal was done that that was the best bit of business he'd ever done. "He'll be out of the game within two years," said Mee, referring to a suspect knee and Kennedy's battle to keep his weight down, something Paul would constantly struggle with. Kennedy, of course, went on to play for another decade, winning three European cups and five league titles with the Reds.

Roger wasn't the only one who fancied Paul as a striker.

"Don Howe told me at the time," says Leon, "that Paul was one of the best young forwards he'd seen."

"We thought we'd found the new John Radford," admits Howe, preferring to draw parallels with Kennedy's brawny Arsenal strike partner.

To others, Paul's conversion to forward came as something of a surprise.

"Really, Paul was not quick enough to be a centre-forward," says brother Lee. "His brain was quick enough but his body wasn't."

"He played in midfield for the school," confirms Steve Gorham. "He scored a lot of goals from midfield. He wasn't a striker at school ever. I was shocked when I saw him as a centre-forward because I never, in all the years I played with him, I never saw him play centre-forward."

Mark Richardson agrees with his friend. "He was a midfield player so when he went to Arsenal and they put him up front, I was very surprised. I thought, 'What are you doing, Arsenal?!'"

"I think it was probably because he was a big, powerful lad, you know," comments Nicky Law. "At sixteen we were both six foot two and thirteen stone."

"I think if they'd left him in the middle they really would have had a find on their hands," says Leon. "That's what I think

47

anyway."

If opinion was split as to Paul's best position, what was clear to all was that he was being fast-tracked towards the first team. Within the space of a year he had gone from promising schoolboy to within touching distance of Division One football.

"For a Saturday fixture, the team sheet would normally go up Friday lunchtime," John Devine describes. "Training would be from ten to eleven thirty – it would be a short day as you'd be expected to rest ahead of the game – and the list would go up in the first team dressing room. For a midweek trip abroad you would have to know the week before as you'd obviously have to be prepared."

However, for his first assignment with the senior side, notification of Paul's last minute inclusion would reach him via a rather unexpected source; the *Metropolitan Police Service.*

"We never had a phone then at our place in Lucey Way," Lee explains, "so Arsenal sent the police round! The coppers came in and said Arsenal needed Paul urgently, that they needed Paul to fly out with the squad that night so my old man went running round Bermondsey trying to find him!"

****

It's probably fair to say that, even though it was home to Germany's first ever national champions back at the turn of the twentieth century, the old East German city of Leipzig didn't provide the backdrop for all that many English teenage football daydreams back in the 1970s. Leipzig was once one of the jewels in the unified German crown, with its association with some of the world's finest classical musicians in Bach and Wagner and its resplendent sites such as the Monument to the Battle of the Nations, marking the halting point of Napoleon's European-wide sweep one hundred and sixty five years before. However, by the time the Gunners arrived for the second leg of their U.E.F.A. Cup first round tie on 27th September 1978, the municipality had long since been disregarded by its communist masters.

And certainly the mist, incessant rain and faulty lift which entrapped most of the Arsenal players prior to kick off and meant the players had to trudge up and down three flights of stairs to their third floor dressing room at half-time, all did little to impress its visitors.

But Paul Vaessen would always have fond memories of Leipzig because it was against Lokomotiv that, just six months after signing as an apprentice, the sixteen year-old would make his first-team bow.

Full-back John Devine was part of the Arsenal squad which flew to East Germany.

"I had a fairly good friendship with Paul, you know? We always seemed to get on quite well together. He was a very friendly, bubbly lad. He had a great smile, he had a magic smile. I always remember him having a big cheesey grin on his face when he came in to training. He was a bit of a joker around the place, you know? A confident, chirpy lad, a very bubbly character.

"But my memory of Paul around the time of his first-team debut is that he was a bit more reserved. Coming into the first-team he would have been aware of the fact that he was in amongst the stars, you know, Pat Jennings, Liam Brady, Frank Stapleton and all the others. So he would have been more reserved. He was a bit cocky and confident when he was coming through the youths and reserves but coming through to the senior squad, moving up to the first team was serious business and he would have been a bit different."

Graham Rix is in agreement.

"I think he might have been a little bit lairy with people of the same age but with us senior players he showed the utmost respect. He was a good lad. There was no doubt about it, I liked him."

"We always had a good relationship with the young kids coming through," states Liam Brady. "Paul was one of the young kids trying to make his way at the time. Paul was a big lad for one so young, a big strapping lad, a big, strong centre-forward, decent in the air. He was a nice lad and he looked like he was going to have a decent future in the game."

With the Gunners coasting to a 7-1 aggregate victory, Paul was brought on for the final fifteen minutes in place of David Price.

Lee remembers it well.

"We knew when he went out there that he was a substitute.

STUCK IN A MOMENT

We listened to it on the radio, there wasn't that much live TV back then. As the game went on into the second half I remember my old man saying, 'That's it, he won't get on now.' But he did, right at the end, and we were all jumping up and down in the living room."

"We spoke about it when he got home," says Leon. "Obviously he was pleased but there was no real merriment on his part. He was not one to boast. He was actually at times quite an insular person. Obviously when he was with his friends or family he would open up – he wasn't a loner or anything like that - but as I say, on his own…

"And he didn't brag. He just got on with what was in front of him."

And what was now in front of him was looking very promising indeed.

****

There would be another brief appearance – and a home debut - in the next round against Hajduk Split at Highbury but, although there was a place on the bench here and there, for the main part the season was spent in the shadows.

Islington Gazette, Friday 27th October 1978:

Arsenal 1 Southampton 0 (Football League Division One)

Missing against Southampton were Malcolm Macdonald, Alan Sunderland, David O'Leary, David Price, John Devine and the inclusion of Kevin Stead and Steve Gatting for their first full outings with 17-year-old Paul Vaessen on the substitutes' bench made for a very odd-looking Arsenal line-up…

With Frank Stapleton and Alan Sunderland firmly established as the club's first choice strike partnership – the pair would go on to play together in fifty three (eighty-eight percent) of

Arsenal's sixty fixtures during the 1978-79 season – and with Malcolm Macdonald to return from injury, first team opportunities for Paul were going to be hard to come by.

Consequently, Paul would find himself a fixture in the reserves, occasionally stepping back to help the youth side out. He was, after all, still only seventeen, still only an apprentice.

Nicky Sullivan played with Paul in the second string as well as the youth team.

"He was a big lad, a strong lad. He was always much bigger than everyone else. To be perfectly honest I think his physical strength made him shine. But he had two great feet, a good shot with both feet and he was determined. He worked ever so hard at his game. He was a determined lad. I wouldn't say he was one of these kids that skillfully shone but it was sheer guts and determination that got him through. He made it because he was big and he was strong and he could hold it up. I mean, his control for a big lad was excellent. And because of all that he got into the reserves quite young and he was always on the verge of things."

Islington Gazette, Friday 6th October 1978:

Arsenal Reserves 3 Bristol City Reserves 3 (Football Combination)

COACH Ian Crawford gave his youngsters a "rocket" after they were trailing 3-0 at the interval against Bristol City at Highbury on Saturday - and it worked wonders!...

Six-footer Paul Vaessen, who went on as a substitute in Arsenal's triumph against Leipzig, blasted home a rocket shot from the edge of the box much to the delight of Crawford.

Said Crawford: "Although originally a midfielder Paul has done a great job for me up front. His goal was a cracker and I feel he can go right to the top."

Doing his best to help him get there was Paul himself. He was now taking advantage of opportunities to ingratiate himself with the senior pros.

51

"Maybe it was because he liked older people but sometimes you thought 'What are your motives, Vas?'" says one former colleague.

"One time it was pre-season so we had a double session at London Colney, session in the morning, lunch, session in the afternoon. Well, we were all having lunch, first team, reserves, youth team, apprentices and Vas is off talking to Ian Crawford and Don Howe. So in the afternoon Vas went off on a cross-country run with them. You thought, 'What are you doing, Vas? What are you trying to prove? Are you trying to prove something to yourself, Ian or Don?' The result, of course, was that it made him stick out a little bit from us others. Really, I don't know the right word for it, but he was crawling up their arses a little bit, Vas."

Islington Gazette, Friday 6th October 1978:

Arsenal Youth 2 Derby County Youth 1 (Southern Junior Floodlit Cup, 1st Round)

Paul one to watch!

ARSENAL first team coach Don Howe ran the rule over the youngsters in this tough Southern Junior Floodlit Cup outing at Highbury on Tuesday and he must have been very impressed by striker Paul Vaessen.

The 17-year-old Vaessen who has been converted to the number nine shirt from midfield looks like he could soon be pressing Malcolm Macdonald and Frank Stapleton for their places.

Six-footer Vaessen from Bermondsey, possesses a nice touch of skill and a powerful shot. He is not easy to knock off the ball and was very sharp against an uncompromising Derby rearguard - especially in the first half.

Vaessen tired badly in the second half but coach Roger Thompson reckons he can play even better. "That is not the best Paul has played for me but there is no doubting he can make it big in soccer," he said.

It was Vaessen who headed Arsenal into a third minute lead from a Dermot Drummy corner.

And Vaessen lined up a last-minute matchwinner for substitute Nicky Terry after heading down a Jimmy Cansick centre.

In between, Derby had equalised in the 35th minute through Johnny Clayton...

Paul's reserve team strike partner for most of the 1978-79 season was Brian McDermott.

"With Paul I would have played up front. He would have been the target man more than anything and I was quick and would have been the one who worked off his flicks and his set play. He was the one to hold the ball up and I was the one who just worked around him. I think we had a good little partnership going really. We were quite competitive as well where the goals were concerned. He wanted to outdo me and I wanted to outdo him, not in a bad way, in a good way."

It was an argument McDermott usually won, not that either one of them was what you'd call prolific. During the previous season McDermott, a pacy, lively forward who could also operate on the wing, had hit fourteen goals at all levels to Paul's five. This season would see returns of seventeen and ten goals respectively.

Islington Gazette, Friday 26th January 1979:

Look out for McDermott and Vaessen

WATCH out for the names of teenage forwards Brian McDermott and Paul Vaessen. For they are pushing for places in the Arsenal first-team squad and could eventually save manager Terry Neill big money in the transfer market...

Six-footer Vaessen from Bermondsey came on as a sub in the UEFA Cup against Leipzig when still aged 16 and followed that up with a last-minute appearance against Hajduk Split at Highbury.

A big future is predicted for Vaessen whose father used to play for Chelsea and Millwall but he guardedly declares: "I'm not expecting too much at the moment and am just taking things as they come. I don't want to be disappointed."

Vaessen who is of Dutch origin, is trying to improve his game by working harder. "Everybody on the coaching staff is pushing me to do better."

McDermott may have been ahead in the goal stakes, but it was Paul who was making the headlines.

Islington Gazette, Friday 22nd February 1979:

Arsenal Reserves 1 Leicester City Reserves 1 (Football Combination)

Vaessen justice

A SUPERB Paul Vaessen goal in the 85th minute made sure that Leicester did not commit daylight robbery in this Football Combination game at Highbury on Saturday.

Vaessen calmly chested down a great cross field pass to the far post from Brian Sparrow and hammered home.

Yet earlier it was a nightmare for the Gunners regarding their finishing and Brian McDermott could quite easily have had five or six goals.

McDermott, Vaessen and Mike Pittaway suffered agonies as three shots hit the bar and two crashed against uprights.

After a goal-less first-half Leicester edged in front from a corner.

The first of his intake to gain first-team recognition, Paul was now ready to go that extra step with his all-important first start for the senior side.

Against, of all teams, Chelsea.

****

I reckon I was no more than six months old when it happened.

54

They just seemed to appear overnight.

I was used to laying all alone in my cot in my small, claustrophobic bedroom.

But I wasn't alone any more.

A large group of men, some of the toughest, ugliest and hairiest brutes you were likely to come across in the early seventies, were glaring silently and menacingly down at me from above.

Storey.

McLintock.

Radford.

George.

Rice.

Armstrong.

Graham.

Wilson.

McNab.

Simpson.

Kennedy.

Kelly.

Enough to give anybody a bad night.

But they were not there to give me nightmares.

Quite the opposite.

They had been deployed by my dad to protect me, look over me and guide me along a certain path in life, namely the one which lead to Avenell Road, London, N5 1BU.

And it worked.

It's just that it took a little time.

The 1971 league and cup 'double', celebrated in that poster Dad had put above my cot, came a little too soon for me, Charlie George's second half belter against Liverpool in the F.A. Cup Final coming just eighteen days after I was born.

But by the time of Arsenal's next triumph eight years later, I was ready.

The 12th May 1979 goes down as the day of my awakening, the day I was Arsenalised. It was the day I sat down with my dad and watched an Arsenal match for the first time.

I was immediately smitten with the brilliant yellow of our second choice colours, matching perfectly, as they did, the glorious sunshine of this cup final afternoon. I succumbed to the sorcery and wizardry of Brady, the dashing of Stapleton, the afro of Sunderland and the reassuring presence of Jennings. And I was captivated by the drama of the last minute victory which my dad and I played out over and over again in the back garden afterwards.

It was the day my dormant Arsenal feelings were released and as I lay in my bed that night with my 1971 godfathers still looking over me, I started planning my new life.

Dad started buying me *Scoop* and *Shoot!* magazines. I kept scrapbooks. I obsessively filled *Panini* sticker albums, only really caring over the Arsenal pages, and compulsively collected *Topps* bubblegum cards. Up alongside the 'double' winners went a new poster of the victorious 1978-79 squad courtesy of the *Daily Mirror* and back Dad came from work one day with an armful of programmes he'd been given by a bloke at work which I then studied so as to familiarize myself with the names of every Arsenal player.

And one of these, although it didn't feature that often, was Paul Vaessen.

Like me, Paul was just a spectator for Arsenal's triumph over Manchester United. Like 1971 had for me, 1979 came just a bit too soon for Paul. He was there at Wembley, though, as were all of Arsenal's reserves and apprentices. Cup finals were a day out for all the staff at the club.

However, just two days later Paul would make the starting line-up for Arsenal's final Division One outing of the season, a trip to Chelsea for whom, of course, he could so easily have been featuring.

The powerful and profligate Chelsea of the twenty-first century, ranked in 2012 as the seventh most valuable club in the world by Forbes Magazine, is unrecognisable from the bankruptcy-threatened outfit of the mid-to-late seventies. This stark contrast is conveyed perfectly by the matchday programme supplement for Arsenal's visit to Stamford Bridge, speaking to us from another age:

WE begin tonight's match with an apology to Chelsea and Arsenal supporters alike – in the form of regret that, for economy reasons, we have been unable to produce a completely new programme for a fixture that was originally scheduled to be played on January 1. It was snowed off that day and, again, postponed on March 21 because of Arsenal's involvement in the F.A. Cup.

In the days before Chelsea's financial difficulties, we would have compiled a fresh programme for tonight, but in prevailing circumstances we could not afford to scrap the original issue, and we hope you will understand the situation…

Chelsea were back then a team put together on a shoestring, a hotchpotch of youth team products such as Tommy Langley, Steve Wicks, Clive Walker and, perhaps the most prominent of all, Ray Wilkins, plus aging veterans including Peter Osgood and Ron 'Chopper' Harris. For another – Peter Bonetti – the Arsenal fixture would mark the last occasion on which he would keep goal for The Blues, his six hundredth football league appearance.

And as Bonetti made his final start, so Paul would make his first.

Manager Terry Neill's decision to rest Frank Stapleton and Alan Sunderland not only opened the way for Paul but it provided Malcolm Macdonald, Arsenal's top scorer in the previous two seasons, with the opportunity to test out his knee which had been badly damaged in the League Cup encounter at Rotherham just four games into the season.

Playing in the Chelsea side that evening was Gary Chivers. He remembers Paul as a young schoolboy training with the club.

"He came down to Chelsea, I think he must have been about thirteen. I do remember Paul. He was a tall lad for his age and, I'm not being funny, but you could tell he had some nice skill about him. He was a decent player. He was a very vocal lad, he was very chatty, a bouncy chap and he was a nice fella. I knew he went to Arsenal and that he signed for Arsenal because word gets around. I knew he was doing well in Arsenal's reserves and obviously he got his first team chance.

"I played in that match against Arsenal. We were already relegated so there wasn't a lot to play for except pride. We'd obviously had a crap season but I was intent on just playing well and doing well because I was a youngster breaking into the side.

"Anyway, it was a Monday night – we still had to play Manchester United on the Wednesday – and I played alongside Micky Droy at centre-half so I would have been playing opposite Paul."

"I remember that game because I was played out of position on the right side of midfield," recalls John Devine. "They were trying me out there.

"Anyway, we were sort of hung over because we'd just won the cup. It was a very, very poor game."

Islington Gazette, Friday 18th May 1979:

Chelsea 1 Arsenal 1 (Football League Division One)

On Monday they (Arsenal) completed their league programme with a 1-1 draw at Chelsea - Malcolm Macdonald scoring their leveller seven minutes from time.

Weakened Arsenal gave runouts to John Devine and 17-year-old striker Paul Vaessen.

Arsenal fan John Adams was at the match.

"I have been an Arsenal supporter since age seven and I remember Paul making his league debut at Stamford Bridge on 14th May 1979. It was the Monday evening after Arsenal had beaten Man United at Wembley to win the F.A. Cup 3-2 after the very late Alan Sunderland winner.

"It was the last game of the season for Arsenal and a Chelsea fan lent me his season ticket and I was directly behind Terry Neill's dug-out. I remember the Chelsea staff including manager Ken Shellito congratulating him (on winning the cup). Chelsea had already been relegated but they still had to go to Old Trafford for their final game.

"Arsenal fielded lots of reserves that night, which turned out to be the final match Malcolm Macdonald ever played. He had to retire due to a knee injury but he did not know that on the night. Brady, Rix and Sunderland were rested.

"I saw that Paul Vaessen was in the side and I thought, 'Two Bermondsey boys in a First Division match!' (I am fifty and lived in Bermondsey until aged thirty-six) as Trevor Aylott was playing up front for Chelsea and he got their goal in the 1-1 draw…I remember the match was not at all competitive and Pat Jennings laughing to Sammy Nelson when he conceded the goal."

Paul had a quiet match by all accounts and was unable to make much of an impression. But had it not been for some good manners on Paul's part things could have turned out quite different.

"Malcolm got the goal," says Leon, "but Paul said to me afterwards that he should have got that one. The ball came across and Malcolm shouted, 'Leave it, Vas. It's my ball' - which I guess he was entitled to do as the senior pro - and stuck it in the net. But Paul said he could have stroked it home himself. He was a bit put out about that one."

Islington Gazette, Friday 25th May 1979:

Home-grown kids best policy for success

With European competition in the Cup Winners' Cup next season the Gunners are anxious to add experience to their first-team squad with the signing of several top quality players.

But the cold truth is that they cannot compete with the big money that is available abroad...

So Neill is set to have to take a back seat in moves for the big names of soccer. Unless he is prepared to lower his sights, Arsenal are going to have to revert to what has made them successful in the last decade...home-grown players.

The only problem in that direction is that Arsenal could have to wait another 12 months to reap the reward of their new wave of talent and that could mean the difference in them losing out in the honours race...

Commenting on the chances of the Young Ones making it at Highbury, (Roger) Thompson added: "Next year is going to be very important for them. By the end of next season we could have five players ready for the first team."

And battling for those places could be Robbie Johnson, Chris Whyte, Mike Pittaway, Nicky Law, Dermot Drummy, Paul Davis, Brian McDermott, Brian Sparrow, Raphael Meade and Paul Vaessen.

Some of them will fail; some of them will become household names and some may even have love affairs with Arsenal.

STUCK IN A MOMENT

4
The Edge of Glory

"I am here for a purpose and that purpose is to grow into a mountain, not to shrink to a grain of sand."

Og Mandino

Roger Thompson likes to tell a story.

"We had a terrific scout at Arsenal based out in Dublin. He discovered Liam Brady, David O'Leary and John Devine. We used to have them over as schoolboys for a couple of weeks during school holidays, at Easter, Christmas and then in the summer. They used to train with the youth team at London Colney.

"Well one time this scout – his name escapes me – told Bertie Mee, who was manager of Arsenal at the time, that he had Brady, O'Leary all ready to come over but that one of the others had got injured and wouldn't be able to come. So he was stuck with a spare plane ticket. Well, rather than waste the ticket he told Bertie that there was this other young lad he knew of. He was a bit raw but he thought he'd send him over."

That young lad was Frank Stapleton.

And I for one am grateful Frank made that journey because by 1979, having witnessed his headed goal in that F.A. Cup Final victory over Manchester United at a sunbaked Wembley Stadium, he was my favourite.

And he wasn't a bad one to have.

I was only eight years old but you didn't have to be a genius to recognise that Frank was one of the very best strikers around.

And there was quite a bit of competition too at the time. Amongst others, there was Trevor Francis at Nottingham Forest, Andy Gray at Aston Villa, West Bromwich Albion's Cyrille Regis, Joe Jordan of Manchester United, Everton's Bob Latchford, Peter Withe at Newcastle United and John Wark of Ipswich Town.

61

"He was definitely one of the best around at the time," continues Roger. "His strength was in the air. He was unplayable in the air, he was incredible. And he worked at his game one hundred and ten percent. He would always be the one who would volunteer to come in in the afternoon to do extra training, to work on improving his foot skills. He was a good, honest lad, very much a family man, as he still is today. He was a great pro, he worked at keeping fit, he was always fit and his time-keeping was impeccable. A terrific pro who really just wanted to do well."

Former teammate Brian Talbot agrees.

"He was a very, very good player. He was good in the air, a one hundred percenter who worked his socks off for the team. He was unselfish and was an excellent team player. Really, he was top, top quality."

"He was a great team player, he was very easy to play with," confirms Stapleton's cohort Alan Sunderland. "When I first came into the side after I was signed from Wolves in November 1977 I played on the right side of midfield. Then when Malcolm Macdonald got injured at the beginning of the following season I was pushed up front and me and Frank just clicked. Like I say, he was just so easy to play with."

There was, therefore, probably nobody better than Frank from whom Paul could learn his trade.

But at the same time, Frank's excellent form and understanding with Sunderland was restricting Paul's first team opportunities.

"It was always going to be hard for Paul," comments John Devine. "He was seen primarily as understudy to Frank Stapleton but Frank was one of the best strikers in the business. He worked extremely hard, had fantastic heading ability and held the ball up and shielded it better than anyone in the league at that time. He was also, of course, a great goal scorer. He had Paul beaten in all departments really so it was always going to be difficult for Paul to break through. Paul therefore only really got a chance when there were injures or suspensions."

"I suppose you could say Paul was my understudy," says Stapleton. "When either I or Alan Sunderland didn't play they automatically brought him in. He was a nice lad. He was still trying to break through. He just wanted to do well, no different really to anyone else at that age. It was early days for him so he wasn't what you'd really call a regular member of the squad but he started travelling with us to provide cover in case someone fell ill over night or that sort of thing. In those days we only had a small squad and there was only one substitute. Like I say, he was pushing to get through, he was only seventeen, eighteen then but he became part of the lads, joining in the banter in the dressing room.

"Holding the ball up, that was his forte. He wasn't blessed with pace. He was a strong, physical lad, he was big but he was never going to be quick. Whether he would have gone on to be able to score twenty, twenty-five goals a season, well, we'll never know."

It was an injury to Sunderland which presented Paul with his first break of the new 1979-80 season.

By then Paul was a fully-fledged pro having signed his first professional contract in the close season at the same time as Nicky Law and another young burgeoning talent, Paul Davis.

"I came up against Paul in quite a few school and district competitions," recalls Davis. "I remember he was physically big at that age and that he was a good player. Then we just ended up at Arsenal together."

"We went up to Arsenal again to sign on," recalls Leon. "And again there was Terry Neill, Don Howe, obviously Paul and myself in the office. It was 14th July 1979.

"Once Paul had put pen to paper, Don started up, you know, 'Now you've got your spot in the dressing room, we're expecting lots of hard work and commitment' etc. You know, typical Don. But give him his due, Terry broke in and said that that was all very well but it was paramount they encouraged Paul's natural ability.

"I was so pleased, seeing him sign on with such a good club. It was a good moment for me. I thought, 'He's away.'"

"We were all so proud of him, so very proud," says Maureen. "He was a Bermondsey boy done good, wasn't he?"

As Paul was signing on, Malcolm Macdonald was on his way out. It was a portent of things to come for Paul.

"If I had one criticism of clubs at that time it was with regards to the treatment of players when they were released," relays Macdonald's close friend Roger Thompson. "On the day Malcolm

63

left, Fred Street, Terry Neill and the club doctor, Len Sash, all looked at his x-rays. They then called Malcolm in to Fred Street's office and basically told him he was never going to play again. He got up and left, walked down the corridor and as he went down the steps of Highbury, he didn't know whether to turn left or turn right. He was totally lost. He was totally confused as to where the rest of his life was going to take him. In those days players were trained for football, not for anything else. It took Malcolm a while to find his feet as a person again."

At least for Paul, Macdonald's departure meant less competition up front.

Islington Gazette, Friday 10th August 1979:

ARSENAL striker Malcolm Macdonald...quit soccer last week because of a troublesome knee...

Macdonald reluctantly gave up his 12-month fight to recover his fitness on the advice of a specialist after his right knee which has had three operations reacted on Arsenal's pre-season build-up in West Germany...

Despite Macdonald's departure, manager Terry Neill makes it clear he is not rushing into getting a replacement.

Although Arsenal have been connected with Yugolsav international Miodrag Kutadie, Peter Ward (Brighton), Derek Johnstone (Glasgow Rangers) and John Geddes (Ipswich), Neill is content to rely on promising youngsters like Paul Vaessen until he swoops for Mr Right.

Despite accompanying Stapleton et al on the first team squad's pre-season tour, Paul was back in the reserves when the new season came around. Scoring seven times in eight matches during September and October – his best spell as an Arsenal player – including one in Ted Drake's testimonial at Craven Cottage and another in the 10-2 reserve team victory at Queens Park Rangers, Paul was again attracting attention.

Islington Gazette, Friday 17th August 1979:

Vaessen could go Dutch

IT IS early days for Arsenal's teenage striker Paul Vaessen but there is a possibility that because of his Dutch origin he could represent Holland at international level in the future.

But Vaessen, who is not 18 until October, is not looking too far ahead and setting targets.

He is content to make gradual progress although he has already made his League debut in the final League outing of last season against Chelsea and came on for 15 minute spells in pre-season warm-ups against Munich and Duisburg. He was also one of the substitutes for the Charity Shield at Wembley on Saturday.

Six-footer Vaessen from Bermondsey admits he has enjoyed his "taster" outings in the first-team but adds: "I don't want to boost my hopes too much. I just want to take things as they come."

Vaessen is built on the lines of former Gunner John Radford and possesses the same touches of skill. He started his development at Highbury as a midfielder but for the majority of the last campaign he was used up front.

Although it is more fashionable these days for youngsters to plump for the less hostile region of the middle of the park, Vaessen does not mind being used as a target man.

"I don't mind playing up front as long as I'm enjoying myself," he says.

With the sudden retirement of Malcolm Macdonald and the smallness of Arsenal's squad, Vaessen is set to get more chances to progress in his career.

In the reserves, Paul renewed his partnership with Brian McDermott who had also hit a rich vein of form and, having made his first team debut as a substitute in the League victory over Bristol City in March, was also catching the eye of manager Terry Neill.

Islington Gazette, Friday 2nd November 1979:

Young Ones stake claim

DON'T forget young reserve strikers Brian McDermott and Paul Vaessen.

That was coach Roger Thompson's reminder to the critics who declare that Arsenal have no cover for first team pair Alan Sunderland and Frank Stapleton.

Teenagers McDermott and Vaessen have been grabbing the goals that have been responsible for the reserves great unbeaten run this season.

Says Thompson: "They would not let Arsenal down if they were called up for first team duty - they must be two of the most talented strikers in the country."

Brian McDermott (18) and Vaessen (17) had a taste of first team action in the last campaign when called up as substitutes…

Vaessen is a striker in the mould of former Gunner John Radford. He is 6ft and 12½ stone - hard running and very skillful.

Thompson calls him a gentle giant. "Paul has the best chest control of the ball in the club. He is strong, two-footed and very good in the air. He just needs to push himself a little more. He could become a very good player…"

Vaessen added: "I'm quite happy at my progress at Highbury but I would grab a first-team chance with both hands."

And that's exactly what Paul did when later that month he was drafted in alongside Stapleton for the visit of Brighton & Hove Albion in the League Cup fourth round replay.

Arsenal fan Emilio Zorlakki was there.

"It wasn't until he appeared alongside Frank Stapleton in that League Cup replay that Paul made an impact. Both strikers bagged a brace apiece and the crowd seemed genuinely pleased that young Paul had done so well in the 4-0 win."

66

Daily Mail, Wednesday 14th November 1979:

Highbury's new hero

Two-goal Vaessen smooths the way as Arsenal stroll it

Arsenal 4 Brighton 0 (League Cup 4th Round Replay)

ARSENAL'S ludicrously easy passage into the last eight of the League Cup last night was notable for one thing only: the two-goal show of rookie striker Paul Vaessen.

While hapless Brighton scour the British Isles for a striker, Arsenal have found one in their locker-room and he's cost them nothing. Vaessen, 18 last week, has a Dutch grandfather and comes from Bermondsey. Technically, he could play for Holland if he wants to.

He had played only one full League game before last night's fourth-round replay but his inexperience didn't show. He is an embryonic John Radford, tall, strong and purposeful.

Superb

That and his superb chest control make him an ideal target man, and having him in the side made a considerable difference to Arsenal's pattern of play in the absence of the injured Alan Sunderland.

Twice he brought roars from the 30,351 crowd when he turned and flashed in shots when the chance didn't seem to be there.

Brighton, with 15 goals conceded now in five games, were suckers for the far-post cross. All four goals came that way, with Frank Stapleton setting the pattern with a firm downward header in the third minute from Vaessen's right-wing cross for the first of his two.

But instead of piling forward with their usual urgency, some Arsenal players became casual.

Liam Brady, stirring himself from the lethargy, struck the bar

67

in the 39ᵗʰ minute, and from the corner that followed, John Devine crossed for Stapleton to head his second.

Arsenal were much more determined in the second half. Vaessen's first goal in the 55ᵗʰ minute was a far-post header from Brady's cross and his second in the 79ᵗʰ minute a blindside run and header from Devine's cross.

Said Arsenal manager Terry Neill: 'I am pleased for him. He is a big strong lad but he has a lot to learn.'

"I was at that match," says Leon. "They were two easy headers really, or rather he made them look easy. It was just like I'd taught him in the park. Any time the ball's going to come over, move away, go to the edge of the box, stand back and let the centre-half wait for the ball in the box and then, as the ball comes over, either cut in front of him or get up behind. That game in the League Cup against Brighton at Highbury, Paul did it exactly, he did it brilliantly."

Islington Gazette, Friday 16ᵗʰ November 1979:

Carry on Vaessen!

TWO-GOAL teenage new-comer Paul Vaessen is set for a further taste of first-team action for Arsenal against Everton at Highbury tomorrow (Saturday).

Following Vaessen's super start - he also laid on a goal for Frank Stapleton - in the League Cup against Brighton on Tuesday, manager Terry Neill now has the breathing space to give his injury victims more time to recover.

Neill was considering recalling John Hollins but he is likely to give him a little longer to get 100 per cent fit. Skipper Pat Rice and striker Alan Sunderland are ruled out for another two weeks.

But it was Vaessen, just 18, who became the talk of the North Bank fans with his display in his first full game at Highbury.

In the absence of Sunderland, six-footer Vaessen proved a superb stand-in. Admittedly, he has still got a lot to learn and the opposition was not up to much but as Neill pointed out: "You've still got to beat sides like Brighton and Paul played a leading part. We are all delighted for the lad. It was an encouraging start and he has now got all the incentive in the world to go and get better..."

Paul followed up that fine performance against Brighton with another impressive display against Everton in the League four days later. Frank Stapleton refused to accept the plaudits after his brace, instead talking enthusiastically about Paul and the fact that he may have just saved Arsenal half a million pounds in the transfer market.

Paul was clearly starting to make an impression on his first first team colleagues.

"He got very friendly with the first team players like Graham Rix and all these, he got friendly with them very quickly," states first team coach Don Howe. "He was a Londoner and he could chat away to anybody. He was always friendly. He used to come in, join in the banter. He got on well with all his team mates. He got on well with all of them, all of the staff. He was very open.

"He did things in a nice way. He couldn't have behaved any better. He was respectful, he was no trouble at all. I thought he just had a nice personality. There was no problem regarding Paul. He just came in, got on with it, did his work, did it the best he could, we'd have a chat if we needed to and off he'd go."

"He was a happy-go-lucky, easy-going lad who lacked a little bit of drive, needed pushing a little bit in training," says Paul's manager Terry Neill. "He was laid back but presented us with no real problems."

"He was good in the dressing room," Brian Talbot recalls. "He mixed well with the lads. Obviously he was a cockney and cockneys always have confidence. He knew he was a decent player and he wasn't fazed by playing with the first team."

"He was a bit cocky," says Alan Sunderland, "but not too cocky, though. He was a nice kid. All the young kids are cocky when they're coming through because they're confident in their own ability. And he had all the signs that he was going to make it. He was a nice kid, a nice kid."

Pat Jennings agrees. "He wasn't like a flash lad. To get into the team at that time obviously he was confident but he wasn't flash. He looked as if he was going to be a really great prospect."

Paul also impressed veteran John Hollins who had joined the Gunners in the summer.

"He was a lovely, innocent kid who just loved his football, wanted to be taught, wanted to be part of the team. Everybody liked him. He was a good lad."

The senior pros were also beginning to appreciate Paul's playing qualities.

"He might not have been the quickest," says Graham Rix, "but he had decent feet. He knew what he was doing and he could lead the line. And he was a nice player to play with because you'd play it in, he'd give it back, a bit like Frank Stapleton."

Islington Gazette, Friday 23rd November 1979:

Alan back for 'Pool?

Manager Terry Neill hopes to have regulars Alan Sunderland and John Hollins back on duty to face the Mersey men at Highbury tomorrow (Saturday)...

If Sunderland fails to recover in time, Neill won't hesitate to give another runout to promising youngster Paul Vaessen.

Says Neill: "We should not expect too much too soon from Paul but he is physically strong and would not let us down. He has not done badly with two goals from two games. I would not be scared to include him against Liverpool..."

Even though the reviews were encouraging, Paul found himself back amongst the reserves when Alan Sunderland was passed fit to resume first team duties against Liverpool. There he teamed up once again with his chief collaborator and partner-in-crime, Nicky Law, and the pair of tricksters who had a penchant for putting *Deep Heat* in their teammates' underpants and cutting up their socks, were still more than game for a laugh.

"That's how I remember Vas," says reserve team colleague Dermott Drummy. "Mop haired, denim jacket, playing air guitar in the dressing room to *Thin Lizzy's 'The Boys Are Back in Town'*. A bit of a headbanger with a little bit of a rebellious streak but we got on great. It just seems like yesterday really."

Far from being funny, however, Nicky Law was finding some of Paul's off the field tomfoolery increasingly disturbing.

"We were best mates," says Nicky Law, "but that was one of the differences between us, I suppose. The drugs. Paul was at it all the time but I had just one experience and it absolutely frightened the f--king life out of me and I never did it again.

"There was this nightclub in Deptford. I went in there one night with him and had a few drinks and I was absolutely f--ked. He said, 'Come here, I'll sort something out.' Now I was pretty naïve and foolish really but he said, 'Have a go at this,' and I took a dab of it with my finger. Well, I only had a bit and I was knocking them back like I'd never get a drink again! I couldn't get it down me quick enough! It must have been speed because it would have enabled you to do things that normally you couldn't physically possibly do.

"And I paid big time for that. I was in bed all the Sunday and my mum had to ring in on the Monday and Tuesday because I still couldn't get out of bed! It had enabled me to drink that much. I was in a right tackle.

"But in a way it was a good thing because I knew that never ever would I have ever done it again. As I say, it knocked the shit out of me.

"He was into the weed too. He was always on it, always on the smoke. When we used to go out in the day he was on it, you know. Thankfully, I wasn't.

"He came in to training plenty of times under the influence too. On the Saturday when we used to go over to London Colney for our youth games he'd be pissed then. He'd obviously been out drinking or something. Sometimes he'd be sat there and he'd be almost moronic, like he was out of his head.

"He used to come over to Catford now and again and we used to go into a snooker hall and play some snooker there. I mean, we'd be in there until four o'clock in the morning playing cards and Paul would disappear every now and then for a piss but it would be the longest piss you'd ever known. He was obviously going in and having a line or whatever.

"I think away from the football and when he was away from me he was obviously moving around in those sorts of circles. After training and games I would drop him off at London Bridge.

Sometimes I'd go back with him to Bermondsey and you could see that he was in with the wrong people, like the chavs of those days. It was just the whole environment, you know, and I didn't feel comfortable in it.

"It's difficult because, like I say, we were best mates but when I went to Barnsley a few years later it was probably a good move for me, not only professionally but because if I hadn't then I might have still been knocking about with him and maybe…"

****

As well as appearing for the reserves, Paul still qualified (by being under eighteen years old at the start of the season) to play in youth team competitions such as the F.A. Youth Cup and the South East Counties League.

"I think," says Roger Thompson, "that the psychology behind putting young players who had had a taste of the first team back in amongst the reserves and youths was to keep their feet on the ground. I would say that, knowing Paul's personality, it would have done him some good."

It also, of course, gave youth boss Terry Burton the opportunity to utilize a senior player and bolster his side for those important youth league and cup clashes.

"He always had a smile on his face," recalls Burton. "There was a cheekiness about him really. He was a typical South London lad and always looking to get up to something or the other, you know? Not in a nasty way but always with that bit of cheekiness about him. He was a real character.

"As a player he was very skillful. It was all about his touch. He could lay the ball off, bring others into the game. I suppose, as Roger says, he was following in the mould of people like Ray Kennedy. Ray wasn't particularly quick but he was a very technical player and could play well with his back to goal and I think that's what Arsenal saw in Paul, a typical centre-forward that Arsenal had produced a few of in that era."

Helping out the youth side, Paul would link up with emerging talents such as Raphael Meade, David Cork and young goalkeeper, Gary Lewin.

"Paul was a year older than me," says Meade. "As I was developing, I started to play with him up front for the reserves. He was a good chap, a good player. He was a different player to me. He was one to hold the ball up. Me, I was quick, making the runs. Paul was a bit more static, a bit slower. But I got on pretty well with Vas really."

"Paul was just pushing for a place in the first team and I was a sixteen year old apprentice," recalls Lewin. "I was a young kid and you looked up to the young pros. He came across as very confident, very bubbly. Typical London lad."

David Cork relays how Paul and company helped him settle in to London life.

"When I came down to Arsenal from Doncaster there was a group of them, the majority of them from London, and they were at it all the time with the jokes and the messing. It was a different world from where I came from. It was so loud and they were all taking the piss out of each other and Paul was one of the front runners. The thing that I enjoyed about it all is that these lads made you feel included, even though they were taking the mickey out of you. Being an outsider, being a bit quieter it helped you acclimatize and eventually you got the humour. It was different but it helped.

"But what I also remember with Paul is that, especially later on, if you were ever alone with him you'd see a different side of him, a bit more serious. He'd want to talk to you about different things, about what your life was really like."

Paul spent the next three months out of the first team but as the season progressed into March, it was becoming apparent that this could possibly turn out to be a mammoth season for the Gunners. Doing well in the League, Arsenal were also through to the quarter-finals of both the F.A. and European Cup Winners' cups where they would face Watford and Gothenburg respectively. Terry Neill would consequently need to draw upon all the resources at his disposal, starting with Paul Vaessen who was called up in the absence of the injured Alan Sunderland for the disappointing nil-nil draw with Bristol City at Highbury on 11th March. Neill retained his services four days later for the 3-0 victory over Manchester City at Maine

Road and the tie in Gothenburg on 19th. The latter was memorable not for the match but, as Leon relays, for an incident which occurred as Arsenal arrived in Gothenburg.

"There was only them on the plane, the players, officials, staff and press. Paul said that as they were coming into Gothenburg Airport they were circling a bit so everybody knew there was something amiss. Then they banked and could see the ambulances and fire engines waiting down on the runway. What it was was that the pilot had gone to put the undercarriage down but wasn't sure whether it was actually down or not because it wasn't showing as such in the cockpit. So he had to fly low so they were close enough for the control tower to get a visual. Obviously the skipper told them all to get into crash positions. Imagine what they must have felt like!"

The Gunners eventually landed and survived to play out a rather dour stalemate against Sven-Goran Erikkson's side but with the first leg having ended 5-1 in their favour, Arsenal were safely through to a semi-final clash with Italian giants Juventus. By now they also knew they were up against First Division champions-elect Liverpool in what would turn out to be one of the most monumental ties in F.A. Cup history.

Before then Arsenal faced three League outings in nine days, Paul playing a part in each one, making the starting line-up for the 1-0 win at Everton where he partnered Alan Sunderland and then coming on as a substitute in the 2-1 loss at Norwich City and again in the 1-1 draw with Southampton on 5th April. Then, just two days later on Easter Monday, came the small matter of a North London derby at White Hart Lane.

Arsenal were in the middle of an absolutely relentless fixture schedule and there were few within the game who seemed sympathetic to their cause.

Daily Express, Monday 7th April 1980:

Brutal to Arsenal

ARSENAL attack a six-day assault course today which ought to be monitored by the Royal Humane Society.

Their coach Don Howe believes that anyone interested in the preservation of human well-being would not have subjected a football team to the pressures his players face this week.

Relaxed

The Gunners meet Spurs at White Hart Lane today, Juventus in the European Cup Winners' Cup on Wednesday and Liverpool in the F.A. Cup on Saturday.

And today they parade their 18 senior professionals to select 11 fit and able to go on duty at Tottenham.

They will be watched from the packed White Hart Lane stands by the Juventus players who fly into Gatwick at lunchtime, quietly relaxed.

Howe says: "If the Arsenal players were horses the RSPCA would already have intervened. It's a crazy situation which is cruel on the players.

"I feel our game against Spurs and our semi-final against Liverpool might have been switched to give us every chance of success in Europe against the Italians.

"We could have played Liverpool any time in the last two weeks and there would have been no trouble finding an alternative date for the Spurs game.

"We want English teams to succeed in Europe yet we seem to put as many obstacles as we can in their way."

Arsenal will almost certainly be without Sammy Nelson and David Price today and manager Terry Neill might make other changes to rest key players for the ECWC semi-final.

Dino Zoff and company would witness a superb Sunderland strike at Tottenham and, as if by way of a warning, they would also see a headed goal by a young, lanky kid with a bubble perm who they'd never heard of.

"I remember," says Liam Brady, "Paul playing at White Hart Lane against Spurs in that derby match when we put out a lot of, let's say, squad players rather than first team players because we were playing Juventus a couple of days later and he played and he scored."

Fan Emilio Zorlakki was there. "Paul scored the first goal in our 2-1 win. It was a towering header from a corner at the Paxton

75

Road end to put us 1-0 up. The Arsenal fans were tormenting the Spurs fans with chants of 'Arsenal Reserves!'"

"I remember that," say Jill Smith, Arsenal employee and fan. "We beat the Spurs with six reserves!"

"It was a match that I shouldn't have been at," admits Arsenal supporter Dean Goodman. "A Spurs friend of mine couldn't attend so he let me have his ticket. Unfortunately, it was at the seated corner of the Paxton Road end of the ground in amongst the home Spurs fans.

"During the game, Paul played well, linking fluidly with the other players, in particular I think it was with Talbot and Sunderland."

"Paul played extremely well," recalls John Hollins who played in midfield that afternoon.

Paul's goal may well have had something to do with his dad.

"I was sitting watching the TV and the scores were rolling over and I said to Maureen that I'd love to see 'Tottenham 0 Arsenal 1 – scorer Vaessen.' This is true. Honestly. All of a sudden it rolled over and it went 'Tottenham 0 Arsenal 1 – scorer Vaessen.' That's just how it went."

"He is fondly remembered for being in the right place, at the right time," continues Dean Goodman, "to enable a classic victory that for me was worth the hassle of sitting with the numpties."

It was a pretty poor affair and was probably memorable to most present for the violence on the terraces and the three Molotov cocktails which burst against a wall during the match.

Next up, just two days later, was the first half of a titanic clash with the Old Lady of Turin, Juventus.

It was true she had seen better days. After all, it was not becoming of one of her stature, for one so used to the good life, to be seen scrapping away with her inferiors at the foot of *Serie A* as she had been doing just months before. But that was all forgotten now. Since then she had gathered herself, regained her composure and taken the nation to the brink of European glory. Admittedly, she would probably much rather have been spending the evening competing for the more prestigious, coveted and, thus far, elusive European Cup. But for now the Cup-Winners' Cup would have to do.

La Signora was, after all these years, still *La Fidanzata d'Italia*, 'Italy's girlfriend', having first earned the moniker back in

76

the 1930s when her dominance in the form of five national championships first earned her the adoration of not only Turin but of cities throughout Italy. Meanwhile, over in England, Arsenal's five title triumphs during the same decade had earned them similar national respect but, in contrast, nowhere near the same degree of domestic affection.

Arsenal and Juve had only ever met on two previous occasions, prestigious friendlies played at Highbury in November 1958 and a return match some six months later in Turin. The cordiality of those two meetings was, however, not repeated when the sides came together competitively for the first time as European Cup-Winners' Cup semi-finalists on Wednesday 9th April 1980.

With Nantes and Valencia also in the last four, both sides were in agreement about one thing. "We would rather not have met Arsenal," declared Juve's star midfielder Marco Tardelli on the eve of the first leg. "It is the toughest tie we could have been given."[4]

By the same token, Arsenal knew they were in for a tough evening and were somehow, in incredibly their fifty-seventh game of the season, going to have to find the energy and guile to not only breach one of the most impenetrable defences in world football, featuring the likes of Zoff, Claudio Gentile, Antonio Cabrini and Gaetano Scirea, but at the same time stop the likes of Tardelli, Franco Causio and the original 'white feather', Roberto Bettega, from grabbing goals at the other end. These were, after all, the individuals who had formed the bulk of the *squadra azzura* which had finished fourth in the 1978 World Cup Finals in Argentina and would go on to capture the crown in Spain in two years time.

"The first leg, you know, was a very hard fought game at Arsenal," says Liam Brady. "Juventus, as we expected, played very defensively and we were finding it hard to break them down. The Italians were, after all, the best defenders in the world."

But the severity of *i bianconeri's* negative approach took some by surprise.

"It was a real eye opener," says Graham Rix, "because they were a top, top team, eight Italian internationals and they came to our place and Highbury was, you know, sizzling as you can imagine, close to the pitch which was something they weren't necessarily used to. And they just killed the game, man-to-man marked everybody. Gentile just followed me everywhere, Tardelli followed Brady

77

everywhere and that's how they played and I thought, 'They haven't even come to play.' Eventually, of course, they nicked a goal and went on to get a 1-1 draw."

What also came as something of a shock, however, was the severity and brutality with which their tactics were executed, encapsulated in one particularly memorable tackle. "I remember that Roberto Bettega committed a really vicious foul on David O'Leary after about twenty minutes or so," recalls Pat Mooney who was reporting on his first game for the local *Hampstead & Highgate Express*. "It was really one of those horrible tackles," a challenge which was described by the *Sun* under the headline, 'SAVAGES!' In his post-match interviews Gunners' boss Terry Neill would call the tackle disgraceful and comment to an Italian journalist, "You must be ashamed. It must be difficult admitting you are an Italian tonight," all of which acted to antagonise the Italians in the run-up to the second leg. Somehow, though, Bettega had stayed on the pitch, fortunately as it turned out for the Gunners as it was he who, with time fast running out, nodded into his own net for Arsenal's equaliser after Cabrini's opener had earned the visitors a vital away goal.

Paul was used as a substitute for John Devine on the night but didn't make it on to the pitch when the Gunners took on The Reds of Liverpool in the F.A. Cup semi-final at Hillsborough on the Saturday. There was no let-up for Arsenal as the game ended in an inconvenient draw, necessitating a replay the following Wednesday where an Alan Sunderland goal earned Arsenal a 1-1 draw at Villa Park. And then – for the third time in eight days – Arsenal met the Merseysiders again. This time it was a League encounter at Anfield where the two sides cancelled themselves out yet again in another 1-1 standoff, Paul having another bit-part, coming off the bench to replace Frank Stapleton.

With the fixtures coming thick and fast and resources stretched to the absolute limit - Arsenal would play a total of ten games in April alone - Paul was retained in the first-team set-up to provide much-needed relief and support to first choice strikers Frank Stapleton and Alan Sunderland.

But it wasn't until the evening of Wednesday 23rd April 1980 that Paul's contribution would truly be appreciated.

****

78

London Evening Standard, Tuesday 8th April, 1980:

After a training session this morning, Juventus manager Giovanni Trapattoni revealed that his biggest fear was Arsenal's aerial power…"I am a bit apprehensive about their ability in the air," he said.

And so, as it would turn out, he should have been.

STUCK IN A MOMENT

5
If I Can Dream

"If one advances confidently in the direction of his dreams, and endeavours to live the life which he has imagined, he will meet with success unexpected in common hours."

Henry David Thoreau

If you had happened to turn on your television at 10.30pm on the evening of Wednesday 23rd April 1980 you may have caught the second half of BBC1's production of *King Henry V*. Over on BBC2 you might have seen the mercurial Alex Higgins dispatching Tony Meo 10-9 in the first round of the World Snooker Championship at the Crucible Theatre in Sheffield. Alternatively, you may have opted for ITV where, sandwiched between the news – the world was anxiously awaiting America's next move in the diplomatic crisis with Iran over the 52 Americans being held hostage in Tehran - and an episode of US police sitcom *Barney Miller* starring Hal Linden, you would have found *Mid-Week Sports Special*. Introduced by Brian Moore, the programme featured gymnastics and football. Suitably for St. George's Day, the matches covered involved English sides attempting to conquer formidable foreign opponents, Nottingham Forest travelling to Amsterdam to face Ajax in the European Cup semi-final second leg, and Arsenal visiting Turin for their encounter with Juventus.

I, of course, didn't see any of it. At least I have no recollection of having done so. In fact, it seems that, for whatever reason, I let Arsenal's return leg against Juve pass me by.

There is nothing in the memory banks, nothing in my scrapbooks. Nothing. In fact, I'm pretty sure I was tucked up in bed by nine o'clock. Maybe I was ill or perhaps just completely oblivious to the fact that the Gunners were playing one of their most colossal fixtures in years.

Of course, I may have chosen to ignore the match, too

81

terrified to listen or watch. After all, not many people on the planet gave Arsenal much of a chance. I guess I would subsequently have found out the score from Dad in the morning and felt sufficiently guilty for not having been there for my team.

Somehow, I need to make amends, I need to go back in time and be present, be there. I need to feel part of that historic night. And so I am here at the British Film Institute to put things partially right.

It is here I have arranged a private screening of Arsenal's clash with *le zebre*. And in stark contrast to the bedlam of the *Stadio Comunale* and the general commotion of the Santa Rita district of Turin on that evening some thirty years ago, I am sat in perfect isolation in a viewing booth down in the depths of the BFI Research Viewing Services basement archives at 21, Stephen Street, West London, waiting for the technician to retrieve the tape…

****

"For the trip to Juventus," Maureen recalls, "he wanted his Italian trousers - they had to be cleaned, two pairs - his Italian shoes, his silk shirts. I wasn't allowed to wash or iron them. They had to be sent to the cleaners in case I shrunk them. In my front room I had a big walk-in cupboard with all his shirts, trousers, jumpers, you name it. He had his suits, his Arsenal jacket from Saville Row for when he travelled. Everything had to be kept up-to-date, just so, because I never knew when he was going to come home, throw his keys and money on the table and say, 'Right, I'm off to Italy and I need such and such.'"

Over at the *Hampstead & Highgate Express*, Pat Mooney had a proposition for his boss.

"The second leg was beautifully set up. The first leg was tremendously exciting for me. It was my very first match for the paper. Some time after, I marched into the Editor's office and suggested that I thought it would be a great idea if I covered the second leg. And he agreed! I think we were the only local paper there."

As Arsenal flew out of Luton Airport on the morning of

82

Monday 21ˢᵗ April, David O'Leary and Liam Brady posing cheerily for the cameras with a couple of Aer Lingus stewardesses, the squad were in high spirits despite warnings from Juventus general manager Pietro Giuliano about the unfriendly welcome awaiting them and their supporters in Turin.

"The atmosphere will be very tense," said Juve's supremo. "Feelings have been inflamed by newspaper reports of what was said at Highbury. We fear our fans may be planning something for Arsenal. They are very angry that Juventus players have been called animals. Now we will need extra police to guard Arsenal in their hotel and on the way to the stadium, but we can't protect their supporters. They will be easily picked out by their red-and-white colours and they won't get a friendly reception. The reception for Arsenal's officials won't be too friendly either. They will be greeted politely but coolly."[5]

Arsenal were unable to stay in Turin because there was a motor show on. Instead, they made camp in the bucolic calm of Asti some twenty five miles from the city.

"That's right, we stayed in a hotel in Asti," confirms physiotherapist Fred Street, "which was where Juve had their training ground. It was a hotel with a sports complex attached, up on a hill. We went there with England when we played in Turin in the 1990 World Cup Finals. I think that's where Juve used to go the night before a game."

The following day was spent training at their retreat and then later on there was a visit to the stadium.

"I remember that evening really well," reveals Graham Rix. "I remember that evening we sat down and it was magnificent food, as you can appreciate, and I remember Don and Terry ordering bottles of wine and they came round and poured the wine out for the lads, as if to say, 'It's just another game, chaps. Don't worry about it, you're doing great. It's just another game,' and we all had a glass of wine which was unheard of in those days.

"So we went to bed - I was sharing with Liam - and then the next day – the day of the match - we trained in the morning and got some more sleep."

Back home, the British press were busy reiterating the size of the task faced by Arsenal.

Daily Mail, 23rd April 1980:

Just win or bust!

Arsenal have to succeed where 32 other top European clubs have failed over the last decade if they are to reach the final of the European Cup-Winners' Cup.

They must beat the formidable Italian opposition of Juventus in front of a fanatical Turin crowd.

That is the enormity of their semi-final task here tonight, quite apart from the antagonism lingering from the first leg at Highbury.

Only FC Twente of Holland, in 1975, have beaten Juventus at any time over the last ten years in a European match in Turin.

On the four occasions Juventus have been held at home since 1970, three have been goalless draws – a scoreline which would satisfy the Italians completely tonight for they would be through on the away-goals-rule after their 1-1 draw in London.

'It was never going to be easy here, but, in cold terms we need a 1-0 win. That would be enough,' said Arsenal manager Terry Neill last night...

"I travelled over on the morning," recalls Pat Mooney, "got in bright and early into Turin. It was a really crisp, sunny morning and the thing that struck me was how many Arsenal fans were already there. I did the usual things and got to the stadium quite early, made sure I had my press pass sorted out and all that and the Arsenal fans were in there already. They were high up in the stands, up in the clouds."

Peggy Goulding was there supporting the Gunners. "We were high up, I think as high as you could possibly go."

Peter Kirkwood had also travelled to Italy.

"Where we were, you were supposed to be sitting. We'd been told these were seats but they were like large steps so everyone just stood."

The Arsenal coach left Asti late in the afternoon, arriving at the stadium some ninety minutes before the 8pm kick-off.

"I can remember the black and white shirts and scarves

outside the ground," recalls John Devine, in at left-back for the injured Sammy Nelson. "The fans were really fanatical. There were a few things bouncing off the windows of the coach. It was like that going through the town right to the stadium. I remember that vividly. And we were getting all the gestures, as you can imagine, letting us know in no uncertain terms that we were goners, you know? Obviously, the crowd were in good spirits, the Juventus fans. They obviously thought they had it in the bag. To them the game was done and dusted because of their track record. They thought they would just hold out and they'd be in business."

"There were massive corridors inside the stadium," Graham Rix remembers, "and it was quite a walk to the pitch. Beforehand we went out on to the pitch. Me and Liam were looking at the pitch, at this fantastic, massive stadium around us and Liam actually said to me, 'What about playing here every week?' I said, 'Yeah, not bad.'" Just a few months later Brady would, of course, be a Juventus player.

John Hollins was on the bench. "We got a lovely welcome(!) when we came out but there was good support for Arsenal as well."

"The atmosphere was f--king electric," recalls Alan Sunderland.

"It was incredible," John Devine continues. "The stadium was full and you had all the flares and fireworks going off which was unseen really in English football."

Pat Mooney had been in position for some time and was not necessarily anticipating an exhilarating, open contest.

"If you'd asked me at the time how the game would pan out, I'd have said, well, the Italians will sit back because from their point of view they had no need to attack. They knew a 0-0 would get them through."

Meanwhile, in a small studio in Euston Road, London, commentator Martin Tyler was preparing to watch the live feed of the match on a monitor.

"ITV had the highlight rights and we didn't show very much of it on the programme. I think we only bought the rights to five minutes or something like that. I had been to the first leg. I'm sure that we all left that game, the first game, thinking that that was it for Arsenal. Even within the building that I was in, there was no great thought that there was going to be a story here."

****

The technician is back with the tape.

"Did you know," he informs me, "that Forest played on the same night? Lost 1-0 to Ajax but still went through to the final. I pulled the tape out and watched it myself. Not interested in Arsenal, me."

He is a chirpy chap, you know, 'salt of the earth,' and despite his aversion to Arsenal, he obviously wants to talk more.

He asks me why I want to see the match, am I a journalist, what the score was, was the game any good?

I am impatient to watch the match.

Eventually, he turns to leave but not before he lands a bit of a body blow.

"You've only got the second half there. The first half was never recorded."

****

"Quite frankly," states Pat Mooney, "the first half was pretty poor. I don't think there were many genuine chances."

It was panning out just as Pat and so many others had predicted.

"They didn't really come out and play," recounts Steve Walford who was one of Arsenal's substitutes on the night. "They were sitting back and just didn't want to concede a goal."

"They were playing for 0-0, definitely," agrees Graham Rix. "It was the same as at Highbury, Gentile following me about and it was really difficult because we didn't come up against that very often."

Liam Brady was attempting to pull the strings in the Arsenal midfield.

"We went to Turin with a very difficult task, you know, because Juventus had a great European record. But because it was 1-1 I think it kind of tricked them out a bit. They again played defensively and invited us on."

86

"I couldn't believe their attitude that night," says Pat Jennings. "I couldn't believe their mentality because they were such a good team."

"They had a star-studded team, practically all internationals, all with European experience," recalls John Hollins.

"But we didn't have a bad side either."

****

I am alone.

I get my notebook and pen out of my bag.

I am ready.

I ensure I am concentrating.

I don't want to miss a thing.

In front of me is a rather prehistoric looking VCR. As I insert the tape, put on the headphones and press play, I feel sickly excited. In the same way I became obsessed as a six year old with *Star Wars* before I actually saw it, I feel, I know I'm about to watch for the first time another great drama, an epic, a blockbuster, a grand production about which I already know so much...

EPISODE ONE: A NEW HOPE

Cast

Juventus FC	Arsenal FC
Dino Zoff	Pat Jennings
Antonello Cuccureddu	Pat Rice
Antonio Cabrini	John Devine
Giuseppe Furino	Brian Talbot
Claudio Gentile	David O'Leary

87

STUCK IN A MOMENT

Gaetano Scirea	Willie Young
Franco Causio	Liam Brady
Claudio Prandelli	Alan Sunderland
Roberto Bettega	Frank Stapleton
Roberto Tavola	David Price
Pietro Fanna	Graham Rix

Supporting Cast

Domenico Marocchino	Paul Vaessen
	John Hollins

Produced by

Giovanni Trapattoni and Terry Neill

Directed by

Erich Linemayr

With a soundtrack performed by the supporters of Juventus FC and Arsenal FC and narration by Martin Tyler.

Scenario

The setting is Stadio Comunale, Turin, Piedmont, Italy. The players of both teams – Juventus FC and Arsenal FC – return to the field following half-time to a cacophony of noise. They assume their positions for kick-off, Juventus 'keeper Dino Zoff defending the goal at the tunnel end. Jill Smith, Peggy Goulding, Peter Kirkwood and Vic Wright are amongst the five hundred Arsenal supporters singing defiantly high up in the stands at the opposite end but remain relatively inconspicuous in a crowd of

88

66,386. On the bench is Terry Neill and his staff, and the substitutes including John Hollins and Paul Vaessen. Austrian referee Erich Linemayr restarts the action. Back in South Bermondsey, the Vaessens are crowded round the radio listening keenly to Radio 2's *European Soccer Special*, as are fans Tom O'Brien, Kevin Welling, Simon Scott-Daniels and Gary Humphrey. All are fully aware that Arsenal must score during the second half to have any chance of progressing to the final on 14th May 1980 in Brussels....

****

PAT MOONEY: The second half was the same.

(45th minute)...Real determination is what Arsenal need in this second half...still 0-0 on the night and 1-1 on aggregate which means by virtue of that away goal scored at Highbury, Juventus still on course for a place in the final...Arsenal may not be too dissatisfied with the way the first forty-five minutes went. It was important that they got a foothold on this second leg and didn't give away anything early on and I would suspect we'll see more ambition from them in the second half...

GRAHAM RIX: We kept going, we're trying to score obviously, typical of how we played at that time. We had some good players.

...(49th minute)...Not a classic match in terms of goalmouth incident but a truly fascinating contest between two of the greatest names in European football...

JOHN HOLLINS: The atmosphere was tense, very tense.

...(52nd minute)...Arsenal certainly giving a workmanlike and organised performance, needing a cutting edge now...(56th minute)...Far more cut and thrust, though, about this second half, as indeed it has to be from the Arsenal point of view...0-0 is no good to Arsenal...

TERRY NEILL: It was the most patient performance that we'd played and Don and I felt, rightly or wrongly, that we'd got a button on the Italian's mentality. They'd got the away goal so they wouldn't be coming out that much. So we decided it wouldn't favour us to go gung-ho and them hit us on the break. So we had to display immense patience but we had the team, we had the players.

DON HOWE: It was a very even game, it was very even and tactically we were doing well the way we were playing. At that time every Italian team you played, they played man-for-man and a sweeper and we knew what they would do and that we had the tactics to cope with it.

...(58th minute)...And Arsenal continue to show patience in the early part of their build-up, certainly haven't been guilty of panicking and playing in a lot of high crosses which favour the defenders...

BRIAN TALBOT: What surprised me about the second leg was how defensive they were really, how negative their tactics were. Their tactics from the kick-off were to keep possession, keep the ball and not exploit the situation.

...(59th minute)...Well, Pat Jennings really hasn't been threatened, the contest being fought out in the middle of the field...and Scirea taking his time over the free-kick, helped out by some gamesmanship by Cuccureddu...

BRIAN TALBOT: If they'd had scored a goal it would have been curtains for us.

...(62nd minute)...and the shot skimming over from Gentile!...It's been a rare effort at goal...(63rd minute)...Arsenal caught ball-watching a little and the shot from Prandelli was fierce and true 'til it struck a defender and went behind for a corner...(64th minute)...it almost came for Tavola, a rare skirmish around the Arsenal goal...

BRIAN TALBOT: They were renowned then in the seventies and eighties for being the best defensive players in the world and I think they were accepting that, as long as they held their position and kept their formation, we wouldn't break them down. And to be fair, we couldn't.

...(64th minute)...Here's Brady as Juventus continue to frustrate Arsenal...They're prepared to let Brady have it from these sorts of positions...Now the challenges go in, forcing Brady to play it back to Rix and again it breaks down...(67th minute)...Arsenal don't really have a great deal of natural width in their attack and they haven't been able to get beyond Juventus on the flanks, looking more often to try and work the one-twos on the edge of the box and Juventus really taught the world how to defend against that sort of thing...Anxious times down in that Arsenal dugout...(69th minute)...Here's Brady and there are bound to be gaps opening up for Juventus to try and exploit because Arsenal still haven't solved their problem which is to get a goal...worth reemphasising that 0-0 is not enough. Juventus lead still by the goal at Highbury...(72nd minute)...Price! Zoff had a good view of it from David Price, a rare direct shot from Arsenal and from the sort of range that will suit Juventus. Nothing has been really worked inside that penalty area...

STEVE WALFORD: We had a lot of the ball without really creating anything.

...(73rd minute)...Rix, turns away from Sunderland and another avenue closes up for Arsenal...So often Arsenal forced to just play the ball back and indeed allowed to do that...So here's Brady as Arsenal probe forward again...looking for a chink in this Juventus armour...

TERRY NEILL: The longer the game went on and with the clock ticking down, we had to make some decisions.

LIAM BRADY: We attacked for most of the game but because they were such expert defenders they looked like they were going to see it through. And then, as a last throw of the dice, Terry sent Paul on with about ten minutes to go.

...(77th minute)...We're inside the final quarter of an hour. On the night, Juventus 0 Arsenal 0...(78th minute)...Arsenal looking to make

perhaps a double substitution...and Paul Vaessen is coming on for David Price...

TERRY NEILL: So we threw Paul on and had a quick word about getting some crosses in.

FRED STREET: Well, Don Howe, Terry Neill and me were sat on the bench and it was all over. It was nil-nil so we were going out on the away goals rule. So Don said, 'Let's give young Vaessen a run so he can tell his grandchildren he played in a European semi-final.'
    In those days the trainer did it all, held the numbers up and all the rest, there was none of that fourth official nonsense. You'd hold the number up, call the referee and put the player on. So I'm saying to Paul, 'Come on, get yourself ready,' and he's nervous, getting his socks on and all that and he's taking a bloody age to do it, you know? He was quite funny, a jack-the-lad. I'm not being critical. He was a cockney jack-the-lad, that's what he was, but even jack-the-lads like Charlie George used to get nervous before games and he was all bravado. But, you know, they're performing in front of the public and for a young kid, well, this was a European bloody cup semi-final!
    So anyway I was saying to him, 'Come on Paul! The game will be over if you don't get on in a minute! He'll blow the whistle in a second!'

PAUL: Coach Don Howe sent me on with about fifteen minutes left. I remember him saying, "Go on Paul, knock one in for us." And I replied, "Yeah, okay."[6]

MAUREEN: We could only listen to it on the radio. There was me, my husband, Lee, my dad and a few others.

LEE: It wasn't televised. It was on the radio. We had a few people round and all of a sudden we heard that he was coming on and we all cheered. We were going, 'Yeah! Come on Vas!' My dad said, 'Come on then, get us some beers here,' so off I went to the kitchen to get his beers.

GRAHAM RIX: Terry took David Price off, put Sundy out on the

92

right and put Vas up with Frank.

...(80th minute)...And Fanna pulling it back! And the miss of the game from Tavola! Well, chances really have been few and far between but Roberto Tavola had the opportunity there to put this game out of Arsenal's reach...Meanwhile, they (Arsenal) send for another substitute, Brian Talbot going off and John Hollins coming on...

JOHN HOLLINS: I was brought on to try and shut the door, to try and stop them coming down the left-hand side.

...(81st minute)...The Juventus crowd now sensing triumph...Nine minutes left...Swung in by O'Leary and Zoff, who even though Arsenal have had more possession in this second half, still really restricted to straight forward bread and butter work, catching crosses and fielding a couple of straight forward shots. It really isn't pretty to watch but you have to admire the effectiveness of Juventus...

SAMMY NELSON: I was sitting in the director's box because I was injured and the Italian Manager, Enzo Bearzot, was in the director's box and he came across to me and said, "Oh, sorry about this, apologies." He just left because he thought Juventus had it won at 0-0.

...(82nd minute)...Well, it's got to be a moment of good fortune or a moment of sheer inspiration now for Arsenal...

PETER KIRKWOOD: I can remember Rix went down the left wing. I bet he was no more than about five yards into their half.

GRAHAM RIX: I remember it vividly. I got the ball on the left and Gentile faced me up and I just showed him enough and he bit and I played a little one-two with Frank Stapleton.

...(88th minute)...Rix, working the one-two with Stapleton...

FRANK STAPLTON: Because Paul was playing and Sundy was still playing, I had to move away to the left to try and make some space.

Rixy played it in to me and it was almost going out and I played it first time back to him and he picked it up brilliantly.

GRAHAM RIX: Frank just managed to flick it back in. So Gentile was out of the game and all of a sudden it opened up because people were still man-for-man marking. I ended up running at Scirea and he was a little bit square and I just pretended I was going this way and knocked it to the byline. I didn't see Sunderland or Vaessen or anybody in there. It's similar to the cross I put over for Alan Sunderland in the F.A. Cup Final in '79. We used to practice crossing and shooting and all that with Don all the time and he'd always say, 'The closer you get to the goal line, think more of 'dinking' it to eliminate the 'keeper.' Because, as you can imagine, the 'keeper has to come to his near post, he has to. So then you eliminate him and you never know what's going to happen. So I'm past Scirea and I'm running to the goal line and I'm thinking 'Eliminate the 'keeper, little dink, little dink.'

TERRY NEILL: Rixy was one of the best crossers of a ball of all time.

FRANK STAPLETON: The delivery was fantastic.

PETER KIRKWOOD: You could see this ball go up and down like the arch at Wembley. The ball went up and it went up and started to come down and you're so conditioned that you're going to lose, you think, 'I'll watch the ball'. You're not watching what's going on in their penalty area. As the ball's coming down you suddenly see there's people in there waiting for it.

...(88th minute)...Sunderland waiting in the middle...

ALAN SUNDERLAND: We would do this routine in training. Basically, one would go to the near post, one to the far post. So I went to the near post and Paul went to the far post.

SAMMY NELSON: I had a chair, believe it or not. It was just a chair and I stood up on this chair because I could see that Paul was at the back post and as the cross came over, Dino Zoff - at that time the

Italian national goalkeeper - he was on the near post and the ball came over his head.

GRAHAM RIX: I didn't see anybody, dinked it, and went off the pitch and I could just see Vas rise at the back post, I didn't even know it was Vas at the time.

PAUL: Then it happened. There I was running to the far post with this cross from Graham Rix coming towards me.[7]

JAMIE WINTERTON: When the ball came over, it seemed to go in slow motion. I remember Vas telling me that from the moment the ball left Graham Rix's foot he was absolutely shitting himself. He though, 'F--k! That's mine!' You can tell by the way he heads it. It's like he can't wait to get rid of it!

LIAM BRADY: Paul was always decent in the air and there he was.

PETER KIRKWOOD: And Vaessen just came in and it was almost like two asteroids colliding in space. It was the perfect meeting of the two. The ball dropped, it came down and it was almost as though it just found his forehead and he eased it in.

...AND VAESSEN!! PAUL VAESSEN!   WITH A PRICELESS GOAL!...

LEE: I just jumped up but I was in the middle of a door-way. I went, 'Yeesss!' and jumped up and it was bang! Next thing I knew my dad's slapping me round the chops asking if I'm alright! I said, 'What's happened?' and he replied, 'Your brother's just gone and scored the winner at Juventus, that's all!'

SAMMY NELSON: Unbelievable! I was standing on my chair and I was chanting and roaring like an idiot in the director's box and I looked round and all our directors were sitting down politely clapping!

PAT MOONEY: The ball was in the net but because of where we were, we couldn't actually see. We knew there was an Arsenal head there and that the ball was in the net. And suddenly, in the silence, you could hear what was going on in the immediate vicinity, in the press box.

JILL SMITH: The Juventus crowd were jumping up and down and then it just went so silent. I've never heard a ground as silent as it was.

JOHN DEVINE: Obviously up to the point where Paul came on and did the business, the Juventus fans were all singing and shouting and celebrating. All of a sudden, stunned silence.

FRED STREET: The place went silent. They were out. That was it.

PAUL: I'll never forget the silence when I scored. The fire crackers, the drums, the chanting all stopped. It was eerie.[8]

LEON: Paul said to me as soon as that goal went in Dino Zoff mumbled something to him but apart from that it all went silent. All the fires had already been lit and their fans just walked away.

...*(88th minute)....JUST TWO MINUTES FROM THE END AND ARSENAL'S PATIENCE PAYS OFF!*...

TOM O'BRIEN: I listened to the second leg in my bedroom, *trying* to do homework and my younger sister (now a season-ticket holder) can still remember the big scream of 'GOOAALL!!!' from downstairs when we scored.

KEVIN WELLING: I remember it well. I was in the bath when he scored. I had it on the radio. Superb.

SIMON SCOTT-DANIELS: I always tell people this was my best ever moment listening to the Gooners on the radio or watching on the telly. The background noise from the Stadio Comunale was enormous as they were confident of holding on to the 0-0 that would give them victory. Suddenly, as time ticks down, Rix flings the cross over and Vaessen knocks it in. At this point normally I would bounce off the ceiling at an Arsenal goal but my reaction mirrored the

96

stadium - utter stunned silence. It was as though someone on Radio 2, as it was then, had suddenly found a way to kill the background noise. But in an instant, the fifty or sixty or whatever thousand Italians shut up. It was magical.

GARY HUMPHREY: On the evening of the Cup Winners' Cup semi-final at Juventus, I was busy painting ceilings at the soon to be marital home. The game was on the radio, possibly just the second half as was the fashion in those days. I was cheering the boys on like never before and remember I was just reaching to paint a particularly awkward spot when the words, 'It's a goal,' were uttered. I knew from the deafening silence that it was Arsenal that had scored and the commentator announced Paul Vaessen as the scorer. Unfortunately, just as this was going on, I was celebrating a bit too much and toppled the ladder over. I landed in a heap on the bare floorboards, closely followed by a near full tin of white emulsion and a paintbrush, which proceeded to first cover me and then the floor in mess. Although I was somewhat bruised and shaken, I carried on celebrating and sang and waved my arms in the air.

TERRY BURTON: I wasn't at the game. I was listening to it on the radio at my place, a small terraced house around the corner from Highbury. When Paul scored I remember doing a forward roll across the floor and jumping up in the air! It was an unbelievable moment.

...(88th minute)...ARSENAL CAN HARDLY BELIEVE IT!...AND THE JUVENTUS PLAYERS, SOME DOWN ON THE GROUND...

BRIAN TALBOT: They sunk to the floor. They weren't expecting it. It came at the ideal time because the Italians couldn't then recover. We knew it was all over then, they'd blown it.

...(89th minute)...IT WAS RIX WITH THAT BEAUTIFULLY JUDGED CROSS, ZOFF WAS CAUGHT WRONG-FOOTED AND VAESSEN FROM A YARD!...ARSENAL NOW ON THE VERGE OF PRODUCING ONE OF THE GREAT EUROPEAN RESULTS!...

GRAHAM RIX: Liam ran twenty-five yards to me and slid on his knees and I heard a little voice behind me say, 'Rico! Chippy! This way!', and we turned round and it was Monte Fresco, the Daily Mirror photographer. He was a big mate of mine, Monte, and he went, 'Come on! This way!' and we both turned round and went 'Yeeeaaahhhhh!' That picture Monte Fresco took of me and Liam is one of my favourite photographs ever. It's a fantastic photograph. I looked at that photograph years later and I spoke to Liam about it because in the background there's a Juventus player with his hands on his head and another one in the back of the net, desperate. And Liam said, 'Yeah. You know why. Because we've just cost them a hundred grand a man!'

PAUL RULTON: I knew he was out there. I had spoken to him a couple of weeks before and he said he was doing well, you know? I always remember because me and my dad were sitting there. It wasn't on telly, we had the radio on and you know when you just go all goose-pimply? I was nearly in tears.

...(89th minute)...THEY BIDED THEIR TIME AND WHEN IT WAS REALLY CALLED FOR THEY FOUND A WAY THROUGH! ...

LIAM BRADY: It was fairy tale stuff really, you know?

...(89th minute)...AND NOW TIME IS SUDDENLY ON THEIR SIDE...

JOHN DEVINE: Maybe the substitution was a touch of genius because it changed the pattern of the game and they lost focus for ten seconds which was unheard of for them.

...(90th minute)...WE'RE MOVING IN TO THE FINAL MINUTE...AND ALAN SUNDERLAND WILL BE HAPPY JUST TO HOLD THE BALL THERE...IT WILL BE A JUVENTUS THROW...

JOHN DEVINE: There was no comeback. They kicked off, there were a few passes and then that was it.

...(90th minute)...WELL JUVENTUS, WHO ADOPTED THE PHILOSOPHY OF SITTING ON A GOAL ADVANTAGE IN THEIR OWN STADIUM, LOOK AS THOUGH, AS ITALIAN TEAMS HAVE

BEEN CAUGHT OUT BEFORE, LOOK AS THOUGH THEY MIGHT BE PUNISHED FOR THEIR ATTITUDE...

BRIAN TALBOT: To be fair, I still say this, the players of Juventus - I don't know about the coach, I can't comment on the coach because I don't know what he said to them - but their tactics and their performance, they got the result they deserved, one hundred percent because they approached the game in a very negative manner and when you consider they had seven or eight current internationals, they should have really come up the pitch. You think to yourself, 'Well, if they get the game by the scruff of the neck, we're under the cosh here.' But it wasn't like that at all. We played the game and, if I'm being honest, we didn't create a lot of chances but we played the game.

JOHN HOLLINS: We deserved it, really. We came and took them on and it was a fairly young team actually with players like John Devine, Liam wasn't old, Rixy wasn't old, Paul was only a baby then. Nobody gave us a chance. Believe it or not, I think at one stage our philosophy would have been damage limitation. But the more we played, the better we got and we just kept trying to get the crosses in, trying to get the crosses in, just hoping someone would be on the end of one. And Paul was. An instant hero from that moment on. Whatever way you look at it, he'd put himself on the map.

...(90th minute)...IN ALL HONESTY YOU COULD NEVER REALLY SEE IT COMING UNTIL GRAHAM RIX HERE GOT DOWN THAT LEFT-HAND SIDE...

GRAHAM RIX: It wasn't a case of he couldn't miss. Vas had to get up there and be strong, you know? I mean he's up against Cabrini. He was an international left-back, played for Italy, went on to win the World Cup a couple of years later. He knew what he was doing. And Vas, he was a big powerful boy. That ball's in the air, he got up early, Cabrini's bounced off him and he's knocked it in to the net, albeit from a yard. I've seen people, you know, get nudged out of the way and miss the header. He was in the right place. Maybe he knew what I could do which made a difference to him being in that position.

99

...(90th minute)...HERE'S BRADY AND ALL THE CONFIDENCE NOW COMING FROM ARSENAL...ANYWHERE WILL DO NOW...ANYWHERE FORWARD WILL DO NOW...

PAT MOONEY: John Hollins had come on as a sub as well, for Brian Talbot. You can imagine how frantic the Italians became after Paul scored. But Terry used all of his experience then to run down the clock but also used the experience of Hollins in that hostile environment.

PETER KIRKWOOD: The Juventus defence were so stunned that we'd had the cheek to attack in the 88th or whatever minute. They had this ridiculous clock behind the goal. It was like it was going round in milliseconds. It wasn't counting down 90 minutes. We were standing there trying to work out how it works and how much time there was left.

...(91st minute)...THE REFEREE HAS CHECKED ON THE WATCH AND WE'RE IN TO TIME ADDED ON FOR INJURY AND STOPPAGES...AND ARSENAL HAVE CONTINUED TO SHOW THAT GREAT RESILIENCE THAT HAS CHARACTERISED THEIR PLAY THIS SEASON UNDER TERRY NEILL AND DON HOWE...BUT THEY MUST HANG ON NOW...

PETER KIRKWOOD: All you knew was that you were getting nearer and nearer to 'exit' on this big clock.

...(full time)...AND ARSENAL HAVE COME UP WITH A TRULY REMARKABLE PERFORMANCE!...

FRED STREET: I remember Don turned to me and said, 'Good substitution, that. Good tactical substitution.' And I went, 'Yeah, alright Don. Tell the press that, not me!'

DON HOWE: It was a good win. I think it was a worthy win. The technical side was good and we played very, very well.

ROGER THOMPSON: I was on the bench that night. When the game finished, I went running off in the direction of Vas who was on

100

the other side of the pitch and appeared to be running, arms outstretched, towards me. Well, as he approached me, he suddenly side-stepped me and grabbed Terry Neill! I was f--king gutted!

DON HOWE: Trapattoni came across and shook all of our hands on the bench and said 'well done'.

PEGGY GOULDING: Of course, you can imagine, it just erupted. The Arsenal supporters went absolutely mad.

VIC WRIGHT: It was brilliant, absolutely brilliant. Until after, obviously. We were okay until Paul scored.

...JUVENTUS SO INVINCIBLE HERE IN THE STADIO COMUNALE AND THE GOAL TWO MINUTES FROM TIME FROM YOUNG PAUL VAESSEN TO GIVE ARSENAL A 1-0 VICTORY HERE, 2-1 ON AGGREGATE.

VIC WRIGHT: But then after that, at the end of the game, Paul and Pat Rice brought all the team over to the supporters and the Italians went a bit mad.

PETER KIRKWOOD: Pat Rice did the wonderful thing of coming over and applauding us five hundred up in the corner, pointing us out in the process. That was the worst moment for us because then they all came at us and the riot started. And it was a riot.

FRED STREET: Our supporters went crazy, of course, because we were in the Final but then the place went barmy.

PAT MOONEY: The atmosphere inside the ground before and during the game was fine but afterwards it did turn nasty.

PEGGY GOULDING: There was just wire netting between us and the Juventus fans next door, as far as I can remember. They'd got huge, like, bonfires going. I said, 'God, they're going to set the bloody place alight!'

PETER KIRKWOOD: We were being pushed up the steps. When

you got to the top there was just like a rail around the top. There was no barrier or netting, just an eighty foot straight drop. And as we were being pushed, they were throwing things at us.

PEGGY GOULDING: They threw anything they could lay their hands on, bricks and stones and bottles. I was absolutely petrified. It was the most terrifying experience.

PETER KIRKWOOD: We got right to the top but we had a lot of what you'd call the crazy boys with us, probably 'Clock Enders' and one of them just said, excuse my French, 'F--k it! We're not going to be driven out of this ground!' and they turned and ran at the Italians. And that's when the real battle broke out. One Arsenal fan ended up on the floor and they just jumped up and down on his leg until it broke. What made it worse was the stadium was so steep, like a tower. You know, how Europeans build their stadiums? Then they turned the lights off so we had to come down holding the wall to guide ourselves down.

PEGGY GOULDING: We got trapped, about twenty of us, on the stairwell over to the right. The police came and formed a barricade around us with their shields and everything and they frogmarched us back to our coach.

PETER KIRKWOOD: When we got to the bottom, of course, there's mayhem. We were just walking across when all of a sudden our mate Vic sort of shoved his hand against me and said, 'Step back! There's a bloke running about with a gun!' His only bit of English was, 'I shoot English, I shoot Arsenal,' and he was being chased by the police and they caught him just more or less in front of us, knocked him to the ground and this policeman just got the butt of this gun and went smash, straight into the side of his head. And then there were hundreds of Torino fans shouting, 'We love Arsenal! You have beaten Juventus! We love Arsenal!' Of course, all the Juventus lot had come round for a ruck with the Arsenal and were suddenly confronted by Torino fans who hated them more than we did. Of course, there was a big battle going on between them. There were hundreds of Torino fans and they were like our protectors. They saw us back to the coaches.

JOHN DEVINE: At the final whistle, as we came off the pitch, there was absolute hostility and we were being led off by the police. Things were getting lobbed on, bottles, bits and pieces, shrapnel I call it. And I can remember the devastation of the Juventus players in the tunnel after the final whistle. Some of them were breaking and smashing things in frustration in the corridors of the stadium.

LEON: Paul took a bit of stick from the Italian lads going back through the players' tunnel. There was a little bit of a skirmish, a bit of pushing and shoving. The Italians had obviously got the real hump and said something to him. They obviously knew he was a young lad. But he wasn't afraid to put his hands up, you know?

PAT MOONEY: Afterwards, we found out where the player's entrance was and I managed to attract Terry Neill's attention and got some quotes from him.

TERRY NEILL: This group of players have not had the praise or the appreciation they deserve. Perhaps, after this they will. This must rank as one of the best results any British team has achieved abroad. I'm very happy for the team. We played our usual away game - calm controlled football. It would be nice to say we planned it but that was not the case… As time went on …we had to take a few chances at the back...We have a tremendous group of players and no one gave up.[9]

PEGGY GOULDING: When we got back to our coach, a few of our fans were missing. One of them had lost his ticket before the game and he went up to the police, they pushed him down the steps and he dislocated his shoulder. He never went in to the game. The police were so heavy-handed. Another guy had jumped over the parapit to get away from the trouble and broke his leg. There wasn't a window left in the coach, they were all broken and, driving along, the curtains were flying out. They drove us to the airport and the coach driver, I don't think he sat on his seat the whole time! As he was driving he sort of kept standing up and singing for Arsenal! We got a lot of abuse as we were driving along. They obviously knew who we were because of the broken windows. They were out and out animals, they really, really were. They couldn't take defeat.

103

PETER KIRKWOOD: In our coach we were told to pull the blinds down. I don't know if we lost any windows. We might have been lucky because when you looked out I think we were one of the inner two coaches and then there were coaches either side. The coaches were going four abreast, belting eighty miles an hour down this motorway to the airport.

JOHN DEVINE: I do remember that Paul was obviously delayed because he was the superstar for the moment and I do remember that we got shepherded on to the bus because there were so many fans throwing stuff at the bus. It was a pretty scary moment. It was so volatile. It was crazy, madness. It was bricks and stones and fruit and bottles and everything getting thrown, and we just wanted to get out of there, you know? It was pretty nasty.

BRIAN TALBOT: I think it was frustration and they were disappointed with their team because I'm sure all of their fans were coming to the stadium expecting them to win the tie.

JOHN DEVINE: I was probably most relieved. I gave the penalty away in the first leg. I was trying to play the ball back to Pat Jennings but I left it short and Brian Talbot ended up having to go and retrieve it and brought Bettega down. Between the two of us we made a right mess of it. It was just one of those things. I just needed the ground to open up. So anyway, with that still fresh in the memory I was the one most eager to shake Vas's hand when he clambered onto the coach. We shook hands and I said, 'Thanks mate, you saved my skin!'

PAT MOONEY: I got a lift with one of the Arsenal supporters' coaches to the airport. We were late but they held the flight for us.

PETER KIRKWOOD: When we got to the airport there was a big delay and I said, 'What's happened,' and they said, 'We've got to wait for the people reporting from hospital,' and they were being pushed in wheelchairs, the bloke with the broken leg came in, still smiling and our one o'clock flight left at about four o'clock in the morning. And there were no facilities in those days. You couldn't get a drink or anything. It was dire.

PEGGY GOULDING: We never felt safe until we were actually on the plane. It was the most terrifying experience of my life. It's as clear in my mind as if it happened yesterday. It was terrifying, absolutely terrifying.

JILL SMITH: I always remember when we got back at the other end everyone whistled the theme tune to *Bridge Over the River Kwai* because there was so much blood and so many injured. All you could hear as everyone was walking through the airport – it was deserted apart from us - was the theme tune to *Bridge Over the River Kwai*!

PETER KIRKWOOD: When I got back home in the morning people came up and were asking, 'Oh, you're still walking, then. You're alright?' It was as if we were coming back from a war zone!

JILL SMITH: To this day it is still the most frightening experience I have ever found myself in and as I travelled with England for many years as well as Arsenal, that is saying something!

MAUREEN: Paul said afterwards the players, they all got drunk, they had a good laugh as usual.

PAUL: The champagne was out. We sang and laughed. The adrenalin buzz was fantastic. A few of the lads were driving around the hotel grounds on a tractor at four in the morning without a stitch on.[10]

FRANK STAPLETON: After the game the adrenalin was still going. I don't know about tractors but I do remember – it was the funniest thing - that John Hollins and Alan Sunderland found a little bike in the hotel we were staying at in Asti. It was a family run hotel and they had this little bike and John Hollins was just bloody going around in and out of the rooms on this bike at about four o'clock in the morning, waking everybody up!

ALAN SUNDERLAND: In the hotel afterwards there was a little child's moped and Johnny Hollins was riding around the corridors between the rooms! We were celebrating! We were nearly in two finals!

JOHN HOLLINS: We did enjoy ourselves in the hotel that night. We took over the bar. We had a really good time and rightly so. It was an unbelievable result.

PAT MOONEY: We got in to Luton early on the Thursday morning and I remember the adrenalin was still flowing.

JOHN DEVINE: What a moment for Paul, you know? A young lad, coming on at the end, doing what he did. He was a hero.

BRIAN McDERMOTT: I was ill at the time so I didn't travel with the squad but I do remember it was just a massive, massive performance. If it had been a game today it would have been seen live on telly all over the world. That goal was great for the club obviously but also for all of us who were being brought through the ranks. We really knew better than anybody what it meant to Paul to score that goal. You know, you didn't go to a place like that and win. Only very, very rarely did that happen.

GRAHAM RIX: Vas was just so excited. And I was just so pleased for the kid because up until now he'd just played bit parts. But to do that - the first time Juventus had been beaten at home by a British team in a European match, last minute goal scored by a young kid who's come through the ranks - it was absolutely fantastic for the kid. I was so pleased for him, Vas. And I think that kept him on a high for a long, long time. A long, long time.

...off-air...Martin Tyler: "It was Vaessen, wasn't it? I've never seen him play...I just went on the back of his shirt..."

PAUL: Last night I had a dream that I would come on and score the winning goal. I can't believe it has happened.[11]

LEON: I was elated. But I was almost sort of expecting it, expecting that something might happen, you know?

The scene shifts to London. It is a bright Spring afternoon and the sun is flooding through the patio doors and into the living room of a flat in South Bermondsey. Light catches a black and white photograph in the hands of a woman sitting on a sofa. In the picture her eldest son is celebrating, elated. Outside, the dogs are barking to be let back in. Two African Gray parrots are swearing at each other in the hallway. In the background is the faint sound of a crowd singing, 'There's only one Paul Vaessen' to the tune of *Guantanamera*.....

MAUREEN: The manager was over the moon, he said, absolutely over the moon with him. And I remember him saying, he said, 'I think I've got there, Mum. I think I've made it.'

Roll credits

STUCK IN A MOMENT

6

Hero (Just for One Day)

"I awoke one morning and found myself famous."
Lord Byron in 'Letters and Journals of Lord Byron' by Thomas Moore (1830)

There was much confusion in the Stadio Comunale on the night of the match, including in the press box. Pat Mooney recalls, "One of the English journalists turned around and said, 'Who's Paul Vaessen?' Several were asking each other. One of the things I had with me was the Arsenal Handbook and I suddenly produced this in the press box and I was flavour of the evening, everybody's best friend because it had the vital stats in it."

"Usually subs in those days, certainly for English clubs, were kids you'd never heard of," says Fred Street. "They'd be sitting there waiting for their chance, nervous, frightened. And so you rarely used them apart from injury, you know, because they weren't top notchers usually, although a few clubs like Liverpool did have better players. That was the normal thing, that the kids on the line were new subs who were coming in for a chance and you were giving them a little taster. You might give them ten minutes at the end if you were winning easily."

Relatively unknown until the evening of 23rd April 1980, by the time Paul arrived home the following day his celebrity had spread way beyond the borders of South Bermondsey as his name and picture adorned the back, and some front, pages of newspapers across Europe. Indeed, it seemed that the world's attention had suddenly fallen upon Lucey Way, London SE16.

"Within ten minutes of scoring that goal," Lee recalls, "there were press outside the front door, cameras going, wanting interviews."

"I do remember all the papers and the pictures the next day," says Gerry Avery. "You think to yourself, 'Yep. I know him. That's my mate!' It was brilliant. It was absolutely brilliant."

109

Some of those pictures showed Paul heading in the winner, others Paul's arms outstretched in celebration.

On his back is the number thirteen.

Another of Paul's secondary school friends, Mark Richardson, remembers exactly where he was when he heard of Paul's success.

"I lived in Deptford and I was in my bedroom which was downstairs and I heard screams coming from the living room, 'Mark! Mark! Quick, get here!' from my mum and dad. I rushed upstairs and there it was – it was on the ITV news – and I just couldn't believe it. You know, at that age, it's not often you see somebody you know on the news."

Having stayed the night in Asti, Paul made his way home with the rest of the Arsenal party on the morning after the match but not before satisfying the press at the airport. They were waiting for him again back in Luton.

"He was mobbed at the airport when he got back," says Lee.

"I do remember getting off the plane at the other end and Paul being absolutely enveloped by press reporters, as you can imagine," John Devine recalls.

"I remember he got a hell of a lot of publicity at the time," agrees Brian McDermott.

Daily Express, Thursday 24ᵗʰ April 1980:

GREAT GUNNERS!

Super sub Vaessen shatters Juventus

PAUL VAESSEN, a teenager with a Cockney accent and the blood of a Viking, earned himself a place in London football folklore last night.

The Bermondsey boy with the Afro perm achieved a stunning victory for Arsenal.

For 77 minutes Vaessen sat with the rest of us as a restless, nervous onlooker as Arsenal endured the ultimate frustration of Juventus' negative football in this European Cup-Winners' Cup semi-final.

Manager Terry Neill then took the gamble of pushing on a young man who has been a professional for less than a year and played only a handful of games.

But Vaessen popped up at (the) far post with just two minutes to go to nonchalantly head home Graham Rix's delicate chip...

London Evening Standard, Thursday 24th April 1980:

Brady & Co salute Vaessen

A LONG career stretches before Paul Vaessen, but he knows that there is unlikely to be an occasion he will treasure quite as much as the night he scored the goal that put Arsenal into the European Cup-Winners' Cup Final.

The amiable curly-haired 18-year-old received the ultimate accolade when his teammates, many established international stars who would cost millions in the transfer market, stood to applaud him aboard the Arsenal team coach last night...

Satisfaction

But for Paul Vaessen, Arsenal would be out of the Cup-Winners' Cup. His priceless goal two minutes from the end of a frustrating semi-final second leg, gave Arsenal a 2-1 aggregate win over Juventus, and means that they now go to the final in Brussels on May 14 to meet Valencia...

I was sure that Arsenal would become the first British side to win in the Stadio Comunale but as the electric clock above the terracing mercilessly ticked off the seconds, I was beginning to have doubts.

Then Graham Rix collected a pass from Liam Brady. He played a one-two with Frank Stapleton and raced to the line, brushing off the inevitable challenge from an Italian defender.

"I really had no idea if we had anyone in the middle," recalled Rix, "but I could see Zoff, their goalkeeper, at the near-post, so I decided to hit a high ball to the far post."

As his centre arced over Zoff, he did not realize that Vaessen,

111

a 77ᵗʰ-minute substitute for David Price, had already seen the potential of the cross.

"I could see the ball coming over as I made a run for it," said Vaessen, whose father, Leon, was a half-back with Millwall and Gillingham...

As Vaessen turned in triumph, Rix sunk to his knees on the edge of the Juventus area. Later, he sat in the bath in the dressing room and said: "That goal gave me more satisfaction than the winner in last year's F.A. Cup Final."

Arsenal applied themselves with a ferocious commitment and finally their industry wrecked the Juventus marking system. "It's nice to be pleased for yourself, but even nicer to be pleased for the others, especially when they've worked so hard and so honestly," said Neill.

"I think the win against Juventus must rank as one of the greatest achievements by an English team abroad."

It was their 61ˢᵗ game of the season. In the last 18 days they have drawn with Southampton, beaten Spurs, drawn at home to Juventus, drawn three times with Liverpool and, now, beaten the Italians.

On Saturday they are at home to West Bromwich Albion - Rix took a nasty kick on the knee - and on Monday they meet Liverpool in the second FA Cup Semi-Final replay. My money, I think, will again be on Arsenal.

They were in an indestructible mood in the early hours of this morning as the team bus ferried them back to their hotel in Asti.

It was a great night for Arsenal, for the seasoned players like Jennings, Rice and Hollins, for those saying goodbye, like Brady, and for those, like Vaessen, saying hello.

It was his fourth first-team goal of the season and no doubt soon he will be back in the reserves. "But he's got a big future," said Neill. "He's a boy with a lot of potential and I want to make sure he fulfils it."

From Luton Airport, Arsenal headed back to North London where, around midday, there was another photo session for Paul out on the Highbury pitch.

Most notable of all the photographs which appeared in Friday's editions was an almost poignant image of Paul by photographer James Gray which appeared in the *Daily Mail*. It has Paul in the foreground, gazing almost wistfully off into the distance as the famous Arsenal clock stands proudly in the background.

Time was ticking away.

"Obviously when he got back to South Bermondsey he went home first," says Jamie Winterton. "After that, he came straight round and me, my mum and him sat and watched him on the telly getting interviewed when he got off the plane."

Steve Gorham also had his TV on. "He was interviewed on what was probably *Thames at Six*. I remember it well. I remember sitting indoors having my tea and thinking, 'F--k me! Look who it is!' I was laughing because he had a terrible perm, terrible!"

"He came round to my house in the evening," recalls David Palmer. "We went out for a beer. Watching your friend score the winning goal on telly felt brilliant to me. I asked him how he felt and he said, 'I just feel like *Roy of the Rovers*. I've got no other way to describe it. Everything is just brilliant.' And we went out and celebrated his good times."

"Next day, I got up first," says Maureen. "I could hear all this chanting and I thought, 'Where's all that coming from?' Well, when I got down to the front door and had a look, I saw the crowd. I'd never seen so many people, all outside with banners and chanting. And that's considering it was a Millwall-supporting area!

"I went up to his bedroom and I said, 'Are you going in to training?' He said 'Yeah' and I said, 'I don't think you are!' He said, 'What do you mean?' and I told him to have a look out of the window. He said, 'Oh my God! I didn't want all this!' You see, he didn't like all the fuss. Anyway, when he came to leave he couldn't get out of the door. There were hundreds of people out there, photographers, press. We've had to phone the police to come and escort him out. He'd have got mobbed. It was frightening. We just couldn't believe it."

"It took him by surprise," says Leon of the attention, "and from what I could see, it didn't change him."

"When he came home from Turin," Maureen continues, "Paul was ecstatic. He was absolutely gob smacked but he didn't let things, his success, the fact that he was playing for the Arsenal, go to his head or anything like that. He didn't make much of it himself at all. He wasn't the sort of person who would let his feet leave the ground. He never really bragged about being at Arsenal or things like that, you know? He just took it all in his stride. He was still the same. Nothing could faze him."

Lee also noticed little change in Paul.

"He was obviously over the moon when he got back. But the next day, bang! It was back into training. There wasn't long to celebrate. Anyway, as far as he was concerned that goal against Juventus, that's what he was there for, that was his job. So I don't think it changed him as a person at all."

"I don't think football got to him in a big way in terms of making him forget where he came from," suggests Arsenal insider Vic Wright. "I think he always had his feet on the ground, always remembered where he came from and always remembered the people who spoke to him and saw him."

It is something confirmed by close family friend Barry Clubb.

"You'd never have known what Paul did, that he played for Arsenal, unless you asked. They hardly talked about it at all."

Meanwhile, his son John was up to mischief.

"I remember when he got back from Italy to Lucey Way we were over on a visit and Paul had left his suitcase open and me and Little Lee, obviously being kids - we were only thirteen, fourteen - went in and had a rummage through his case and found whatever Juventus shirt it was that he had.

"After, all the local kids used to go up to his place at Lucey Way, knock on his door and get an autograph. Kids at school used to do it and they used to sell them to other people."

"I sold loads of autographs," Lee confides. "I used to sell them for 25p a go.

"After Juventus he was under a lot more pressure. There was a lot of publicity, a lot of hangers-on. All these third, fourth and fifth cousins were coming out of the woodwork, people we hadn't seen in years, all wanting to be part of it, to be part of the family. One day they're crossing the street to avoid you and the next they're at the front door with bunches of flowers. My dad told them where to go. 'I won't be so polite next time,' he'd say to them."

As a result of his endeavours in Turin, Arsenal showed their gratitude in a couple of ways, firstly by arranging for a huge colour television to be delivered to his house in South Bermondsey, and

114

secondly through the awarding of a win bonus which Gerry Avery remembers Paul putting to good use.

"I think, if I remember rightly, and I'm not sure about the sums involved, but the win bonus helped Paul buy a nice little sportscar."

"It was an Alfa Romeo GTV," says Lee.

"He loved his cars," Maureen reflects. "He had a little runabout to begin with then the nice cars came. He had an Alfa Romeo, he had a Jag. His Jag was nice."

"He loved coming around the flats in his latest cars," recalls friend Adam Rutherwood. "Jaguar, Fiat X19 or the Alfa Romeo he bought from his bank manager."

"I was sitting in class one day at school," says Lee, "it must have been about midday, and Paul pulled up in this XR4 sports car he had. He was all tanned up and he had these white leather shorts on. Well, the school emptied. People were going, 'Look! It's Paul Vaessen!' and running out of class. He'd come to see some of the teachers. He signed a few autographs and then he said to me, 'Come on, take your tie off. We're off to see David Bowie!'"

Paul may have been grounded but there's no doubt he did relish some of the trappings of his success. Friends remember a lads' holiday to Malta, for instance, where he took delight in the fact that he was recognized abroad, signing bank notes for admirers.

And there was more.

"He used to get letters from girls," Lee reveals, "asking if they could come over and do whatever to him. Yeah, he took up the offers and I had a few of the cast-offs. I was only about fourteen or fifteen at the time but I gave it my best shot. He liked his women. He was a pretty boy, always tanned up. He got fined half a week's wages by Don Howe once for sunbathing.

"Well, this one night he came back home with two birds and woke me up and asked me to look after one of them. I told him I was knackered but he wouldn't have it. So I did my best and I was laying back when all of a sudden he appears at the door, obviously looking for some more action, with a full-length mirror and nothing on but a pair of green wellies!

"But the thing is he just wanted to play football. It was all about the football. From the age of ten he'd been playing football seven days a week. He just loved to play. Paul didn't care about the money or the lifestyle. They came as part of the package. He didn't go into football for the fame or the money. The fame was irrelevant. The money was irrelevant. He just wanted to play."

****

Paul's fifteen minutes of fame were over and despite his recent achievements, Paul was under no illusion about his position in the squad. With Frank Stapleton and Alan Sunderland both fit, he was not anticipating – at least publicly - any involvement when Arsenal played West Bromwich Albion at Highbury on the Saturday following the triumph in Turin.

With another massive encounter with Liverpool coming up in two days time, however, Terry Neill put out a slightly weakened team against the Baggies, giving Pat Jennings, David O'Leary, David Price and Graham Rix all a well-deserved rest. Jennings' deputy, Paul Barron, made a rare appearance in goal and there were starts for Steve Walford and John Hollins. And Paul was rewarded for his European exploits in midweek with a place in the starting line-up alongside, unusually, both Stapleton and Sunderland.

As a triumphant homecoming, the match was something of an anti-climax as the Gunners had to strike late again, snatching an equaliser three minutes from the end after Cyrille Regis and man-of-the-match Peter Barnes had combined to put Ron Atkinson's West Brom 1-0 up in the twentieth minute. Paul justified his inclusion, though, collecting a pass from Liam Brady and putting over the inch-perfect cross from which Frank Stapleton scored a trademark header.

Although retained in the squad, Paul sat out Arsenal's next engagement, the second F.A. Cup Semi-Final replay with Liverpool at Villa Park on Monday 28th April. With Kenny Dalglish pouncing in the third minute of injury time to cancel out Alan Sunderland's strike just fifteen seconds into the contest, the tie remained at deadlock. That meant another replay on the Thursday, a major annoyance for Arsenal secretary, Ken Friar, and his Liverpool counterpart, Peter Robinson. Friar pleaded unsuccessfully with the Football Association to consider putting the Cup Final, scheduled for Saturday 10th May, back to 31st May in order to allow the successful semi-finalist sufficient time to get organised in time for the big day. Arsenal's fixture congestion was stretching them to the absolute limit. It was also threatening administrative chaos.

"We have four League games left," said Friar, "and have still to arrange dates for three of them. We have to make arrangements for moving ten thousand to twenty thousand people to Brussels for the European Cup-Winners' Cup Final on May 14 and, just to add to our problems, that is the day of the national strike."[12]

Already, a fourth replay at Bramall Lane had been penciled in for the Bank Holiday Monday of Cup Final week but in the end it wasn't required as Brian Talbot's solitary goal finally prized apart the two giants and put the Gunners through to a Wembley date with Second Division West Ham United. It had been the longest running semi-final saga since 1899 which, Brian Glanville pointed out in the *Sunday Times*, was a time when "England's leading clubs did not, into the bargain, have to play the Football League Cup, a European competition and 42 League fixtures."[13]

And there was no special secret as to what was keeping the Gunners going. "It's character," said Don Howe after the replay victory. "They want to win, they want to graft and when you've got that, you've got a chance."[14] Captain Pat Rice concurred. "It's team spirit, you know, and that is the main thing. We realise we're all in it together."[15]

Paul was not involved at Highfield Road but was back in the starting eleven when Arsenal returned two days later for a league match with Coventry City.

It wasn't pretty. Michael Eaton, writing in the *News of the World* on Sunday 4th May, described the match as "tedious" and "third-rate entertainment" played out in front of only 16,817 fans. He scored Paul's contribution, and that of the majority of the under-strength Arsenal side, at 5 out of 10 and that was despite scoring the 87th minute winner after Brian Talbot had worked his way into the left corner and played the ball back for Paul to fire in. Indeed, the standard of the match was such that it had some observers debating as to whether the Football League should fine Arsenal for fielding a team including five reserves or punish Coventry for losing to them. Terry Neill was, nonetheless, pleased with what he had seen from his "other first team" and confessed, tongue in cheek, that after this win he wasn't sure now which was his best eleven.

With the Cup Final looming, Paul was clearly in manager Terry Neill's thoughts, retaining his place up front for the 0-0 draw with Nottingham Forest at Highbury just five days before the clash with the Hammers.

"I think Paul had convinced himself he was going to get on the bench at least for the F.A. Cup Final," recalls Steve Gorham, "and I remember him being awfully disappointed when he missed out. I remember talking to him about that and him being absolutely choked."

"We did wonder if Paul should have been substitute for the F.A. Cup Final against West Ham," says supporter Emilio Zorlakki. "Full-back Sammy Nelson substituting the other left-back on the day, John Devine, was in my opinion done on a sympathy basis as Devine had played in the semi-final against Liverpool (in place of Nelson). However, many fans felt this was a waste of a substitute and a defender was hardly going to change the course of a game that we were losing."

Arsenal put in a tired display as they lost 1-0 to a rare thirteenth minute Trevor Brooking header.

"We didn't perform particularly well in the F.A. Cup Final," recounts Brian Talbot. "We had a four game saga with Liverpool. We thought we'd done the hard job. We were playing a team that we knew on paper we were better than, but on the grass on the day they deserved to win.

"And then four days later we went to the European Cup-Winners' Cup Final and lost on penalties to Valencia where to be honest it was a very mediocre game but we did actually create maybe the two best chances of the match but we didn't finish the game off. We were not fresh and it all caught up with us and I think on the night we didn't have a lot of good fortune, we had a lot of bad luck and that's what happens in football."

"This time," continues Zorlakki, "as in Turin, Paul was a substitute, but out of the two subs allowed Arsenal only used John Hollins in extra-time. Who knows what might have happened if Paul had got the chance. It might have even changed his life."

"To me, they should have played him in that final," Leon contests. "As far as taking penalties was concerned, he'd have had no problem with that, no problem whatsoever."

Fan David Collins travelled out to Brussels and stayed in the same hotel as the Arsenal squad.

"The night after the game we were in the hotel bar and at some point during the evening I ended up standing next to Paul Vaessen. I turned around and asked him how he was feeling and he expressed that he was very disappointed that he hadn't got on in the game, especially as the game had gone into extra-time. He was very, very disappointed."

Arsenal's season, which had promised so much, was now petering out.

"Every Arsenal game that season was a huge game," says Pat Mooney. "They lost the Cup Final, lost the Cup-Winners' Final, beat Wolves 2-1 and then they had to beat Middlesbrough in their last game of the season to qualify for the following season's U.E.F.A. Cup. They lost 5-0."

Paul was a sub in the last two fixtures.

"The thing that blew us away," remarks John Devine, "was the semi-finals against Liverpool and Juventus. Every game was a massive game, all top pressure games."

"With all due respect, it wasn't just Coventry City at home. It was Tottenham, Juventus, Liverpool, Liverpool," says Graham Rix.

"They didn't come any bigger," Devine continues. "It was remarkably intense, the pressure was phenomenal. And by the end of it we were absolutely shattered, we were absolutely drained. And remember we only had one substitute at the time and we had a small squad so a lot of the players played sixty-plus games that season. Brian Talbot played in every game. He had a remarkable engine."

"We would literally travel back from a game at Villa Park or wherever," recalls Rix, "arrive back in the early hours of the morning and pile into this pub, the *Chaseside Tavern* in Winchmore Hill. The owner, Jack McGowan, would keep the place open for us so we could have a few beers and he'd lay on some food. Then we'd literally be off to the next game. That was the case with Juventus. We went out. We won in Turin. First British team to do so. Last minute goal. Brilliant. Young kid scores it who's come through the ranks. Absolutely brilliant result. And then we went back to the hotel and had a quick beer and got ready for the next game."

"And that's how it was," maintains Devine, "play, rest, maybe some light training, play, rest…"

"I think in those days players accepted it," says Brian Talbot. "We got on with the job in hand. You've got to be lucky, obviously, with injuries. We never had a big squad at Arsenal, never. We didn't have the luxury that they have today. I think it all caught up with us. From being a fantastic season in terms of winning things, we ended up with nothing."

"Everybody played their part," Sammy Nelson insists, "even if you only played two games or half a game you were part of it so it didn't make any difference. I think if you reflect on today, you know, you have a squad of about thirty to forty players, we didn't have that availability. So we tried our best, we gave our best. Everybody did."

"We had a small squad of about fourteen, fifteen," Alan Sunderland agrees. "All the other big clubs had big squads. But we were playing practically the same team, the same players, week in, week out. By the end of the season we were knackered. We played seventy f--king games that season. We had John Devine, Steve Walford, Steve Gatting as our reserves and that was it really. Paul came in as maybe our sixteenth man."

****

If there was to be an abiding image of Arsenal's 1979-1980 campaign it would perhaps be that described by Ken Jones of the *Sunday Mirror* after the final whistle against West Ham at Wembley.

"Scattered around...like severed daffodils on a green meadow, were the yellow shirted men of Arsenal. Beaten, tired men."[16]

But now was the time for some much needed rest and the chance to reflect upon what had still been a great season, albeit four games too long. Thoughts turned to the future and even with Liam Brady's imminent departure to Juventus, there were still reasons for optimism at Arsenal. One was the club's determination to deflect unwanted interest from Turin in striker Frank Stapleton, chairman Denis Hill-Wood defiantly declaring that there wasn't enough money in the world that could buy him. The other was the emergence of new talent such as Brian McDermott, Paul Davis and, most notably, Paul Vaessen.

It had been a good campaign for Paul. Still within his first year as a professional, he had, owing to his exploits in Turin alone, already written his name into Highbury – and Torino - folklore.

"I remember the goal like it was yesterday," says Steve Gorham. "We all remember that goal and the accompanying perm!"

"After Turin, everyone thought he was on his way to the top," reflects friend Adam Rutherwood.

Even Don Howe seemed upbeat.

"Young Paul's contribution can hardly be forgotten as he came on as a late substitute against Juventus in Turin and headed our winning goal. That must be a great boost for the lad. Now he has enjoyed a good introduction to first-team football he must work harder to establish himself. He has proved he can score some outstanding goals and has the makings of a top-class player."[17]

Indeed, as the close-season arrived, things were looking good for Paul Vaessen. And what was most encouraging of all was the fact that, at just eighteen years of age, time was on his side.

STUCK IN A MOMENT

7

Stars Crash Down

"Great talents are the most lovely and often the most dangerous
fruits on the tree of humanity. They hang upon the most slender
twigs that are easily snapped off."

Carl Gustav Jung

It is a sunny day in June 1980 and a happy, handsome young professional footballer is standing on the steps of Arsenal Stadium signing autographs for a group of schoolboys. The fledgling striker from London has just held a press conference in the Arsenal boardroom and, following his recent achievements, is the talk of the town. Although only really just starting out, in the opinion of most commentators he has the world at his feet.

"I think now I've set myself up for life," he proclaims as he beams away for the cameras.

But it's not Paul Vaessen.

Instead, Clive Allen has just become the fifth million pound player in English football history, the first million pound teenager, Arsenal's record signing by far. Despite Paul's recent contributions, Allen was acquired from Second Division QPR as a long-term replacement for Malcolm Macdonald and with quiet uncertainty over the future of Frank Stapleton in mind. To Paul he represented serious competition and was perhaps a reminder that he still himself had much to do. As the *Islington Gazette* rather harshly put it, "If Arsenal had a problem last season, it was a lack of support up front for Frank Stapleton and Alan Sunderland but the acquisition of Allen will now end that problem."[18] To Terry Neill it all made good business sense. "Clive is still only aged nineteen and could be with us for the next decade. He is also able to get plenty of goals and that's what this game is all about – putting the ball in the net."[19]

Paul could have felt disconcerted, intimidated by Allen's arrival but he didn't.

123

"You've got to understand," explains Lee, "that it was all or nothing with Paul. He had complete and utter faith in himself. He had a confidence in his own ability which was pumped into him by his old man from an early age. His attitude would have been, 'Well, if he's worth one million pounds, then I'm worth two million pounds.' He'd think, 'I'll just work my way through him' and 'If I'm flying, in top form, he won't catch me'. He wasn't worried. He was loving it. He was just riding the waves. He was playing for one of the best clubs in world football. Even if he was only a sub, he was loving every moment of it. He just wanted to play football. He loved football that much."

As it worked out, of course, Allen was not much of an obstacle for very long. He didn't last the projected decade. He barely lasted 270 minutes, failing to score in three pre-season friendlies in August against Glasgow Rangers, Aberdeen and Vasco da Gama. Less than two months after signing for Arsenal, Allen was transferred to Crystal Palace along with Paul Barron in exchange for Kenny Sansom and £400,000.

Why?

"We brought Clive in," recalls Alan Sunderland, "and tried him up front with me and Frank in those pre-season matches, all of which we lost. We'd been playing 4-4-2 up until then and had been doing okay and I can only think that with Clive in there as well Terry saw something he didn't like, that it didn't seem to be working."

"Don't get me wrong," says John Devine, "Clive Allen was a gifted player, a quality player but all three of them playing up front, it didn't seem to work."

Conspiracy theorists, however, have another explanation, maintaining that the whole business was contrived, a sham, that QPR chairman Jim Gregory wouldn't sell Allen directly to Palace so Arsenal agreed to act as go-betweens.

John Devine has his suspicions.

"Even though he hadn't slotted in straight away, there's no way a player gets transferred out within eight weeks of joining. Everybody was bemused by that one. Maybe there were other forces at work, things going on behind closed doors."

"I wouldn't like to comment," Alan Sunderland continues, "about whether the deal was concocted or not but I must say, in my opinion, you can't really tell a great deal after just three pre-season friendlies."

To Terry Neill it was quite simple.

"There was nothing wrong with Clive Allen at all but priorities very, very quickly started to change. Sammy Nelson was beginning to struggle with a knee injury and then the opportunity came for Kenny Sansom and also to reward Paul Barron who'd been a very good and conscientious deputy for Pat Jennings.

"In a perfect world I'd have loved to have kept Clive Allen but financially it was good business as well. When you've been brought up by the club, you treat the club's money as your own. I was at the sharp end. I could have bottled it and done nothing or I could have said, 'Right, we're saving the club a hell of a lot of money here and we're getting the best left full-back in the business.'

"It was a hell of a shock for Clive but, as I say, when you're at the sharp end your job is to make decisions and you live or die by them and you accept that."

What made losing Allen that much easier to take for Neill was the realization that he did have plenty in reserve, what with Paul, Brian McDermott and Raphael Meade all coming through. He was also, following Liam Brady's departure, more determined than ever to tie Frank Stapleton down to a new deal with the club.

Whatever the reason for the recent shenanigans in the transfer market, the drama was played out whilst Paul was on youth team duty for Arsenal in Holland.

Islington Gazette, Friday 15th August 1980:

Arsenal kids are toast of Europe

ARSENAL'S kids beat the cream of Europe over the weekend in Holland.

The young Gunners won the Ajax 80th anniversary under-20 tournament defeating Feyenoord 6-0 in the final.

Arsenal also put paid to Ajax 4-1 in a competition that included Real Madrid, Anderlecht, Hamburg and FC Hague.

Declared coach Roger Thompson: "My biggest thrill in charge of the youngsters was when we finished runners-up in the Football Combination last season – but this was definitely our best *tournament success against some of the best and strongest clubs in Europe."*

Ironically, Arsenal struggled to qualify with draws against AZ67 1-1 and Real Madrid 1-1. It all depended on Real Madrid's result with AZ67 – and they got beat 2-1.

Arsenal then went on to crush Ajax and Feyenoord. "We seemed to get better as the competition went on," added Thompson.

He thought that Arsenal looked stronger at under-20 level compared with the European clubs which augured well for the future – especially as the same players could one day be competing against each other in senior competition.

Arsenal's three strikers Raphael Meade, who hails from Hornsey Rise, Paul Vaessen and Brian McDermott were the main reason for their success. They all scored hat-tricks – and Meade ended up top scorer with five goals.

It was Paul's only ever hat-trick for Arsenal.

"Arsenal had a good crop of youngsters coming through," Leon reflects, "what with Paul, Brian, Raphael Meade, Chris Whyte, Paul Davis, Danny O'Shea and a few others."

Islington Gazette, Friday 15th August 1980:

More stars on production line

ARSENAL'S future looks safely assured along a well-worn and successful path.

That is mainly their youth production line that has been responsible for so much of their success in the past 12 years.

Just like the "double" year of '71 when nine of their squad were youth products, Arsenal's recent FA Cup and European Cup Winners Cup Final sojourns owed much to the Highbury Academy.

The new wave for the 'eighties have already made their mark.

Supporters saw glimpses of Paul Vaessen, a powerful six-foot striker from Bermondsey, in the last campaign.

It was Vaessen who came in as a late substitute to head the vital goal against Juventus that clinched a European Cup Winners

Cup Final date...

    Manager Terry Neill...said..."Paul Vaessen has gained experience and the games he has played has let him know what it is all about."

Paul's accomplishments of the previous season had clearly raised expectations. "This could be a great season for him," stated the 1980-81 *Official Handbook*[20] and indeed things started off well when Paul came in in place of the suspended Alan Sunderland for the first two league games of the season – a 1-0 victory at WBA and a 1-1 draw at Highbury against Southampton.

    "He did well," says Leon. "There was even talk that he'd done well enough to keep Sunderland out of the side."

Hampstead & Highgate Express, Friday 22nd August 1980:

    Such has been the form of his (Sunderland's) replacement, young Paul Vaessen, Neill may be tempted to leave alone the team which has secured three points from their opening games.

    Neill was particularly pleased with Vaessen's display against Kevin Keegan's Southampton on Tuesday evening. "Vaessen is improving all the time," said Neill afterwards. "The kid is serving his apprenticeship and I'm pleased with him."

Unfortunately for Paul, he was back in the reserves the next day and that's where he stayed for the next three months, his best spell coming in November during which he scored five times in four reserve team outings playing alongside Raphael Meade.

    It was early December when Paul was recalled to the first team squad, appearing as a substitute in the 1-1 home draw with Wolves and the 2-0 defeat at Sunderland. Next up was Manchester United and Paul was back in alongside Frank Stapleton in place of Alan Sunderland who was again suspended.

London Evening Standard, Friday 19th December 1980:

Arsenal call for Vaessen

ARSENAL bid to boost their flagging championship prospects by drafting Paul Vaessen into the attack for tomorrow's big First Division clash against Manchester United at Highbury.

Arsenal, who will again be without suspended striker Alan Sunderland, have won only one of their last six matches.

Vaessen, who played in the opening games this season when Sunderland was also banned, is recalled to the team along with England's Graham Rix, who has recovered from the heavy cold that kept him out of last week's 2-0 defeat at Sunderland...

Arsenal, unbeaten at Highbury this season, have the same number of points as United.

Sunday People, Sunday 21st December 1980:

Swinging Gunners

Arsenal 2 Manchester United 1 (Football League Division One)

IT was a real swinging affair at Highbury. In fact, there was so much talk about in-swingers after the match, it was more like Lords!

Rix started it all with a corner kick that swung so viciously, Stapleton and Bailey were still rising to meet it when it curled into the top of the net.

And United's defence was mown down by the Rix crossfire again, when he put a perfect inswinging centre on to Vaessen's head.

He had only to nod his thanks to put Arsenal two up and the game, seemingly, beyond United's grasp...

Reason then, one would think, for a good Christmas.

****

128

Christmas 1980 could have been a bit of a disappointed for me. My favourite gift, the electronic shooting game, *Tin Can Alley*, didn't last long. Neither I nor my dad could knock over a tin can to save our lives and so, concluding that the rifle wasn't shooting straight, we reluctantly returned it to *Woolworths*. As they didn't have any more in stock to replace it with, I had to choose something else from the store and so plumped for an *Evel Knievel Stunt Cycle* set.

It was one of the best decisions I have ever made, something the family cat would not, however, agree on as the bike sped after her throughout the house, day after day. I loved my Evel Knievel, not just because of the resemblance of the action figure to the late Elvis Presley, but because of his buoyancy, his optimism, enthusiasm and his apparent indestructability. He thought he could do anything in the world. He could leap over toy cars and buses, soldiers, Action Men. He could tumble intrepidly down the stairs, get up and do it all over again. He was never fazed and just didn't know when he'd had enough. He just wanted to jump, loved to jump.

But with time, things started to take their toll. Evel showed a previously hidden brittleness and as he grew increasingly embattled, signs of a fallibility started to show, cuts and blood stains appearing on his body and white jumpsuit, albeit courtesy of a red felt tip pen.

Unfortunately, the cuts and blood on Paul Vaessen's wrists that Christmas Day were real. The happy-go-lucky Londoner was also showing signs of vulnerability.

There had been speculation for years. The first hint that something had happened came in 1985 when Terry Neill revealed in his autobiography, *Revelations of a Football Manager*,[21] how one Christmas morning he had discovered an unnamed player who had failed to show up for training, at their home, their wrists slashed after a domestic argument.

Kenny Sansom then wrote in his book, *To Cap It All*, in 2008 that, "there were rumours circulating that one of the Highbury boys had attempted suicide and Paul's name had been linked to the drama. How true these rumours were I still don't know."[22]

Confirmation comes from the author Jon Spurling who interviewed Paul in 1994 and who I met at the Emirates Stadium at an evening function a few years ago. We excused ourselves from the laughter, the clinking of glasses and the general hubbub of the

129

opulent Diamond Club and took up a couple of seats outside in the empty, silent stadium overlooking the magnificent perfection of the brightly lit Emirates pitch. It was there that Spurling corroborated the not-so-secret dark secret, revealing to me that he had it on very good authority – including from Paul himself – that it was indeed Paul who attempted suicide that Christmas Day.

It was not exactly a surprise but it's still something of a shock. I know it sounds a bit daft but, as I have said before, I consider myself to have grown quite close to Paul, that I have become a friend, an ally. There are some parallels in our lives and because of that I feel empathy towards him.

What this episode showed was that beneath the confident exterior we have seen from Paul up to this point, there lay a more sensitive interior, a fragility which would be severely tested at various times throughout his career and lifetime.

"There were underlying weaknesses in Paul," agrees Lee. "He was susceptible to things. He was also easily led. For instance, if he hadn't had his football, he probably would have ended up in crime because when he was fourteen he was going out nicking motors. And like the drugs. He'd been doing weed and speed as a schoolboy. Then he stepped it up and when he was sixteen, seventeen, making his breakthrough at Arsenal and was earning a good wage, he'd go and blow it on a line of coke. In that way, he was weak, vulnerable.

"You've got to remember that there was a lot of pressure on Paul. From thirteen, fourteen he'd be over in the park with our old man. He'd be pushing him forward, always pushing him forward. He had high expectations of Paul. Don't forget, Paul made his debut at sixteen. You don't see that all that often. Now he was playing for one of the biggest clubs in the country.

"Where Paul's personality was concerned, I think what made things worse was that he was an extremist. That was instilled in him by our dad. He used to say, 'If you're going to be a thief, do something big, rob a bank. If you're going to play football, play for the best club in the world.' So everything he did in his life, football, drugs, he really went for it. So later on in life when he was low, he wouldn't just say he was down. He'd talk of suicide."

His reaction to a domestic quarrel may not, then, simply have been to walk away, to sleep on it but to take more drastic action.

Paul, aged 8 months.
(Source: Maureen Vaessen).

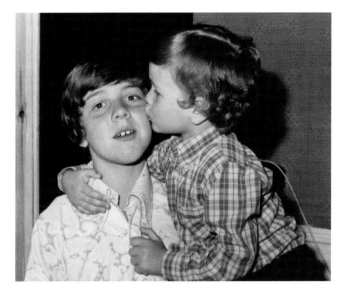

"Life as yet untouched by tragedy." Paul and Lee in the late sixties.
(Source: Leon Vaessen).

Paul (front row, centre) with team mates and the Blackheath U-16s Cup. "Football was his life. He knew from an early age he was going to be a professional footballer and that was that". (Source: Stephen Underwood).

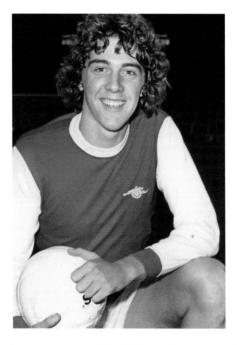

"Paul is a tremendous prospect with all the attributes required to make it to the top." Paul aged fifteen in September 1977.
(Source: Andrew Franks).

Paul's accomplice, Nicky Law. (Source: Arsenal FC).

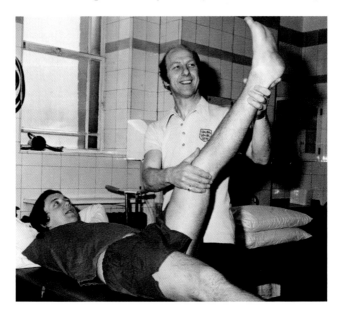

Richie Powling gets treatment from Fred Street as he recovers from a
cartilage injury – January 1977. (Source: Getty Images).

Tommy Caton in action for Arsenal in 1983. (Source: PA Images).

"It was all over a lot sooner than I had envisaged," says Warwick Bean
today. (Source: Author).

Paul in action at White Hart Lane, April 1980. (Source: PA Images).

Despite his suspect pace, Paul bursts through the WBA defence during an encounter in April 1980. (Source: PA Images).

"There aren't many people in their entire lives who get a glorious moment like that, that no one can take away." (Source: PA Images).

"I'll never forget the silence when I scored. The fire crackers, the drums, the chanting all stopped. It was eerie." (Source: PA Images).

Paul slots the ball past John Lukic for the winner against Leeds United in January 1982. (Source: PA Images).

Paul tries to build up his left knee in the gymnasium at Highbury in 1982. (Source: Getty Images).

Paul, by now retired, marries childhood sweetheart, Sarah, in September 1983. (Source: John F. White Studios).

"He loved Jack to bits, he really did". (Source: Maureen Vaessen).

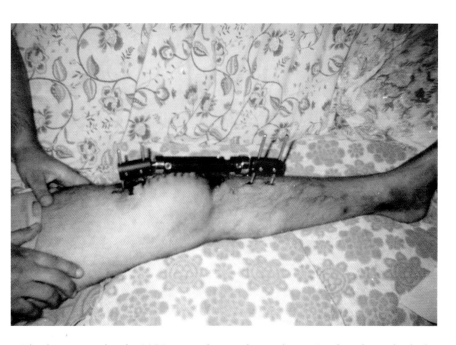

The last operation in 1997 proved a turning point as Paul took to alcohol and drugs to escape his ensuing depression. (Source: Maureen Vaessen).

Brother, can you spare me a dime? Paul and Lee in happier times.
(Source: Maureen Vaessen).

Standing proud: Maureen returns to Arsenal for the first time in twenty five years. (Source: Author).

"You silly bastard, Paul. You silly bastard." Maureen at Paul's memorial in Rotherhithe, South East London. (Source: Author).

Fortunately, what we do know is that his drastic action that Christmas Day was unsuccessful, maybe only half-hearted, a gesture, a cry for help because he played a full ninety minutes for the first team during their 2-2 draw at Crystal Palace on Boxing Day.

And peace had been made with his partner, Sarah, by then, even though Paul was probably fighting more with himself than anyone else. After all, it's hard to imagine Sarah clashing with anyone.

"She was a lovely lady," says Lee, "I couldn't fault her. She was tall, slim, had lovely long, fair hair. She was very well spoken, well brought up. She lived on the Pepys Estate in Deptford where my Nan used to live. Paul used to bump into Sarah when he used to go visiting our Nan. They also drank in the same pub, *The Madhouse*. Some of the top bands of the day, like *Squeeze* and *The Clash* used to drink in there."

"She was lovely, absolutely lovely," agrees Maureen. "And she was very kind, always buying me presents. She called me 'mum' and really was like a daughter to me. She was very bubbly, very pretty and really was part of the family."

So perhaps things were not so bad for Paul Vaessen. He had a beautiful girlfriend, a great job, money, a nice car. And things were back on an even keel.

For now.

There would, however, be more trying times ahead for the young couple, more challenges just around the corner.

****

The next drama involving Paul came on 10th January 1981 at Goodison Park where he once again showed his penchant for scoring winners, particularly late ones.

Paul's last-gasp header in a 2-1 win over Everton not only allowed the Gunners to enact revenge for the 2-0 F.A. Cup defeat at the hands of the Toffees the previous weekend but also ensured Arsenal remained just four points behind Division One leaders, Aston Villa, who had beaten champions Liverpool in the day's big top-of-the-table clash.

****

"Even though he was back in the reserves after that, things seemed to be going pretty well," says Leon. "And then everything stopped."

Islington Gazette, Friday 6th February 1981:

Heatbreak for Vaessen

ARSENAL'S young goalscoring protégé Paul Vaessen could be out of action for the rest of the season because of a serious knee injury.

Vaessen was carried off in the 43rd minute of Arsenal's Football Combination derby against Spurs at White Hart Lane on Saturday after a heavy tackle.

On Tuesday he had an operation at St. Mary's Hospital, Paddington, to repair damaged knee ligaments.

Vaessen has proved a capable stand-in striker for Frank Stapleton and Alan Sunderland and has scored some key goals in his first team appearances.

This season he has been on the verge of a regular first team spot.

Manager Terry Neill commented: "It's very disappointing for the lad - he's been doing so well and now this."

"He'll have his leg in plaster for six weeks and it will take him some time to regain match fitness. It's possible he could be out for the rest of the season but we don't like to think like that. We prefer to take things as they come."

"It was an unfortunate incident – the knee was damaged when Paul went into a heavy tackle."

"I actually played with Paul when he damaged his knee really badly at Tottenham in that reserve game," recalls Sammy Nelson. "I'd got out of the first team and bang, it really was a bad, bad tackle, a dodgy tackle."

Maureen believes it was intentional.

"I think they were out to get him, two or three players, in

that match. They were out to pull him down because he was getting a little bit of publicity and I think he went down a couple of times and it was the third time they pulled him down that he did the damage. They pulled him down and that was it. He said he heard it crack and that he knew straight away that it had done a lot of damage."

"He went over in a heap, sat up and the pain hit him and he was sick," says Lee.

Fred Street was Arsenal's physiotherapist at the time.

"I remember when he did his left knee in the reserves at Tottenham. He tore his knee badly so we brought him in on the Sunday at the club and I had no doubt; the cartilage was torn and so were the ligaments. It wasn't one of these wait and see jobs.

"Nigel Harris was our consultant then. He'd been the Arsenal consultant for years for surgery and I'd arranged it so I could ring him up on a Sunday morning from the club and say, 'Look, I've got this player here,' and book a bed. It was almost, you know, whatever you say we'll do and I said, 'I've got this lad here who needs surgery on his knee and he needs the ligaments sticking back.' And he said, 'Bring him in tomorrow to St Mary's, I'm doing a ward round at twelve o'clock. Go to the ward, tell the sister and they'll put him in a side room and I'll see you then and then we'll probably get a bed arranged for tomorrow evening.' So we're down at the hospital the next day, saw the sister, she put us in a side room.

"So we're sitting in this side room and Nigel Harris is doing his rounds on the ward. Now, this was still in the days when surgeons were gods. They've got an army of people with them, you know, secretaries, assistants, junior doctors, students, all walking along behind, listening to his every word, like with old James Robertson-Justice in the Dirk Bogarde 'Doctor' films. And Nigel Harris was very much in that mould. He was wartime. He was that age and I'd known him since the fifties. But he'd got that rather distant, remoteness even with patients, even in the private world. The players all knew him as 'Nigel the Knife' or 'Chopper Harris' because players don't give respect to anyone. You get respect in a sort of affectionate, disregarding way. They're off-hand with you but don't mean it.

"So Paul's there, he's a young player, he's nineteen, he's laying on the table. And this particular injury is a very easy one to diagnose, you know, you put your thumb right on the ligament and it's 'Oww!' and you know what you've got, pretty much. This was in the days before scans, this was. Now you'd scan it to make sure before you look inside but the old method was pretty conclusive.

"So Nigel's here, looking over his glasses. I said, 'This is Paul Vaessen, Mr Harris. He's got a medial ligament for sure for me and I think he needs surgery.' So Nigel feels it with his thumb and Paul goes, 'F--king hell, leave it out Nigel!!' I thought, 'Oh Christ!' And there's all these people standing there, this team of assistant doctors who wouldn't say boo to him, looking at each other, probably bursting to laugh. Nigel never batted an eyelid, just looked over his glasses. That was Nigel. Never gave it a second thought."

Arsenal Programme v Middlesbrough, Saturday 28th February 1981:

Although we have had a difficult season by way of injuries we have a reasonably clean bill of health at the moment except for Paul Vaessen who is recuperating from an operation on knee ligaments, and we are hopeful that Paul may have a game or two before the end of the season. We all certainly wish him well for the speediest possible recovery. It came at an unfortunate time for Paul, but then you can say that of any long lay-off for any footballer, but it is something the professional player has to live with.

"He did everything in his knee," says Lee. "Cruciate ligaments, the medial ligament and cartilage. It was a bad injury.

"But whilst he was in hospital he had loads of visitors. Raph Meade came in one day with a lovely present; six cans of *Special Brew*! He said, 'Here, get that down your neck. That'll cheer you up!' Paul said, 'Don't you think I'm in enough bother already?!'

"He actually got sympathetic cards and letters from Tottenham fans who had been at the game and had actually heard the crunch as he went over.

"He went off to America for a couple of weeks with Sarah for some r and r. They went to Florida. Paul paid for all of it out of his own pocket. It wasn't like nowadays where the club will pay to send you somewhere. He saw consultants, specialists while he was out there. He had a bit of a set-back when he jumped into some water which he thought looked about six foot deep but was actually only about two foot deep. He really jarred his knee and it blew up.

"He was out for the remainder of that 1980-81 season and the prognosis from the doctors wasn't good. They doubted he'd be able to make it back to the same level he'd been playing at. But Paul was determined to prove them all wrong. I remember him sitting at home after he got out of hospital. He was in plaster from his toes to his nuts. Me and my dad were sitting there and he said, 'You two watch', he said. 'I guarantee you I'll be back in that first team within a year. I'll get back in if it kills me.' He truly believed he could defy those doctors. He didn't take any of their advice. They told him he needed to rest up but he'd say, 'F--k them, what do they know?' and off we'd go to our local park, Senegal Fields, which is where the New Den was later built, for a work out. We'd been going down there since I was a kid. It was basically a big field with a canal running behind it. They never cut the grass there or anything like that but we didn't care. I was always sat in goal. I'd have Paul firing these rockets in to me, knocking me back into the goal.

"Anyway, here we were and Paul would have this harness he got off the back of a lorry and he'd tie two car tires to it and go off round the park dragging them along.

"We'd also go down the Arsenal doing weights in the gym. He put in so much work. That pre-season he did extra work after training, running up and down the stands, doing weights. He was putting in double time training and he built his knee up again. He worked so hard during that summer, I don't think people really realise how much work he put in, how determined he was. Again, it was all or nothing with Paul. He went at it full pelt, fully committed. I've never seen anybody try so hard for something, fight so hard for something.

"Of course he did have his down moments. I sat up with him as he cried some nights. At other times he'd be angry, frustrated with his body. He also got worried that somebody was going to take his place at Arsenal. Who wouldn't? So when he was down, I'd drag him back down to Senegal Fields and pretty soon we'd be kicking the ball about to each other."

"He wasn't too bad whilst he was recovering," says Maureen. "I think he knew how bad it was but he was not the sort of person to sit around and mope. He had his friends, his brother and family. He played video games on TV with Lee, went for walks around the park with his brother and he also visited the Arsenal. His dad spoke to him quite a lot. I didn't understand things like football matters but it did not stop me worrying over him. I worried tremendously over him."

****

By the time the players reported back on Tuesday 28th July 1981, Paul had made sufficient progress that he was included in pre-season training. There were, however, some words of caution from Don Howe.

Arsenal Official Annual 1982:

THE RISING STARS OF ARSENAL: SIX OF THE BEST –
Don Howe's pick of the Arsenal youngsters

Paul Vaessen

Paul was a bit unlucky with injury last season after getting a few goals in the First Division. He's got over a nasty injury, and we've got to be patient with him. At the same time he himself has got to get over this knock. He had a pretty severe knee injury but John Devine had a similar injury and got over it. So that is a good example for Paul.

It's now a question of time, and Paul regaining confidence.

8
Beginning of the End

"It is easy - terribly easy - to shake a man's faith in himself. To take advantage of that to break a man's spirit is devil's work."

'Candida' by George Bernard Shaw (1898)

My three boys were in the lavish living room, bouncing up and down on the sumptuous white leather sofa.

I was having kittens.

Now, I know that they are good, respectful boys but they get excited and I was terrified, terrified their *joie de vivre* would overflow and result in something valuable, irreplaceable in this pristine Hampshire home getting broken.

And Graham, who I'd spoken to on the phone a few times but had only just met several minutes before, had been so cordial, so trusting, I thought, inviting us all in like this.

The plan had been that my wife would just drop me off and I would come in and interview Graham whilst my wife and boys went off to the beach or a restaurant for a while. Graham, though, had insisted that we all come in.

So the boys got a briefing.

'This is Mr Rix. He is one of Daddy's heroes. Don't touch any of Mr Rix's things unless he tells you you can.'

Some of Mr Rix's most valuable things are in his office. It's a mini personalized museum. There are England shirts, including one he wore during the 1982 World Cup in Spain, framed on the walls. There are England caps, photos and his 1979 F.A. Cup winners medal which he proudly shows off to the boys.

All of this is, of course, evidence of the good times. But with the ups came the downs, including that decisive, saved penalty in the European Cup-Winners' Cup Final against Valencia in 1980. Then there was the time he was chinned by Wolves defender, Bob Hazell,

137

in front of the North Bank during a match at Highbury in the late seventies. And perhaps worst of all was the heckling, the jeering and rejection by his own supporters a few years later.

It's a beautiful day in early June so we sit outside in the sunshine in Graham's immaculate garden.

"I got severe stick from our crowd," Graham reflects. "It was around the time that Arsenal got the disc jockey or announcer to start reading out the players' names whilst you were warming up before kick-off. You know, 'In goal, number one, Pat Jennings...at right-back, number two, John Hollins...' that sort of thing. Then they'd get to number eleven, Graham Rix, and there was this section up in the East Stand, I got absolutely pelted by them. They were booing me and there I was on the pitch thinking, 'We haven't even kicked off yet!' And my ex-missus was sat in the stand with her head in her hands.

"It does affect you, getting that sort of stick. It affects you big time. For example, a ball would be pinged out to me and I'd be thinking, 'Okay, I'm going to play this into the front man with the outside of my left foot.' All of a sudden the ball would be coming to me and I'd be thinking, 'I'm going to miss it, I'm going to mis-control this here.' And that's because the seed of doubt had been sown in my head.

"You see, when you're a footballer, people tell you where to be, what to eat, what to do with your money, where to stand at a free-kick. They tell you all that. Nobody tells you how to handle being famous, if you like, how to handle the pressure that goes with doing your job in front of forty thousand people. Nobody explains that to you. You're going to make mistakes and unless you're of a tough mentality, you could struggle.

"I'm lucky. I didn't like it but I could handle it. I've had so many kicks in the bollocks my mentality today is that there's always somebody worse off than yourself.

"I think how you react, it's down to your grounding, the way you were brought up. My parents, they'd hammer me all the time. Dad would say everything's crap. Even when I was twenty, twenty-one he'd say, 'You tackle like a poof.' And yet, when I was twenty-four, twenty-five, twenty-six and I was getting that stick from the Arsenal punters, my dad would watch me play and he'd phone me up and say, 'You were the best bloody player on the pitch today, son.'

Because he knew at that time I needed a boost. He knew when to cut me down, he knew when to give me a boost.

"The other thing that helped me was I actually had a long chat with a guy called Chris Bradnam. He used to play tennis – he was a young player at Wimbledon – and was now into coaching. He was a friend of my ex-missus and he said to me, 'When you run out on to the pitch, what's on your mind?' I said, 'Well, I want to show everybody I'm the best player on the pitch.' He said, 'Nightmare. You should be going out on to the pitch thinking, 'I'm going to do my job today.' Set yourself a little bit of a lower target, do the easy things so if your first attempt at a forty yard pass doesn't come off you can still think to yourself, 'Well, I'm still doing my job for the team.'

"I think Vas needed that talk. You know, 'The lads love you, you hold it up, you lay it off to a team mate, you get in the box. That's all we're asking of you.' The problem was the crowd was angry that Frank Stapleton had gone and Vas was thinking, 'I'm following Frank Stapleton, I've got to do a fancy flick, I've got to beat a man...' You've got to be tough mentally and I just think that Vas, although he was a strong boy, mentally I'm not sure he was that strong."

Before we leave a couple of hours later, I ask Graham if he wouldn't mind signing some photographs for me. In one of them Graham is leaping on Paul after the final whistle at the *Stadio Comunale* during what were, for Paul, happier days.

The days before the injury.

The days before anyone had ever heard of Winterslag.

****

By the time the little-known Belgian side arrived in North London at the beginning of November 1981 for their UEFA Cup second round, second leg tie with Arsenal, there was a suffocating cloud of pessimism and despondency hanging over Highbury. The Gunners seemed to be going backwards at a time when they could so easily have been amongst the title challengers.

139

"There was this little period," explains Graham Rix, "a little bit like at Manchester United with the Nevilles and Beckham and Scholes and Butt coming through. We had a similar situation at Arsenal. We had Liam, Frank - world-class players – O'Leary, myself, John Devine and underneath that Vas, Paul Davis and Chrissie Whyte. We had a really good, good young squad. But they needed to add to it. But instead of keeping that squad together they allowed Liam to go and, with all due respect to him, Peter Nicholas came in, a good pro but a worker. Then Frank goes the following season, similar situation to Liam. They didn't offer him enough money and in the end, when they realized he was prepared to leave, they were bending over backwards for him. But the damage had been done. And I'm not being disrespectful to them, but they brought in John Hawley, as nice a person as he was, and Ray Hankin. When Ray Hankin arrived he was sixteen stone. Don Howe was coach and I said, 'Don, he's a little bit heavy.' Don replied, 'He's been in a health farm for three months!' I mean, he couldn't run!"

As Paul would later say himself, "When Arsenal let Liam and Frank go, the atmosphere around the club went flat, to be honest. Everyone tried to put a brave face on things, but when your two best players leave, and you replace them with the players Terry Neill brought in, you know there is a problem."[23]

Without Stapleton, Arsenal had scored just seven times in their first eleven league outings and subsequently occupied a lowly seventeenth place in Division One. They were playing some pretty discouraging stuff in front of a dwindling Arsenal public increasingly disgruntled by the team's poor start to the season and by a perceived lack of ambition from a club seemingly unable to hold on to its major stars. The biggest noise in the half empty Highbury house was invariably the sound of slow hand-clapping echoing around the old stadium.

And as if that wasn't enough, things were buzzing over at White Hart Lane where Cup-holders Spurs were serious title contenders. Attracting all sorts of plaudits for their swashbuckling style, Tottenham had managed, unlike Arsenal, to hold on to their prize asset, Glenn Hoddle, during a summer of speculation. And perhaps most frighteningly of all they were even proving a success in the hit parade with their exquisite collaborations with *Chas & Dave*.

It was into this setting that Paul was attempting a comeback.

He also had to contend with serious competition for Stapleton's place in the side from Brian McDermott, Raphael Meade and Hawley. But there was initial encouragement from club chairman Denis Hill-Wood when he declared, "There's no reason why a youngster like Paul Vaessen shouldn't develop to replace Stapleton the way Stapleton developed when Malcolm Macdonald had to retire."[24] However, it was McDermott, who had impressed during pre-season, who got the nod when the opening day of the season came along, Paul coming on as a replacement for John Devine during Arsenal's depressing home defeat to Stoke City.

Paul steadily felt his way back in the reserves until the middle of September when, with Alan Sunderland suspended again and Hawley ineligible, he was brought in to start for the first time in eight months as Arsenal travelled to Greece to take on Panathaniakos in the first round of the U.E.F.A. Cup.

"It's great to get another chance," said Paul. "I'm very excited. If I do the same in this match as I did the last time I played in Europe then I'll be well pleased."[25]

But it was another youngster, fellow Londoner Raphael Meade, who stole the headlines when he scored with a spectacular overhead kick with his first touch having come on as a substitute for Paul whose, "legs seemed to have gone,"[26] according to manager Terry Neill.

It was, perhaps, an indication that Paul wasn't perhaps yet ready.

****

It was difficult to spot many similarities between Arsenal and their U.E.F.A. Cup second round opponents, Winterslag, other than that they were both struggling in their respective leagues. The two clubs were, in reality, worlds apart and occupied opposite ends of the footballing spectrum.

Formed in 1923, Winterslag, flatteringly nicknamed *De Vieze Mannen* - the 'Dirty Men' - had played for most of its history outside the Belgian top flight. A small, friendly club based in the town of

Genk with a population of only 65,000, Winterslag were accustomed to playing their home matches in front of crowds of just a few thousand. A club with no honours and no money, the extent of the chasm between them and their famous, aristocratic English opponents could be gauged by a quick glance at the matchday programme and the pen-pictures of those lining up for Winterslag on the evening of Tuesday 3ʳᵈ November 1981:

Jean-Paul de Bruyne: Goalkeeper. A twenty-year-old Belgian who has always played for Winterslag. Third choice last season but the new manager has given him his chance and he has taken it. Works as a coal miner.

Patrick Houben: Right back. Twenty two years old and Belgian. Solid, strong, quick and reliable he likes to attack and gets the odd League goal. Now employed as a miner.

Mathy Billen: Centre back. Twenty eight year old Belgian. A former left back who liked to attack he was converted to do the marking job by the new manager. Good in the air, he goes up for set-pieces. Works as a miner.

Eric van Lessen: Centre back. The veteran of the side being thirty three years old and Belgian. Captain of the team and regarded as the brains of the side he always goes up for corners and free kicks. Manager of a local bank.

Paul Lambrichts: Left back. Twenty seven years old and Belgian. Excellent in the air he was a centre back until switched this season. Vigorous, quick and full of energy but thought to be a bit too impetuous. Off the field is a teacher.

Roger Albertsen: Midfield. Twenty four years old with fifteen full caps for Norway. Helped them beat England recently in Oslo. A full-time professional.

Luc Thys: Midfield. Nineteen years old and Belgian. Signed from a local amateur club in 1980 and is now a key man in the engine room of the team. Probably the most popular player with the fans who admire his ball skills. Unfortunate to be unemployed at the moment.

Pierre Denier: Midfield. Twenty five years old come November, and Belgian. Transferred to Winterslag from a local amateur club in 1974 and now works as a clerk in a warehouse.

Karel Berger: Forward. Thirty years old from West Germany. A full-time professional with Winterslag, he joined them from Fortuna Cologne in 1978 and still lives in Cologne.

Carlos Weis: Midfield. Twenty three years old with full caps for Luxembourg. Began with Spora Luxembourg but was signed in 1979 from FC Metz in France as a full-time professional.

Guido Davids: Forward. Twenty six years old and Belgian. Engaged in 1978 after being released by Royal FC Standard-Liege. A teacher off the field.

For KFC Winterslag, who would only exist for another seven years before merging with neighbours FC Waterschei Thor in 1988 to form the new club, KRC Genk, their U.E.F.A. Cup pairing with Arsenal would be the pinnical of their history.

For Paul Vaessen, it would represent the lowest point in his Arsenal career.

Times, Wednesday 4th November 1981:

Now is the Winterslag of Arsenal's discontent

Arsenal 2 Winterslag 1 (UEFA Cup Second Round, Second Leg)

Arsenal, who had sought release from their domestic headaches in the fresh, rejuvenating air of European competition, found the treatment curtailed at Highbury last night. The sad truth is that having walked headlong into an early goal by their opponents they were simply not quite good enough to overhaul a Belgian side containing eight part-timers.

When eventually they did find some rhythm and menace it

143

was too late to prevent Winterslag advancing into the third round of the Uefa Cup at their expense on the away goal rule and an aggregate of 2-2. Arsenal's spirit, in the end was willing but their flesh, particularly in attack, is embarrassingly weak. Terry Neill, their manager, will be under even greater pressure now to spend, spend, spend in the transfer market...

Arsenal's impotence in attack, now without Sunderland, who failed a test on his injured calf, was highlighted by Vaessen, the replacement. His sleepy manner, topped with an abject failure to do little right, made him the butt of Arsenal supporters' frustration. The cheers that greeted his substitution were heartless and severe on a young man who was the toast of Highbury two years ago when he headed a semi-final winner against Juventus in the Cup Winners' Cup...

Paul would tell Jon Spurling some years later, "It was very strange - the thing with the crowd...The night of the Winterslag game - I have to say that at the time it was complete and utter humiliation."[27]

"Arsenal fans have had a reputation of being good to their own," says Spurling, "and yet history shows that, say with Jon Sammels in the 1970-71 season, it doesn't always happen. I wasn't old enough to remember what happened to Sammels but I've never heard a crowd before or since treat a player like they did Paul Vaessen. The crowd were just horrendous. They were booing him around the stadium. You could hear it echoing right round. It was an eerie night. I think the crowd was 23,000 in a ground which could hold 58,000. It was less than half full. It was just depressing but it was depressing at Arsenal in those days. If I was to select a worst ever Arsenal performance in my lifetime, I think that would have to be the night."

Playing alongside Paul that evening in an inexperienced front line also including Raphael Meade was Brian McDermott.

"I remember playing against Winterslag with Paul," says McDermott. "I think he'd been injured and he came back and whether he was right or not I don't know but he got a real unfair reaction from the supporters. He did get a lot of stick on that particular day which was unusual for the Arsenal crowd, to give one of the home-grown boys a bad time like that, especially when you

144

consider the goal against Juventus. It was surprising really. They were shouting "Vaessen off". I've never heard that before. It was very unusual."

Family friend John Clubb was in the crowd.

"It was the one and only time - and I've been going to Arsenal since 1981 and have spent probably ten, twelve years of that travelling around the country going to games – it was the one and only time I've heard a crowd singing negatively about their own player. I've heard players booed and you get mumblings for some, but they were chanting, 'Vaessen off, Vaessen off, Vaessen off.'

"I would have been about twelve, thirteen and I'd say that, at that time, it was probably the most distressing thing I'd known because, well, I knew him so I took it personally."

Lee was also there.

"They had to drag me out of the North Bank that day. I went mad. I remember this bloke about six yards away started up first. 'Vaessen off, Vaessen off.' He was standing there about eighteen stone, eating a meat pie, never done anything physical in his life. I turned round to him and said, 'Excuse me, what do you mean?' He said, 'He's no good. He's finished.' That started me off. I said, 'You don't know what he's been through.' I started punching every Arsenal head I could find. I was biting people. A few fans gathered round me, knew I was his brother, saying, 'Come on now, son' and 'Sorry' but I told them all to f--k off. None of them realised how much work he'd put in to get back."

"The barracking he got was bad, really bad," continues Brian McDermott. "Even when you were playing, you noticed it. It culminated in the manager bringing him off the pitch."

"I mean that game, it was dreadful," says Jill Smith. "I wanted to slide down in my seat, it was so embarrassing and when he came off, because I was sat by the tunnel, you could see he had tears in his eyes. It was dreadful. It was awful. I could see he was virtually crying when he went off the field and it was so uncalled for. I would say it was the worst I think an Arsenal crowd have been to a player other than Jon Sammels."

"Can you imagine?" asks Lee. "Can you imagine 23,000 people telling you you're crap, when only eighteen months earlier you were top of everyone's Christmas card list?"

"That just shows you how fickle football is," says Leon who

had also been at the game having seen in the *London Evening Standard* that Paul would be playing. "You know there's a saying in football that you're only as good as your last game. It's cruel but that's the way it is."

"Without being harsh on Paul," agrees Terry Neill, "it's the same for everybody. I mean, you know, that's the game. You're a king one week, you're a bum the next. We've all got to deal with it."

"After he was substituted," continues Leon, "I went down to see him in the dressing room. I found him in floods of tears."

"I just wanted a hole to open up and swallow me," Paul told the press the next day. "I don't know why the crowd picked on me," he said.[28]

"For some reason," comments Jon Spurling, "it was Vaessen the crowd really turned on and I don't know why that was."

Don Howe remembers the fixture well.

"What I would say is we were all poor that night. We put in a shocking display. I think everybody just took it for granted that because they were a Belgian team who nobody knew, everybody thought we were going to beat them five-nil. It worked out a little bit different. They were quite clever tactically. We misread them.

"It wasn't down to one player. It was down to the entire side. I can't think of one player that night who I thought, 'Well, they played okay.'"

"The thing I remember about that game," says John Clubb, "is that, even though Paul was having a bad game, you couldn't pick out anyone else who was having a good one."

"It wasn't just Paul," confirms Kenny Sansom who was in the Arsenal side that night, "but obviously Paul being a young lad, expectations on him were going to be high."

"Whenever something's going wrong with the team," states actor, journalist and Arsenal enthusiast, Tom Watt, "the first reaction is to find an individual to blame. It's human nature for supporters to want to blame someone, one person, whether it be the manager or a player."

And something clearly was going wrong with the team. In Paul, still adjusting after returning from a lengthy lay-off, they had found a convenient scapegoat.

"Maybe," opines Jon Spurling, "it was because he got to such a high, scoring that goal away at Spurs and then scoring against

146

Juventus. Maybe this raised expectations amongst the fans. Maybe we thought he would be the next big Arsenal star."

Certainly there are those who feel that Paul's moment in Turin, happening as it did so early in his career, was a tragedy rather than a triumph.

"I think pretty quickly," Spurling continues, "after the injury he lost his pace and the Arsenal fans were frustrated because Stapleton had just left and Brady had left. Arsenal fans were angry, they were angry because we were only two players short at one point of a championship-winning team. Suddenly we were a long, long way short."

Paul himself agreed.

"The problem was that the Arsenal crowd of that time was a fairly unsettled one. Many were pissed off that Liam and Frank had gone. Suddenly the good feeling was gone. It was a case of 'Why isn't Vaessen as good as Stapleton? Frank wouldn't have done that' if I messed up a chance. Their patience with me had vanished."[29]

Fan Peter Kirkwood concurs. "It was bye-bye to Stapleton, bye-bye to Brady. It was like the break-up of the side and anyone who came in then, if they weren't a big name, they had five minutes to score or that was it."

"It was a bit like with Jeff Blockley, for example," says Tom Watt. "Jeff Blockley replaced Frank McLintock in 1973. Jeff Blockley was no Frank McLintock and was never going to be a Frank McLintock. So the stick he took really stemmed from a poor managerial decision, to let Frank go."

"So we looked to Vaessen," Spurling continues, "to suddenly not just be a promising kid but to actually be the finished article and it didn't happen because he had lost his pace and very quickly you could sense the crowd's frustration."

"I did not start going to Highbury until 1982," reports Arsenal fan and journalist Barnaby Phillips, "but my brother was a regular on the North Bank during the miserable 1981-82 season when we could not score and struggled to get 20,000 into the ground. I remember him coming back from matches and saying that Paul Vaessen was one of the players who was regularly getting barracked by the crowd (Paul Davis and Brian Talbot were others). 'Vaessen shit' was the chant from the North Bank. I was surprised, as Vaessen

147

was such a young, home-grown player, and was the hero of Turin."

"You could see he'd lost half a yard of pace," remarks Lee. "He couldn't twist and turn. I went to his first couple of reserve team games when he came back. I remember my dad saying, 'Look at that poor sod.' He was struggling for pace, he'd lost half a yard of pace and he couldn't open up. Every time he took the ball down on his chest and went to turn you could see him wincing."

"It was clear he wasn't the same player he was before his injury," agrees Leon, "although I have to say I think they brought him back too early. That's my opinion anyway."

The change in Paul was easily explained. He was experiencing pain in his left knee every time he trained, every time he played. It was something that would stay with him for the rest of his life.

As Paul said to Jon Spurling, "What they (the fans) didn't know was that my knee injury…was already restricting my movements on the field."[30]

"He said his knee was like a rusty old gate in terms of the actual noise it made inside," recalls Spurling. "He said it was like a burning inside his knee, it was so hot, because it was bone on bone. His shock absorbers – the cartilage – had gone."

"He could just about get through games," says Maureen, "but it was the after effects, his knee swelled up. He used to go up in his old bedroom and I used to hear him crying up there, it was hurting him so."

"After that Winterslag game he always looked as though he was playing within himself," says John Clubb. "Whether it was the Stapleton thing, the injury or psychological I don't know. But there was just this undercurrent every time he played and, you know, from my point of view I got nervous for him before each game because the feeling you got from that Winterslag game was that ninety percent of the crowd didn't like him at all."

"He was never one of those players that the crowd seemed to take to," agrees Jill Smith.

It all acted to have a devastating impact on Paul who, by his own admission, didn't have the strength to deal with it.

"Some blokes are born to play football. I'm not simply referring to their talent - I'm also talking about mental toughness. I've never been the strongest of people."[31]

148

"Vaessen said to me that he was never really cut out to be a footballer because he was a sensitive guy," recalls Jon Spurling.

"He definitely was very sensitive," says cousin Jackie Line. "He had a conscience and was always very respectful to his elders, always very polite. He loved family and he wouldn't speak ill of anyone. I imagine the barracking from the crowd would have bothered him greatly."

Vic Wright went out with the players after the Winterslag game.

"It was David O'Leary's stag do. Vas was absolutely gutted. But it's the same old thing at Arsenal. If you get booed the boys get behind you. The crowd may get on your back sometimes but the players - your mates - they get behind you. All the boys spoke to him, David O'Leary, Brian Talbot, Willie Young. You've got a few of the boys out with you, they try and bring you out of it, you know, like 'You've got to take the rough with the smooth. Get your head up. Forget it. It's a one-off. Don't worry. Next time you score they'll forget all about it.' But if it's the first time you've been booed, it's very hard, you know, and you're thinking you're playing for the club that you love and you've come through from the youth team, the reserves and you're thinking, you know, is this for me or not?"

"At the time, fellas like Graham Rix and Kenny Sansom would tell me to ignore the barrackers, and go home and forget it," Paul would disclose years later.[32]

Graham Rix reveals, "I would have probably said something to Vas like, 'Hey. I like playing with you, so f--k them. When they cheer you just put your arm up and get on with your job and when they boo you just don't take any notice of it. Don't get too high, don't get too low.'"

"Barracking happens and that's one of the things you've got to try and deal with," Terry Neill points out. "You don't get carried away when you have a little bit of success and you don't get suicidal when things are not going your way. Life owes us nothing. There's nothing you can do and it will continue in the future. And if you don't understand that, you're best to get out and get a proper job."

"It destroyed him," says Lee. "It destroyed his faith in football. He was wrecked, destroyed. He was never the same after that. It ruined him. It destroyed his pride, his self-confidence. I remember after one match he came home in his Jag. He was living in Lee Green with Sarah at the time but on this occasion he came home to us. I was fiddling about with my bike. I went up to the car and tapped on the window. He was just sitting there with his head in his hands. It was obvious he'd been crying because his eyes were all red and everything. Eventually he got out and went straight up to his room. He was inconsolable. He didn't come back out of his room for a day. He knew then that that was it."

More than ten years later Jon Spurling found Paul still very bitter towards Arsenal fans.

"He hated Arsenal fans. He loathed and detested Arsenal fans because of what had happened to him. In fact, initially he didn't want to do the interview with me because he knew I was an Arsenal fan. He said, 'You're the guys who destroyed me.'

"The thing is, we were never fully told what the extent of his injury was, how bad it was. Bring things forward thirty years to Arsene Wenger, he would have protected Vaessen and you probably wouldn't have seen him for a year. But that was Arsenal at the time. The club was under pressure from the fans. Terry Neill was under pressure. Everyone was under pressure, pressure, pressure, pressure. They had to win and Paul was supposedly the next big thing and, you know, it didn't work out that way and after just a few more games Vaessen just seemed to fade away."

But Paul wasn't quite finished yet.

****

Manager Terry Neill had tried every combination he could during the 1981-82 season in an attempt to get a new partnership with Alan Sunderland going, to get some goals. Neill tried John Hawley, Brian McDermott, Raphael Meade, even Graham Rix - Ray Hankin came and went too – but none of them had made the position their own. So after some impressive performances for the reserves, Paul was recalled to the side in the New Year after a three month absence. He went on to enjoy his best ever run of games in the first team. But with the Arsenal public still edgy at the time, Vaessen's reappearance only acted to agitate them further. The booing, the

150

groans and the grumblings had not gone away.

Neither completely, though, had Paul's ability:

Sunday Mirror, Sunday 31ˢᵗ January 1982:

Viva Vaessen!

Arsenal 1 Leeds United 0 (Football League Division One)

A Paul Vaessen goal five minutes before half time enabled the Gunners to end their Leeds hoodoo – and ease the Highbury goal famine.

This was Arsenal's first League win at Highbury against Leeds in nine attempts. But they made hard work of it.

Vaessen, the London boy with the continental name, brought into the side in a bid to boost the worst home scoring record in the First Division, obliged with his first goal of the season.

Hesitant

He robbed hesitant Trevor Cherry out near the left touchline and left the Leeds defender sitting on his backside as he went on to calmly roll the ball wide of the advancing John Lukic.

The roar that greeted the goal showed how desperate Arsenal fans were for a score.

Arsenal manager Terry Neill admitted, however: "There are still problems scoring goals."

But he praised 20-year-old Vaessen. "It was Trevor Cherry's ball but Paul persisted and was a good example to everybody. He put him under pressure and finished nice and coolly."

Disbelief

The goal made up for Vaessen's boob after 23 minutes that had the fans howling in disbelief.

He beat the Leeds offside trap, but on his own in the penalty area and with only Lukic to beat, he booted the ball hopelessly wide...

The Gunners, who have still only scored a meager six League goals at home this season, deserved their win, but they scarcely looked like Championship challengers...

As well as scoring the winning goal, Paul left his mark on the match - and on one Leeds United player in particular - in an altogether different way.

"After the match," Lee recalls, "Paul came round and said, 'Dad, you know Kenny Burns?' My old man said, 'Yeah, what about him?' Paul said, 'I laid him out in the tunnel.' He was so blasé about it, so matter of fact." Burns, a notoriously uncompromising Scottish hard man who was later described by his former Nottingham Forest boss, Brian Clough, as the ugliest player he'd ever signed, had marked Paul a bit too closely during the match.

"Apparently Kenny had been trying to terrorise Paul during the first half," Lee continues. "He was digging him in the ribs, pinching his arse, grabbing him by the bollocks, giving him verbals and all that. Paul never complained, never said anything on the pitch but when they were half way down the tunnel and out of view of the referee, Paul turned around and went bang! Take that. He nailed him. They had to pick him up off his arse. When Paul got back to the dressing room, the players were all going, 'Good old Vas! Go and give him another one!' That's how Paul told it anyway."

Three days later Paul was on the scoresheet again.

Islington Gazette, Friday 5th February 1982:

Vaessen for victory

Arsenal 2 Wolves 1 (Football League Division One)

NO ONE was happier than back-in-favour striker Paul Vaessen after this gritty victory at Highbury on Tuesday night.

Vaessen scored his second goal in two games to clinch victory for the Gunners – and lift them into the top five in the table for the first time this season.

Indeed, Terry Neill's mean machine are now hovering just three points behind the leaders Southampton. Their position, though, is largely due to their thrifty defence which has only conceded 16 goals in 21 league games.

Once again Arsenal were in charge but could not score.

Graham Rix broke the deadlock after 66 minutes when he raced onto a Paul Davis pass and shot home from 25 yards.

Wolves veteran Ken Hibbitt snatched an equalizer ten minutes later.

Then it was left to Vaessen, turning smartly in the box and knocking the ball over the on-coming goalkeeper, Bradshaw, for the 81ˢᵗ minute winner.

Terry Neill was obviously pleased.

"The lad has done very well since he came into the side and it's up to him to stay there."[33]

Pleased, maybe, but not convinced, as one could tell from his comments following the stalemate at Sunderland in Arsenal and Paul's next match.

"We've got one of the best teams around - and if we get a striker we'll really be in business,"[34] said Neill as he continued to court the likes of Stoke's Lee Chapman, Coventry's Garry Thompson, Tony Woodcock of Cologne, Celtic's young striker Charlie Nicholas and even Diego Maradona of Boca Juniors.

"Believe it or not," says fan Emilio Zorlakki, "the Arsenal fans were giving Paul a hard time as, in spite of scoring fairly regularly, he was struggling to impose himself in matches."

Paul soldiered on with appearances against Notts County, Middlesbrough (played in front of a paltry Highbury crowd of just 13,738) and Manchester United. There were, however, no more goals.

Paul got one last opportunity, lining up alongside Alan Sunderland for the visit of high-flying Swansea City on Saturday 27ᵗʰ February 1982. It didn't go well, with former Gunner, Ray Kennedy, who Paul was once likened to, scoring the first goal in a 2-0 victory for the visitors. The *Hampstead & Highgate Express* reported the following Friday that Paul "never looked the part."[35] He was replaced by Raphael Meade after 58 minutes, his chance gone.

It had been his 27ᵗʰ start for the first team. It would also be his last.

STUCK IN A MOMENT

****

"I don't remember too much about my brother's twenty-first birthday party," says Lee. "My dad bought a case of *Special Brew* and after I'd had about three cans, I was blotto, I was out of the game. I was sick all over Paul's new £400 velvet curtains. He went mental. 'You little bastard!' he shouted. I was only about fifteen at the time. It was the first time I'd got drunk.

"The other thing I do remember was that there were quite a few Arsenal players there. Kenny Sansom was there doing his Norman Wisdom impersonation and having everybody in tears."

"Kenny was the life and sole of the party," Maureen agrees. "He had us in stitches with his jokes and impressions."

For cousin Jackie, the party had more sinister undertones. "My uncle, my mum's brother, Wally, he said to me that one day Paul went round and asked him to take him to pick up some stuff for the party. So Wally said, 'Alright, where do you need to go?' Paul said, 'I need to go to Deptford to get some coke.' So they drive to somewhere in Deptford, pull up at this house. Wally gets out and opens the boot, Paul goes into the house, comes out and Wally, who's expecting to see some crates of drinks, says, 'Where's the coke?' Paul just patted his pocket.

"With Paul and the drugs, I don't know why it was," Jackie continues. "Maybe it was earning all that money all of a sudden. Then, maybe, with the injury, he just got some comfort from it, from the drugs, I don't know."

9

Scrapheap City

'What'll we do with ourselves this afternoon?' cried Daisy, 'and the day after that, and the next thirty years?'

'The Great Gatsby' by Scott Fitzgerald (1925)

My instincts were telling me to stand perfectly still, pretend it wasn't happening and it would go away, it would pass.

Standing still was not a problem. I couldn't have moved if I'd wanted to, we were so packed in. It was January 1983 and the George Wilson Stadium, home of Bishop's Stortford Football Club, was filled well beyond capacity for the F.A. Cup Third Round Replay with Malcolm Allison's Middlesbrough. The children in the crowd had filtered their way through to the front of the terracing and I could see friends from school sitting cross-legged along the touchline in scenes you'd never see today.

What had put the wind up me was the conduct of the Stortford fans, the chanting. I just wasn't prepared for it. It was so antagonistic, so loud and so rude.

"Who the f--king 'ell are you?" they were shrieking at the 'Boro end. I'd never heard anything like it before. I'd only ever been to one football match before, the 1981 F.A. Trophy Final between a Stortford side boasting Arsenal 'double' winner, John Radford, and Sutton United which had been played in a pretty friendly atmosphere at Wembley Stadium. This was something altogether different. It shattered my perceptions of Bishop's Stortford as a respectable, middle class, conservative Hertfordshire market town. This behavior was something more fitting of neighbouring new town, Harlow in Essex.

I was there with dad and I was dying of embarrassment. As far as he was concerned I'd only ever heard one swear word before. I had once said to him that I thought the *Boomtown Rats* were crap and had been severely admonished. Now here we were amidst this

155

uncomfortable chorus of profanities.

Stand perfectly still, pretend it isn't happening and it will go away, it will pass.

Of course, I understand now why I was there. It was not only a momentous occasion for Stortford, it being the first time they had reached the third round of the F.A. Cup in their 108 year history, but it was also part of my graduation into adolescence. It was a bit of toughening up for an introverted, quiet mummy's boy, a bit of masculine bonding between father and son. But perhaps more than anything, it was a crucial step in my evolution as a football fan.

Soon I would be ready for Highbury.

And it was just over a year later, to mark my thirteenth birthday, that I made my Arsenal debut. The Gunners beat Leicester City 2-1 with late goals from Tony Woodcock and Paul Davis. But it was Charlie, Charlie Nicholas, I'd been longing to see.

Charlie was my darling, there was no doubt about it. Like thousands of others desperate for something exciting to happen to Arsenal again, I was captivated from the moment he set foot in North London in June 1983 with the promise of sex, goals and rock n' roll. He was Arsenal's new pop star, their first celebrity footballer since Peter Marinello in the early seventies and having scored a colossal 52 goals for Celtic during the previous season, he was Europe's hottest property. Just by endorsing Arsenal ahead of the likes of Liverpool, Manchester United, Inter Milan and Torino, Charlie had put Arsenal back in fashion. And pretty soon his disciples on the North Bank were sporting diamond earrings, wedge haircuts, leather trousers and listening to the likes of *U2* and the *Psychedelic Furs*, all in homage to their new messiah. Arsenal were back in vogue again, they were relevant again and I quickly became infatuated, obsessing over Charlie the same way my sister was preoccupied with John Taylor of *Duran Duran*. I built a shrine to Charlie in the corner of my bedroom, I meticulously kept scrapbooks dedicated to Charlie and documenting his every game, goal, movement. I stopped just short of stalking him.

I'm not sure what they made of it at school. I rather think they saw my fixation on Charlie as confusing, bizarre and, of course, a bit gay. But I didn't mind. I felt no embarrassment, no shame. I was mad about the boy. I looked up to him like an older brother who I aspired, but didn't have the guts, to be.

And as I sat for that very first time in the East Stand, Upper Tier in the Spring of 1984 mesmerised by the razzmatazz surrounding Prince Charlie, I and no one else for that matter knew or cared what had happened to Paul Vaessen.

Paul had actually been released by Arsenal in the early summer of 1983, just as Charlie was arriving from Scotland. Two twenty-one year olds heading in entirely different directions and for one I was frankly far too mesmerized with who was coming in through the front door to really register Paul's low-key departure out through the back.

The truth is he had long since been forgotten. His final season at Arsenal, 1982-83, constituted something of a lost year. Paul obviously didn't feature that prominently in manager Terry Neill's plans with half a million pound strikers Lee Chapman and Tony Woodcock brought in during the summer from Stoke City and Cologne respectively. Paul failed to make a single appearance for the first team, the nearest he got being the pre-season photo call when he was selected to show off Arsenal's new controversial green and navy blue away strip alongside John Hawley and John Devine. All three models, as well as the unpopular colours, would be out of Highbury by the following summer.

There were three appearances in reserve team pre-season friendlies – Tooting & Mitchum away must have provided something of a contrast to the heights Paul had reached in Turin – and Paul would make his final appearance for Arsenal on Tuesday 21st September 1982, coming on as a substitute for the reserves during their 3-1 defeat at Brighton & Hove Albion. Paul spent the rest of the season trying to get his knee right. There were two further operations, more specialists, more rehabilitation. But as well as coping without the cartilage, arthritis had begun to set in and Paul had been diagnosed with a degenerative knee joint. With his other knee starting to give him trouble as well, things were getting worse, not better and it was becoming quite obvious he couldn't go on.

Not that we knew. Paul Vaessen had long since slipped our minds. I couldn't have told you where he was, what he was doing, whether he was even still at the club or not.

Out of sight, out of mind.

These were the days long before the internet, tweeting, blogging, *Arsenal ClubCall* even. For updates on players you relied almost exclusively on the press and the matchday programme. And it was in the latter, for the visit of Luton Town on Saturday 27th August 1983, amidst the optimistic columns devoted to debutant Charlie Nicholas, that the following was disclosed:

Voice of Arsenal

Unfortunately, centre forward Paul Vaessen has had to give up the game completely because of recurring knee trouble - a harsh reminder that there's a lot of pain to go with the glamour. We wish him well.

That was it.

Lee recalls the pain.

"No matter how hard he tried he couldn't get that knee working again. He had two further operations and they told him, 'Look, Paul. If you play football at any level again you'll be a cripple. You'll be in a wheelchair by the time you're thirty-five.' He went over to America to Florida to recuperate for two to three weeks. He got advice there too which was basically that he should stop playing football – any sport really. He was basically warned by every doctor and surgeon he spoke to that he'd be a cripple by the time he was thirty-five, forty."

"Paul was devastated when Arsenal said they were going to release him," says Maureen. "A bit of Paul died that day."

"He took it so badly," Lee continues. "He was suicidal. He was on the edge, very, very close to pulling the plug. I remember the day he packed up, the day the doctors told him he couldn't play any more. He came home and just sat on the edge of the sofa and cried his eyes out. He said, 'What am I going to do now, Lee? What the f--k am I going to do now?' I just couldn't console him. He could not stop crying. I sat there and cuddled my brother all night.

"It used to tear me apart because he was my big brother, the one I looked up to. He was like a superstar to me and here he was, broken.

"You see, all he wanted to do was play football. He used to say if he could get himself a new pair of knees he'd pay Arsenal to let him play.

"There wasn't much help from Arsenal to be honest but

158

that's how things were in football back then. There wasn't a lot of support, no suggestions, no counselling. There was no back-up plan. Paul was a bit bitter about it really. It was a case of, 'Thanks Paul, off you go, good luck.' You couldn't do that to a player these days."

As Paul himself commented in a rare interview in 1994, "I bore a grudge against Arsenal for years, believing they'd basically booted me out on the street and left me to rot."[36]

Paul felt he'd been seduced and abandoned by the football community.

"He obviously had a very nasty injury," says Ken Friar, Club Secretary at Arsenal at the time. "We maintained him for about two years without him really playing that much, we rehabilitated him but at the end of that period it was clear that Paul couldn't play. Therefore, his career had to finish. But that's the risk of being a professional footballer."

"Some of the players wanted the club to put on a benefit match for Paul," says Maureen, "but Arsenal obviously thought better of it."

"People like Raph Meade came around to try and cheer Paul up, straighten him out but he was so down," says Lee. "He used to say, 'If I can't play football, bruv, my life's over. I won't be able to go on like this.'"

10
Yesterday's Men

"You and Skipper and millions like ya are livin' in a kid's world,
playin' games, touchdowns, no worries, no responsibilities. Life
ain't no damn football game. Life ain't just a bunch of high spots.
You're a thirty-year-old kid. Soon you'll be a fifty-year-old kid,
pretendin' your hearin' cheers when there aren't any. Dreamin'
and drinkin' your life away. Heroes in the real world live twenty
four hours a day, not just two hours in a game. Mendacity! You
won't...you won't live with mendacity, but you're an expert at it.
The truth is pain and sweat and payin' bills and makin' love to a
woman that you don't love anymore. Truth is dreams that don't
come true and nobody prints your name in the paper 'til you die."

Harvey 'Big Daddy' Pollitt (played by Burl Ives) to Brick Pollitt (Paul Newman) in
the film 'Cat on a Hot Tin Roof' (1958)

I'm early.

I'm always early for Arsenal.

Ever since I missed the opening minutes – and goals – of a North London derby at Highbury back in May 1985, I have arrived early. And by the same token I have never left a match early, for fear of missing something special at the end.

So I like to get here with plenty of time, to acclimatise to that intoxicating aroma of cigarettes and burgers filling the air; to relish the delicacies of the foot long hotdog stand just outside Arsenal tube station; to browse through the merchandise stalls; to flick through the matchday programme and the latest editions of the fanzines. And to sit and watch everybody else go by doing the same.

I'm sitting now, watching, watching the shoppers going in and out of the flagship store, *The Armoury*.

Arsenal shirts.

Arsenal shorts.

Arsenal socks.

Arsenal slippers.

Arsenal beach towels.

Arsenal curtains.

Arsenal fridge magnets.

Arsenal fluffy dice.

Arsenal nodding dogs.

Arsenal gnomes.

Arsenal anything.

Arsenal everything.

It makes me think back to how I used to have to queue up to get into the confined space which the original *Gunners Shop* occupied along Avenell Road.

Shows you how far we have come, I suppose, although I will always prefer the intimacy, familiarity and uniqueness of Highbury to its modern day successor.

Things always seem better before.

Back then.

Paul Vaessen would attest to that.

And back then, when I started attending Arsenal in the early eighties, legendary 'keeper Jack Kelsey was manager of the compact little shop and Terry Neill was manager of the somewhat larger football club. Thirty years on, I carry on people watching as I wait for Neill to poke his head out of the press entrance next to the superstore and beckon me in. Terry is due to provide expert analysis of today's Premiership clash with Middlesbrough here at Emirates Stadium for Arsenal TV but has agreed to meet with me beforehand.

It would have been easy for Terry to have said no. Terry, and Arsenal as a club, had a duty of care towards Paul and are seen by some, especially Paul, as having been complicit somehow in his downfall.

I'm here with an open mind. I'm well aware of Paul's attitude towards his former club but am also mindful of Arsenal's unrivalled reputation when it comes to class, style and looking after its own.

The press lounge and facilities here are impressive. We help ourselves at the bar to a coffee I get the feeling we're not entitled to and settle down in one of the many, many booths from which reporters from around the world will later be compiling and dispatching their stories.

It is Paul's I'm interested in.

"When I think of Paul Vaessen," Neill tells me, "my first thought is tragedy. Then guilt, a huge amount of regret and guilt. Absolutely. Obviously it was a tragedy with his injury, his knee and you immediately think could I have done more, should I have done more and the answer is always 'yes'. It's always going to be a 'yes', unless you're telling lies.

"I'm very sorry to hear Paul felt he had a gripe against the Arsenal. I'd be very surprised if he had a genuine gripe with regards his injury or his treatment as Arsenal have always been absolutely magnificent on the medical side."

What was lacking was the after-care for a twenty one year-old who had just lost his dream, his livelihood, and who now had to return, physically and psychologically wounded and unprepared, to humdrum society and find something else a lot less stimulating to do.

"But how long do you go on?" continues Neill. "How much can you do for an individual?

"When Paul left Arsenal in the summer of 1983, I had immediate concerns here. We'd just lost two semi-finals. I was under pressure, I was fighting for my life as well and I had other players here to be concerned about.

"But at the same time the first thing you feel is an immense guilt because you'd like to help anybody, whether you've known them, whether you've been pals, whatever they've been, just fellow human beings."

I wondered what would have been in place during Paul's time at the club to prepare him for life after football. Not much, it seems but that's how it was across the board back then. There was, of course, the opportunity to attend college and make coffee tables and bake cakes. And then there was some friendly, worldly advice from the boss.

"The only thing certain when you become a football player is that your playing days are going to end when you're relatively young," explains Neill. "On average, you've got two-thirds of your life ahead of you. Every promising young player I was negotiating a contract with, I'd say to them, 'Look, this is what we're offering you. We think you're a very good player, an exciting prospect but at the same time you've got to think about what you're going to do after.

You need to prepare.'"

But who was listening? Paul, like all the others, was too distracted by the dreams racing through his mind. He just wanted to play and he couldn't envisage a time when he wouldn't be playing. He'd cross that bridge if and when he came to it.

Of course, what didn't help was coming across that bridge a lot sooner than he'd anticipated.

Paul Vaessen was, of course, not the only player ever to have lost his livelihood prematurely. The football community is littered with similar hard luck stories of those who tragically couldn't live with their heart break, who couldn't adjust to the banality and drudgery of everyday life, who discovered all too soon how fragile and fickle the world of football can be. For some the end of a career marks the beginning of an infinitely more difficult chapter in their lives as they face up to the 'living problem' of filling the huge void in front of them. Gone is the structure, the goal of making the team on Saturday, the banter. Some simply find it impossible to cope, replacing one addiction with another.

Look at poor Tommy Caton.

"I remember him as a nice lad, a likeable lad," says former Arsenal colleague Brian Talbot. "He was a big boy, a big centre-half with a tonk of a left foot. But he didn't really fulfil his potential."

Tommy was earmarked as the long-term successor to Willie Young who'd left for Nottingham Forest in December 1981 after one too many disagreements with boss Terry Neill. Neill had since tried various partners for David O'Leary in the centre of defence, such as Chris Whyte and Colin Hill, but none had grasped the opportunity. They seemed to be nothing but stop-gaps and it wasn't until the recruitment of Tommy at the end of November 1983 that O'Leary found himself a partner.

Tommy joined Arsenal as one of the great white hopes of English football having been thrown into first team action by Manchester City boss Malcolm Allison at the tender age of sixteen and going on to become the youngest player in football league history at nineteen years and five months old to notch up one hundred games.

Tommy perhaps endured his footballing nadir whilst still at City when he was turned this way and that by Ricky Villa in the 1982 F.A. Cup Final Replay at Wembley. But disaffected with life at

Maine Road following City's relegation at the end of the following season, Tommy jumped at the chance to join what he thought to be a more stable club and a more settled atmosphere.

Distinctive not only for his abilities but also his huge blonde afro, the popular Liverpudlian had caught Terry Neill's eye long before he was able to secure his services.

"I was aware of Tommy Caton since he was the age of sixteen at Manchester City," recalls Neill. "He was a bit of a prodigy at sixteen and he'd gone into a bit of a trough playing-wise but I believed he'd still got a lot of natural ability. I'd lost Willie Young so I signed Tommy but a month or so later I was gone so there wasn't much time to get to know him."

What Tommy soon came to realise was that he had jumped from the frying-pan into the fire.

"He was a young lad, big, powerful, a smashing kid," recalls Graham Rix. "I was injured when we signed him and he came down when we lost in the League Cup to Walsall. The management team had asked if I could look after Tommy, so me and Tom sat in the stands." Having beaten Spurs in the previous round and been handed what amounted to a bye into the next round, the Gunners contrived to loose 2-1.

"We were f--king awful," says Rix. "Tommy must have been thinking, 'What the f--k have I joined here?!'"

Two days after signing, Tommy replaced Chris Whyte for the home match against West Bromwich Albion, playing alongside a fresh-faced Tony Adams who was in the side due to an injury to David O'Leary. Tommy and Tony were up against a pretty formidable strike-force in the form of Cyrille Regis and Garry Thompson and they gave the young Arsenal pair a torrid time. The Gunners lost 1-0 and after another defeat at Upton Park the following Saturday, Terry Neill's number was up.

Under Don Howe, however, Tommy managed to cement his place in the side and became a fixture alongside O'Leary for the remainder of that and the following season. As a naturally left-sided player, he even moved over to left-back as cover for Kenny Sansom on occasion, playing brilliantly when the Gunners won at St James' Park in December 1984.

"For a time it looked good," says O'Leary in his autobiography. "Tommy wasn't the quickest. But we went well

165

together. He was a good battler and very few strikers got the better of him in the air."[37]

Pat Jennings agrees. "Tommy was a lovely big lad. Coming down to Arsenal at that age, he was going to go on for the next ten years."

"A lot of people might say, well, Man City are a big club but when you come to the Arsenal it's a different kettle of fish," says close friend and playing colleague Kenny Sansom. "He came here and he was really nervous, you could sense it. But then he found himself, came out with the boys and felt part of it."

"He was a sensitive boy, though," recalls Graham Rix. "At the time there was a little bit of a drinking culture at the club. There was Tommy, there was myself, Paul Mariner, Viv Anderson, Tony Woodcock and we used to go up *The Orange Tree* pub in Totteridge after training. We use to have our initials on our training kit at the time and there was me, Kenny Sansom, Charlie Nicholas and big Tom there one day. Now Tom was academically brilliant. He had 'O' levels and 'A' levels, so he was academically tuned in. But he was a bit thick! So we're having a drink and having a laugh and he's an easy target, he's around a few sharp brains and I said, 'I've worked out what TC stands for on your tracksuit - thick c--t!' Well, he was so angry he drank his beer, put his glass down on the table and ran home - from Totteridge to New Southgate where he lived! Joking apart, though, I loved Tom."

"He'd do anything for anyone," says Kenny Sansom. "Tommy was fantastic, a great kid."

But self-doubt seemed to gnaw away at Tommy and his form took a downturn as he began to get anxious about his abilities, his lack of pace and his popularity with the home fans.

"Tommy was always worrying about things," says Gus Ceasar. "I think he lacked confidence. He was a great player but he always needed someone to reassure him, to tell him things were alright all the time or he would be asking, 'Is that okay, is this okay?' Tommy was always worrying about what people were saying about him or thinking about him."

Things didn't exactly improve with the arrival of coach John Cartwright who didn't rate Tommy highly and after a nervous display in the 3-0 reverse at Southampton in December 1985, he was dropped for Martin Keown when Liverpool were overcome at

166

Highbury seven days later. Losing out to Keown and then Adams, he featured in only two more games that season and not at all under the stewardship of George Graham.

"When I came to Arsenal he wasn't in the side," says Perry Groves. "Tommy was in the reserves and to be honest he never had a chance of getting back in to the first team. It wasn't that George didn't rate him and it wasn't that George didn't like him. It was just that George thought he was too slow. I think his problem was, running in straight lines he was alright but if you looked at him turning he was a little bit on the cumbersome side. Great left foot, great in the air, great competitor, fantastic in the dressing-room, fantastic player but I think George saw him as not being quite quick enough.

"They didn't row, they didn't fall out and his attitude was exemplary. As a big name player stuck in the reserves he could have sulked, he could have moped around but he didn't. His attitude was spot on. Off the pitch, he was like the gentle giant, a loveable lad. He was quiet. He wasn't gregarious, loud, in your face. He was always good to me. I don't think that anybody you'd talk to would have a bad word to say about him."

Graham eventually sold Tommy to Oxford United in February 1987. It was a move which O'Leary felt was "essential for his peace of mind as well as his football." [38]

Soon made captain, Tommy suffered relegation again at the end of the following season and once more with Charlton Athletic in 1990. The following January he injured his foot and despite repeated surgery he was finally forced into retirement in March 1993. By the end of the following month he was dead having suffered a heart attack on 30th April. He was just thirty years old.

"It really saddened me when I heard about Tommy," says Graham Rix. "It was self-induced to an extent," he says hinting at rumours that Tommy had fallen into depression and had turned to drink. "His world had fallen apart."

"I think he'd split from his wife," says Sansom. "I don't think it was just the injury in my opinion. It was loneliness too.

"I went to his funeral. There was a fantastic turn out from an Arsenal perspective. There was a wreath from Arsenal Football Club. There were club directors there, Ken Friar was there. There must have been about twelve players there at least."

"Obviously he had problems," says Talbot. "Some people unfortunately have got problems and need help. Sadly he didn't get it and things went the way they did. It was a shock what happened to him, obviously another one who found it difficult to cope when he had to finish. It's difficult when you can't replace what you had."

There are other Tommy Catons out there, many of whom we aren't probably even aware of. But, of course, it doesn't always have to end this way.

Warwick Bean is a name that will be unfamiliar to the vast majority of Arsenal supporters but it could easily have been very different.

From Tadworth in Surrey, Warwick was a tremendous prospect as a schoolboy. A striker, as opposed to a centre-forward, Warwick had already made his way onto the back of the *London Evening Standard* by the age of fifteen.

"I've still got all the newspapers from that era," Warwick continues. "I was playing for Sutton Schoolboys. They were always the wooden spoons of London football but in my particular year we staggered everybody and got to the London Schools Cup Final for the first time in our history, beating all of the big teams on the way, like Newham, who Alan Curbishley played for, and Harlow, who had Glenn Hoddle. We got beaten in the end by East London but somehow the *London Evening Standard* got hold of it and there I was, being likened to Kevin Keegan!"

Warwick was courted by many of the top clubs.

"I was offered apprenticeships by just about everybody," he says. "I had trials with Tottenham, West Ham, QPR, Chelsea, Crystal Palace. Leeds United wanted me. I also remember going up to Everton but Liverpool wasn't for me.

"I narrowed it down to Arsenal, who I supported, Fulham, where Ted Drake was head scout, and Ipswich who were managed by Bobby Robson and who were absolutely fantastic. My dad said, 'Consider this. If you join Fulham or Ipswich you could become a big fish in a small sea.' I said to my dad, 'Dad, I want to be a big fish in a big sea.' So it was Arsenal."

Warwick signed as an apprentice on 1st June 1974, the same day as Graham Rix. Graham would, of course, go on to win an F.A. Cup winner's medal with Arsenal in 1979 and three years later would represent his country at the World Cup in Spain.

By then Warwick was out of the game.

"Arsenal, they were the most fantastic years of my life. Unfortunately for me I tore a cartilage in my first season around Christmas time 1974. I remember going in to hospital in January the following year to have the cartilage removed. It was an excruciating operation. I was left with bone on bone. It took a long time to heal. In fact, it never really healed properly. About seven or eight weeks after the operation I went to RAF Headley Court which today is famous for the rehabilitation of soldiers coming back from Afghanistan or wherever. They started rebuilding me, rehabilitating me. They then found a big lump on my knee that had to be removed and so it was another God knows how long until I actually got back to playing.

"I came back for the last few South East Counties fixtures of that 1974-75 season. We played QPR away and Southend away and I scored in both games so it was a nice end to the season.

"About a quarter of the way through the following season I had another problem with the knee and ended up in hospital again. I was in hospital for my eighteenth birthday and whilst I was in there having a third operation, Bertie Mee, the Arsenal manager, came and offered me professional terms. I remember him saying to mum, dad and myself that if I could steer clear of injury, I had a great chance of making it. So I signed a two year contract and recovered from that lastest operation and carried on playing mainly for the youth team and some games for the reserves.

"By 1976-77 I was a reserve team squad member. I was nineteen and playing with the likes of Frank Stapleton and David O'Leary. I played a pre-season friendly somewhere in South London and John Radford was playing, George Armstrong was playing, John Matthews, David Price. I think Geoff Barnett was in goal. It was a mixture of reserves and first team players and I basically played like a bag of shit that day. I just couldn't get my leg going. My leg was never quite right ever again. Anyway, we were 2-0 down at half time and Ian Crawford, reserve team coach, gave us a right slagging. In the second half, we came back. I remember it well, not only because it was my last game for Arsenal but because I scored the winning goal with the last kick of the game. I can remember it vividly. I was playing up front with Radford and George Armstrong came down the right wing, cut the ball across and I said to Radford, 'Leave it, leave it Raddie!' and I hit it from about ten yards out into the roof of the net. We won 3-2. I felt dead chuffed but as I did it I felt my knee go and I just knew that I had a serious problem.

"Two days later we met up with the doctors, Fred Street and all of it and they basically presented the facts and said that they couldn't do anything more for my knee. It had got to the stage where I'd play on a Saturday and I'd spend all week on the physio table and then on Friday morning I'd just about make the five-a-side warm-up.

"Ultimately it was my decision to stop. It was black and white, more or less. I wasn't told that I had to stop. I wasn't told that they wanted to terminate my contract. They said I could probably play amateur football or part-time football or whatever and I thought, 'Yeah, from Arsenal to part-time football. No. Not for me.'

"Looking back what probably didn't help was that on Monday afternoons we'd do a fitness session at Highbury. I remember we had to do ten sprints up the East Stand, Upper Tier. We used to race against each other and then after that we had to do ten more with someone riding piggy-back. Sometimes we used to be physically sick. This is not a criticism but an observation many years later, I think doing that probably didn't help my knee. I had damage in the knee and all I was doing was compounding it.

"It was all over a lot sooner than I had envisaged and you know, the realization that your lifetime's dream has come to an abrupt end was quite distressing. I dwelled on it for a long time and was in a no mans land in terms of what I really wanted to do for a long time. I hadn't got a clue what I was going to do at the time because football had been my life. But Bertie Mee told my parents that if I went back to college to get some more 'O' levels, he could get me a place at Loughborough University. It seemed like a good idea so off I went, straight from Arsenal to college.

"I didn't blow it but I just wasn't really interested. To be honest, what I should have done was had a year off, to get it out of my system and then start something new.

"But the real world beckoned, I had to earn some money so I went into sales and was in sales for twenty-odd years. And when I hit forty, I thought to myself there's more to life than being in sales. I fancied running my own business so I bought a pub in Outwood in Surrey and for the second time in my life found something I really enjoyed. It's been a great success.

"Thirty years down the line I've had a total of fourteen

operations on my knee. And I'm still an Arsenal enthusiast. For the first few seasons after I left the club I followed Arsenal virtually every game, home and away. I'm still a season ticket holder today. I actually, as a bit of a laugh, applied for the job of Head of Youth Development at Arsenal in 1998 but Chippy Brady got the job!

"Everybody at Arsenal was brilliant. To the club's credit as far as I'm concerned they gave me every opportunity. I was treated impeccably. I've got no criticism at all with regards to the way I was treated. They were fantastic. They did everything they could possibly do to help me, right down to the medical treatment. I got the same treatment that a first team player would have, same hospitals, same surgeons, which was not necessarily the case at other clubs.

"I had it difficult, I suppose. I've been unlucky. But I've also been fortunate in that I've managed to move on. I'm very relaxed in my life. I played for Arsenal. I had a fantastic three or four years at Arsenal and I'm very, very proud of that. I loved it, loved every bit of it. I wouldn't change it for the world."

As Warwick walked away from Arsenal, Paul was on his way in. There, on the treatment table, he would have found Richie Powling.

Like Warwick, young Richie Powling was in high demand.

"I was fortunate enough that a lot of clubs wanted me to play for them," says Richie. "I'd decided upon Manchester United. I used to go up there every summer holiday and it was really only right at the death that I realised I didn't feel old enough at fifteen to leave home. So in my mind I was going to do my 'O' levels and then go up there at sixteen."

That was when Arsenal, relatively close to Richie's Barking home, stepped in. "It meant I could start straight away."

Richie signed as an apprentice soon after the 'double' success of 1971, his debut coming in a 2-0 defeat at Queens Park Rangers in October 1973. However, it wasn't until two seasons later that he began to establish himself as a first team member, appearing thirty times in the heart of Bertie Mee's defence which spent most of the campaign staving off the threat of relegation. Indeed, it was unfortunate that Richie's tenure should coincide with what turned out to be one of the bleakest periods in Arsenal's modern history.

"He was a little older than me," recalls Graham Rix. "When I was an apprentice he was a young pro. My first game for Arsenal was actually in the reserves. It was the beginning of the 1974-75 season and there'd been a few suspensions and injuries so some of the reserves had gone in to the first team and there was a little void. There were people like Mark Ambrose, Frank Stapleton, Wilf Rostron, Trevor Ross and Richie Powling."

Richie was an atypical footballer. Of rather stocky physique, the former England youth international didn't exactly look the part.

"He wasn't very big," Rix continues, "and he couldn't run very quick. His nickname was 'Tubby Powling' and he had a face like Captain Pugwash but he was such a shrewd, shrewd footballer. He'd read things and nick things and play nice passes. He was a really clever footballer, very highly thought of. He could play full-back, centre-half, midfield. He actually rolled the ball back to me for me to score with my first touch against Leicester on my first team debut, although he put it on my right foot rather than my left! But he was a great kid. I learnt so much off of him. He was such a clever, clever footballer."

The Gunners' fortunes were soon to improve under new boss Terry Neill but Richie was left behind as he fell down the pecking order behind new recruits Pat Howard and Willie Young and the emerging young Irishman, David O'Leary. His problems were compounded when he was struck down by injury just as he seemed to be finding a new niche for himself as a holding midfielder, playing in the first five games of the 1977-78 season.

He never played for the first team again.

"He just faded out of it", says Rix. "He always seemed to be struggling, in and out of hospital."

"He had a cartilage tear initially", says Fred Street, "but he'd got a worn knee that had obviously gone through some arthritic changes. It's what happens with some knees, although it normally happens later on in life. But obviously he'd got some damage in there."

"I spent four years having operations," Richie recounts. "I'd break down and have another operation and break down again, never actually playing. The thing is you do anything at that age to get back. I was fully aware I could be crippled by the age of fifty but you do anything at twenty-five to play. Arsenal didn't know whether it might get better or not but there came a time for both sides really, after four years of it and it not getting a lot better, to call it a day.

172

"I was just a working class kid who felt that I needed to make the conscious decision to become so obsessed with what I'm doing in order to achieve success. The hardest thing I found was, without blowing my own trumpet, being so good, in the top hundred at what you do, and then suddenly becoming a nobody. I don't suppose it's any different to any other trade really. You could be in the top hundred reporters or the top hundred accountants and then find yourself right on the lowest rung of the ladder. I remember sitting down and crying. I was scared because it had been my life. One day everything's going so well. I'd got in the first team at seventeen, I was captaining England at youth level and I was thinking, 'I'm going to do all this and do that. And then...'"

Richie is appreciative of the support and faith shown him by Arsenal. "I signed a number of contracts while I was still injured because, like I say, they didn't know what was wrong with it and to be honest I wasn't on that great money. It was just that I was training every day and night and never seemed to be playing a game. It was pretty hard emotionally and from their point of view I suppose they came to the decision that I just wasn't going to come back."

Confirmation came in March 1981 when midfielder Peter Nicholas arrived from Crystal Palace as a replacement.

Richie relied heavily upon his family and friends – including some he didn't even know he had - when he left Arsenal. And one other thing which helped him through this time was his faith.

Richie says, "Life goes on. I went into sales. One of the supporters was kind enough to get in touch with the club and helped me get into that. You didn't need qualifications either. But then Barry Fry rang me up and I went to work for him at Barnet to see if I could cope on a part-time basis. I was hoping that going semi-professional, training just twice a week, wouldn't be such a chore but I couldn't even play at that level, in truth.

"I found it hard when I first left football. I didn't watch a game for about four years. There was no bitterness, it just hurt.

"I suppose you need a crutch when things aren't going right. For some people it's alcohol, for others it drugs. I became a Christian when I was twenty-one, when I was injured, and it did make life much easier when the thing that I loved was taken away. It helped massively because being a Christian, having that faith, I knew there was something that was more important than football. That certainly

STUCK IN A MOMENT

helped me to cope."

Richie moved in to non-league management with the likes of Tiptree United, Braintree United, Clacton and Sudbury where, as a self-employed sales rep, he is now based.

"I can't complain," he reflects. "I can walk about. It's very humbling when you find out ultimately that there are some people who are far worse off than you are. One of the most important things in my life was football and it was taken away from me. But my faith - nothing can take that away from me."

People respond to adversity in different ways.

Warwick and Richie made it.

Tommy didn't.

Which way would it go for Paul?

11
Heroin

"I don't know just where I'm going
But I'm gonna try for the kingdom, if I can
'Cause it makes me feel like I'm a man
When I put a spike into my vein
And I'll tell ya, things aren't quite the same."

'Heroin' by the Velvet Underground (1967)

The loss of his career hit Paul like a bereavement. Apart from close family he was left alone not so much to get over it – you never get over it – but to simply move on.

Simply.

As Paul told the *News of the World* in 1994, "I was just 21 and, when the doors of Highbury shut behind me, I had no idea what to do. I loved playing and had grown used to the lifestyle of being recognised wherever I went in my home area of Bermondsey. I was on the scrap heap; nobody had any more use for me."[39]

"Where else can you get that high life, that buzz?" ex-England international Kenny Sansom asked me. "You might turn to alcohol and gambling like I did. It's an easy trap to fall into. Anyone who says, 'I wouldn't do that,' I think must be kidding themselves because you don't know, when you're under pressure, you may well do something you shouldn't do."

Richie Powling was one who had an inkling of where Paul might be headed.

"I remember Paul saying once, 'If I wasn't a footballer I'd be a junkie.'"

And six months into his enforced retirement Paul proved true to his word when he ran into some old friends who offered him a way out of his pain and despair.

"I remember the first time I did what's known as chasing the dragon," Paul would later recall. "The heroin turns into oil when

175

heated by a flame under the foil and I inhaled the fumes.

"I was physically sick and turned as white as a sheet. But I took it often enough over two or three weeks to get withdrawal symptoms.

"I had the sweats, the runny eyes and nose, the stomach cramps and the terrible empty feeling that only goes away with another fix."[40]

Paul sunk into addiction, largely because he had no motivation not to. Heroin won by default.

And it wasn't just heroin. Paul took cocaine and downers like benzo-diazapan.

"When he did something," remarks Lee, "he did it one hundred percent, full on. That's how it was with the football and that's how it was with the drugs."

For the time being, Paul had the money.

"He had a bit of money when he left Arsenal," Lee points out. "He had a bit in the bank but not a lot. He was insured through the club for a certain amount so that policy paid out. I think Arsenal also paid up the remainder of his contract. But he didn't earn that much from his career. It wasn't like it is today."

A few of the players like Kenny Sansom helped out with some cash when he left Arsenal but the problem was that, according to Lee, "he was still living the same lifestyle he'd been accustomed to at Arsenal with now no money coming in."

With the heroin alone costing almost £200 per day, Paul's money lasted about eighteen months before he turned up at his parent's place and declared he had nothing left. By this time he was married to Sarah whose suspicions were raised when she opened up a letter from the bank one day asking where the mortgage was. She soon discovered where the money had gone when they went on holiday to America and found Paul's drugs paraphernalia. Sarah and her family decided to keep things from Maureen and Leon, hoping they could help Paul without having to worry them. They lasted almost a year.

"I was oblivious to it, the drugs. I just had no idea. The first time we ever found out," recalls Maureen, "was one Sunday afternoon. Sarah and her mum asked if they could come down to see us. So I thought they were coming down to visit for a bit of tea and all that so I got a bit of salad out and cake and things like that, you

176

know. And they knocked on the door but Paul wasn't with them and I thought, 'That's strange'. I thought they were all coming down. Anyway, they sat down in the dinette and they sat there in silence and I looked at my husband and I thought, 'What's going on?' Then Sarah burst out crying. I said, 'Whatever's the matter, Sarah?' but I couldn't get anything out of her. So her Mum said, 'I'm ever so sorry to have to tell you this, Maureen, but Paul's been on heroin for a year.' They'd been out in Fort Lauderdale. They'd been out there three or four weeks and whilst they were out there they found a load of pills and other stuff and threw it into the sea. That's when they first knew. They'd known for a year but they kept it a secret from me. We'd seen that Paul had been down but just put it down to depression at not being able to play any more and the financial pressures he and Sarah were under. Sarah and her mum thought they could get him straight and protect me, save me the bother. And that's why they came down to see me. They came down to see me that Sunday to tell me he was on heroin. By then it was too late.

"And when she said 'heroin', it hit me. I ran up to my living room and bounced off the four walls. I was punching all the walls. My husband came and gave me a slap round the face to calm me down. We had no inkling, no inkling whatsoever that he was on drugs.

"A few months later - I do remember the day, it was Christmas Day - we had a phone call from Sarah in the middle of the night. We could hear Paul crying down the phone. Sarah couldn't handle it any more. He'd started selling the house. He'd started selling some of the furniture.

"My husband went over and he phoned me and he said, 'I'm bringing Paul back home to stay with us for a little while but be prepared. He's in a bit of a state.'

"I had the shock of my life when he brought him through the door. He was bent over like a little old man of ninety. He had boils and lumps, you name it, all over him. I just sat down in the chair. I had no idea his illness was so bad. You might say that day was the day things got bad for all of us."

It was the end of Paul's marriage. Lee remembers it well.

"That night he split from Sarah, he was back home. My room was next to his and I could hear him crying his heart out. She was the first person he lost. He really loved her. I don't think he ever fully recovered from it."

****

Needing a new purpose in life and some money in his pocket, Paul worked a number of jobs, not that he had been completely idle since leaving Arsenal. Not long after his retirement an offer came in from non-league Fisher Athletic.

Friend Jamie Winterton recalls, "Somebody came and asked him if he wanted to play a few games for the Gas Board so he got himself fit again."

"There was a lot of money being put into Fisher at that time," says Leon, "and they approached Paul. He didn't go begging to them or anything like that. They paid him quite well and he turned out a few times for them."

"I think they may have given him a signing-on fee," says school friend Steve Gorham. "He was still pretty well-known then. I think he was also given a nominal job as a cleaner for one of the fellas in charge there who had a printing company. He literally used to go down, clock on and go home. He didn't actually do any work. I think it was just to do with money."

Lee takes up the story. "The boss there was Dogan Arif, regarded as the head of the formidable Arif crime family who operated out of South-East London. He approached Paul a while after he'd been released by Arsenal and said, 'Look. I'll give you £500 a week, no training, no physical stuff, just turn up on the Saturday, knock a couple of goals in for me, set a couple up and job done.' And that's what used to happen. He'd score a couple or set some up and after about twenty minutes he'd have his arm up, calling to the boss to take him off.

"One time Fisher were struggling for players so Paul shouted out, 'Put my brother on, get him a shirt.' And I came on out of the crowd and played forty minutes in my trainers! That was the one and only time we played together for the same team. But Paul knew where to find me with his thirty, forty yard passes. He still had it."

Jamie Winterton agrees.

178

"He'd like stand in the middle of the park and run the game."

"The problem was," Lee remarks, "that of course it was a lower standard to what he was used to. He was well above the level of the other players. It was a rough old league. The damage he could do to his knees in half an hour was immense."

"I watched him play," says Steve Gorham, "He didn't last long because I think by then both of his knees had gone. He was back playing in central midfield. Obviously his movements were restricted by his knees but he ran the game without moving out of the centre-circle."

Former Arsenal colleague Nicky Sullivan adds, "I remember playing against him in a pre-season friendly. It must have been when he first went to Fisher. He played part of the match and he was hobbling around then."

Richie Powling also encountered Paul again when his Sudbury Town side played Fisher. "It was the last time I saw him," says Powling.

"He was just not the same," Leon reflects.

Lee continues, "He used to go up for headers, come down and his knee would go. Playing non-league, that's what finished him off.

"Another problem was that he was using during the time he was at Fisher. He'd get his gear out in the dressing room after he'd come off. He didn't care who was watching."

"I'm not sure why he left Fisher," says Jamie Winterton, "Probably just couldn't be bothered. Either that or it may have been something to do with drugs."

There were other propositions early on after Paul's playing days at Arsenal came to an end.

"Kenny Sansom, I think, tried to get him to take a job with an accountant," says Maureen. "Someone else tried to get him into insurance but he turned them down. And then he had the chance to go and train youngsters in football over in Malta but he turned that down too. I don't know why. Perhaps because he couldn't play any more, he thought, 'Why should I train others to do what I can't, when my own dream has been taken away from me?'"

Neighbour Sue concurs.

"I asked him once why he didn't consider becoming a trainer. 'I've had that offer', he said. I said, 'But you could still be a

179

part of football, you could give your knowledge to young children'. 'No', he said. 'No. I play or I don't do nothing.'"

"Both me and my old man would say to Paul, 'Why don't you go for your coaching badges?'" says Lee. "Someone would have snapped him up. But his attitude was, 'If I can't f--king well play football, I don't want nothing to do with it.' There was no good arguing with him. He wouldn't even watch football."

But now Paul couldn't afford to turn down many opportunities.

Lee got him a job on a building site.

"After two days he thought, 'F--k this, I'm off.' He didn't stay for very long in any job really."

"My dad offered him work and he worked with my dad on building sites," says cousin Jackie. "My dad used to go and collect him and he was always late and as soon as they'd get on site he would go in to the toilet for ages. He was always in the toilet, he always wanted a sub, always wanted his money at the end of every day. It didn't take my dad long to work out what the problems were."

Leon was still working for the Post Office.

"I put the word around and after a while got Paul a job with the Post Office in the City. He was mainly working inside in the sorting offices. It was hard for him but it was something to keep him occupied and put a few bob in his pocket. It didn't last all that long, though."

Lee thinks he may know why.

"Credit cards and PIN numbers used to arrive in batches. Paul would intercept a credit card, then look out for the PIN number arriving separately. Once he matched them up, he'd go out and spank the card, buying gold, gold chains, rings, trainers, tracksuits and selling them on. People would be getting statements with thousands of pounds of debt on them and they hadn't even received their card yet!

"I think Paul was politely asked to leave. They knew he was at it but they couldn't catch him!

"Another time, Paul got himself a job as a delivery man. He was delivering cookers, fridges, washing machines. Well, he struck a deal with the owner's son to lob a few extra on the lorry each day and he was selling them off on the side. That all went up in smoke, literally. The owner's son set fire to the place because there was an audit coming up and there was so much fraud going on. Paul had a good thing going there. Every job he got, he had a little fiddle going on.

"I got Paul a job as a delivery man once when a girlfriend asked me to look after her flower shop for her," Lee goes on. "People used to come in and order their flowers for new babies, sick relatives, all that and they'd pay in the shop. Then when Paul delivered the flowers he'd ask them for payment again!

"One time we had a huge funeral we were looking after and Paul went off to deliver the flowers in the van. Later, they were ringing the shop, going mad asking where the flowers were as they hadn't arrived yet. We couldn't find Paul anywhere. It turned out he'd had some pretty heavy gear and was stoned, flat out amongst the flowers in the back of the van. We ran that shop into the ground within nine months, we did.

"Another job Paul got was at the *London Dungeon*! He asked the owner if he had anything going and he said, 'Yeah, you can dress up like a monk and stand still over in the corner by that pillar.' People would come right up to him to see if he was real or not, peer right up close at him, lift his hood and he'd say, 'Boo!' and have them pissing themselves. And whilst he was standing there in the dark, of course, he used to dip into the ladies handbags for their purses! Honestly, every job he did he had something going on.

"I had a good job once as a sprinkler fitter which didn't pay bad money at all. One day on site the boss came up to me and said, 'Your brother starts here tomorrow. That was an excellent reference you wrote for him.' I didn't know what he was talking about, what was going on. Paul had only gone and written in to the company saying he was an expert, putting in a fake application and got himself a job as an advanced fitter – more senior and more money than me! He said to me, 'Right, you've got to teach me everything you know in two weeks.' And I did, you know, showed him all the drawings, the equipment. And he got a bit of leeway too because the foreman was an Arsenal fan. He was delighted to have Paul there, you know? He came on site and was going, 'Look. This is Paul Vaessen everybody.' He got all the perks. The foreman put him down for overtime he never did and things like that.

"Even in that job Paul was up to it. At the end of each day, he'd collect up all the copper, iron, put it in a bag and sell it for scrap.

"Our next venture, he was even worse. We went self-employed after a while and had the contract for the *Burton Group*, fitting out all the sprinkler systems in their shops, *Burton's, Dorothy Perkins* and all that. We were working all over the country. Well, whilst we were working in the shops Paul wouldn't just take a couple of tee-shirts, he'd take a whole rack of suits. He'd wait for security to pass, wheel the rack out of the shop and into the back of the van. He would then go off and within the hour he would have sold them on and be back working in the shop. The security guards and shop staff would be thinking, 'I'm sure there was a rack of suits there!' We'd be eyes up to the ceiling, carrying on with our work!

"We nearly lost that *Burton's* contract because me and Paul flooded *Next* in Cheapside in the City of London! We blasted dirty, shitty water all over everything, clothes, leather couches, the parquet flooring buckled. The whole shop was ankle deep. We caused £15,000 worth of damage. Paul was going, 'What are we going to do?! What the f--k are we going to do?!' I'll tell you what we did. We legged it!

"The thing about Paul," says Lee, "is that his philosophy basically was that because he couldn't do the thing he wanted to do any more – play football – then he didn't want to do anything else. He just wanted his knees back. He just wanted to play football.

"Paul didn't stick at any job for very long. He couldn't get his head round it. It was a different world to the one he'd been used to. He'd gone from being at the top of his profession in Turin to getting up at 3am to sort the post.

"He was sat at home one day and I said to him, 'What's the matter with you?' He said, 'Look at me. I'm finished. My career's over, my life's over.' He just wanted to turn the telly off, turn the lights out, curl up into the foetal position and block all thoughts out. He wanted to revert back to the days when he had two good knees."

****

Having Paul back at home was traumatic for everyone. Maureen saw a lot.

"I had to take needles out of him, call for ambulances

because his tongue had turned black. Where he'd taken it, he'd just black out and you'd go in and find him there. One time I got home and he was out of it, he was lying there with the band around his arm and there were needles. I had to call the ambulance and they had to roll him over and pull his tongue out. He refused to go with them to hospital, though. 'No, I'm alright', he said.

"I had drug addicts and dealers at my door, holding knives to my throat asking, 'Where is he?'"

Paul was possibly at his worst while he was staying back with his parents at Lucey Way. Neighbour Sue comments, "All Paul had in his life was that he'd wake up every morning and think, 'Well, how long have I got to go before I have that next fix? I gotta get some money.' It didn't matter where he got it, it didn't matter who he hurt, as long as he got it."

"I tried every approach I could think of," says Maureen. "I was soft on him, caring towards him and then I was tough on him. It didn't seem to matter what I did.

"The family split four ways when we found out Paul was on drugs, you know? My husband was staying out most nights. I don't think he could cope with it. He stuck him up on a pedestal and it came crashing down. It hit him really hard."

Increasingly, Paul was turning to crime to fund his drug habit, admitting, "I broke into commercial premises, thieved from vans and people. I stole anything I could get my hands on. I was in court about half a dozen times and often returned for non-payment of fines. I don't know how I stayed out of jail."[41]

Paul got into debt with some rather heavy local characters and would soon start selling off the contents of his parents' place. He returned to Arsenal on occasion and things would go missing from the dressing rooms.

Throughout all this, Paul seemed to maintain his charm.

"Paul was never anything other than a gentleman with me," says retired police officer Laraine Kempster. "I remember being out on patrol one time, driving along and we went past him in the street. I'm from 'The Blue' myself and know the ground and the people who live there pretty well so I mentioned to my colleague, 'That's Paul Vaessen over there. He used to play for Arsenal.' He said, 'Oh. Paul Vaessen. I've heard of him,' so we pulled over, stopped the car and introduced ourselves. He was telling us about his career and what happened, the injury and all the problems. He was actually nearly in tears talking about it.

"After that, we would always stop and speak. I probably saw him as many times when he was off the drugs as when he was on them. A few times he was so out of it he probably didn't even know I was there. One time we were called to attend an incident and he was there. He was out of his head. I knew he'd recently been in rehab and I said, 'What are you doing back on that?' He just shook his head.

"Paul never gave me any problems. He stood out, in fact, because he was always very pleasant, to me anyway. Sometimes he'd go off on one, like once when I saw him in Custody and he was being bolshy, shouting a bit. As soon as he saw me he'd quieten down."

"The limits I sank to were immeasurable, both towards others and personally," Paul would later write. "Calculating how I could be as nasty as possible to others and myself became an art form, consisting of subtle manipulation and execution of one's knowledge concerning my 'victims.'"

****

The nadir for Paul came on 7th March 1985.

Paul was a cabbie at the time in his Renault 18 Turbo.

"I was living at Lucey Way," recalls Maureen. "I got home from shopping one day when his best mate Paul knocked on the door. He looked terrible. Have you ever seen a black person gone white? Well, he sat on the bottom of my stairs, trembling. I said, 'Whatever's the matter?' He said, 'Paul's been stabbed.'"

"They were waiting for him," says Lee. "They came at him in East Street Market, just between Walworth Road and the Old Kent Road. They knew he'd be going back there, to that area. It was notorious for drugs."

Paul knew there was going to be trouble because there were three of them.

"As he got out of the car," Lee continues, "these three fellas just leapt straight on him."

"For some people fear takes on completely different forms,"

184

Paul would retell. "You either freeze or panic. I panicked. Within seconds I was lashing out wildly with my fists, punching, kicking and desperately fighting for my life. I received a barrage of blows, which seemed like blows but were in fact several deep and severe stab wounds.

"Within what seemed seconds, it was over, my attackers had fled and had left me standing there, blood spurting from a wound under my left arm and me gradually losing consciousness. I knew then for the first time I was in trouble."

"He ran about five hundred yards," says Maureen, "and then collapsed outside a funeral home because his lung had been punctured and he couldn't get his breath. People were just walking, stepping over him. His mate had just happened to come by. He asked Paul what the matter was and he said, 'I think I've been stabbed.' He didn't realise at first. He said he felt like three heavy punches, that he didn't feel the knife. It was a ten inch knife. It went into him three different ways. He was open all the way up."

"There were three wounds," Lee confirms, "and I tell you they stuck that knife right in. They meant to kill him all right."

The people in the funeral home came out and called an ambulance but he wouldn't wait. His friend took him straight up to hospital then came back to let Maureen know where he was.

"It was only the extreme good fortune of one of my friends passing that saved my life," Paul would later recall. "He flagged down a passing motorist, dragged him from his car, put me in it and drove me to hospital. All this, from the time the attack took place until I arrived at hospital, ten minutes, and I still nearly bled to death."

Maureen describes how, "One of Lee's mates ran us up to the hospital. I was called into sister's office. I had been working at Guy's Hospital up until about three months before so I was aware something was wrong, very wrong when I was called in. She told me he'd been seriously stabbed and that he was up in theatre. Anyway, whilst we were in there, there was a phone call. Sister said, 'It's for you, Mrs Vaessen.' I couldn't think of anyone who could have known I was there but I took it and there's this fella down the other end and he said, 'Just wondering how Paul was.' And then I twigged. It must have been the person that had stabbed him. They were trying to find out whether he was alive or not and I just screamed down the phone at him and slammed it down.

"Leon had arrived by now. We'd separated two weeks before and it was the first time I'd seen him since then. He didn't want to come in at first. He was pacing around his van outside for quite a while before he eventually came in.

"It was fourteen hours Paul was on the table. They said, 'He went in fighting, we can tell you that!' Apparently he was shouting, 'I ain't gonna die! I ain't gonna die,' as they wheeled him in."

According to Paul, "Only the efficiency and quick thinking of the staff at the hospital kept me alive. The last thing I remembered was slipping into unconsciousness and having the real fear that I was going to die."

"He had a ruptured spleen, a punctured lung and a ruptured lower bowel," says Lee. "They had to open him right up, break his ribs to get to the bleeding."

"They had to take him straight in, fully clothed," Maureen recounts. "They couldn't even close him up because of internal bleeding. He lost forty pints of blood and ended up having 144 stitches. They came out half way through and called us in. They just said to us, 'Well, we can't even give you fifty-fifty, we can only give you thirty per cent.' I just looked at my husband and I remember he turned round and said to me, 'He might not make it, Mau.'

"Other people had started to arrive by then. It flashed up on *teletext*. News of it was everywhere. The police were there, half my family, friends. Paul's wife Sarah was there, even though they had split. She was in a terrible state."

Lee was the first one to see Paul come out of theatre.

"He looked like the colour of white emulsion. He was laying on one side, where they'd obviously opened him up on the other. I just ran out of the hospital. I was terrified."

Years later Paul would recollect, "One o'clock, that's what the clock said. It took a few minutes to focus, but, after some adjustment and recall of memory, I remembered what had happened. That clock, ticking very slowly, was it one o'clock in the morning or afternoon? How long had I been there? These questions went through my head within seconds of awakening. Then the pain, pain beyond belief overwhelmed me and sent me into a frantic screaming episode. That's when the staff nurse noticed that I was conscious.

"When I came to in hospital," Paul continued, "I couldn't

understand why I was still alive."[42]

"Finally," Maureen resumes, "in the middle of the night they came in and said that we could go in and see him. We were asked to go up to intensive care. I knew exactly where it was because I'd worked there. I also knew what I was in for. They took us in to see him and he was sitting up. He was shaking and he had so many tubes in him. He was sort of semi-conscious. Now, I'm used to seeing people in intensive care but my husband wasn't. He took one look and ran. I could hear him kicking the lift in. He couldn't hack it. As I say, I'd been used to seeing this sort of thing but it was still a shock. I sat down with him, held his hand. His eyes were open a little and he murmured, 'Mum.'

"He was in intensive care for four days. I sat with him for those four days. I didn't leave him, stayed in the same clothes. He was in hospital for three weeks altogether."

"The wounds ran down the left side of my body from my armpit to my waist," said Paul. "Doctors told me it was a miracle my heart, liver and kidney had been missed."[43]

Daily Express, Friday 8th March 1985:

Soccer star is stabbed

FORMER Arsenal soccer star Paul Vaessen was fighting for his life last night after being stabbed during an incident in Walworth, South East London.

Vaessen, 23, whose career was cut short by a knee injury two years ago, needed surgery to remove his spleen. A man is due to appear in court charged with grievous bodily harm.

"I read it in the paper," recalls Kenny Sansom. "You think, 'What are you doing?' but it's easy to say things, it's harder to do."

"When he retired," says former colleague Gary Lewin, "by that time I'd stopped playing and I'd gone to Guys Hospital as a physio so the next time I came across Paul was when I'd heard he'd been involved in the stabbing and was at Guys and I popped in to see him. It was the usual stuff really, you know, 'You alright?', 'What happened?' He was awake, he recognized me but I wouldn't say he was with it. He looked terrible. It was obvious what road he was going down. Then the next thing I heard he'd discharged himself."

"You might have thought the shock of the knife attack would have put me off drugs forever," Paul said in 1994. "But my addiction was so strong I discharged myself from hospital after just three weeks when I should have stayed in for three months. I was so desperate to get my hands on some more drugs."[44]

Paul had already made one attempt at escape from hospital.

"About a week after the stabbing," says Lee, "somebody popped around the house to tell me that Paul had been seen walking down the Old Kent Road! He'd only just come out of intensive care! He was in his hospital gown walking along with his arse hanging out with a tripod, his saline drip, catheter and colostomy bag, looking for some gear. The stabbing hadn't put him off in the slightest. He had just unplugged himself and walked out of the hospital. And believe me, if they did try to stop him he would have just walked straight through them. Anyway, I went down there, to the Old Kent Road to pick him up but the hospital had already come and got him.

"He even worked out how to fiddle the drugs in the hospital. He was on a twenty-four hour morphine drip which was controlled by a timer. Well, he worked out how to turn the timer and pump off and give himself a six-hour shot of morphine in one go so he was out of his head."

Long-term friend Jamie Winterton visited Paul in hospital and had his suspicions that not all the drugs Paul was on were legal.

"That was when I finished with him. I went to see him and you could see he was still on it (drugs), that people were bringing it in for him. I remember walking out of there with Sarah and saying, 'That's it, I can't see this any more.'"

"The police took some names and they went after them," says Maureen. "What exactly happened all came out when we went to court. It was all over £200. Paul was trying to put something right. Paul never got drugs for anybody but himself. He wasn't a dealer, he wasn't anything like that, he just got drugs for himself, for his own use. But this one time he got some for someone else it ended up being dodgy, it wasn't pure. Paul didn't know but they ended up going after him. He said to leave it with him for a while and he'd put it right, get the money back but they didn't give him a chance. They just stabbed him there and then, just stabbed him.

"Paul just went straight back to the drugs," Maureen confirms. "He actually went back to the person who stabbed him. That's why the fella got off. The other two of them admitted being there and they got two years but the one who did it, he got away on a technicality. While the case was going on, the trial and all that, Paul went and got some drugs off of him, the same fella that stabbed him, and that came out in court so they threw it out.

"All the time I was thinking, 'Why me, why me?' In two weeks my life was turned upside down with my husband walking out on me and Paul getting stabbed. I went from eleven stone to seven stone three in six weeks. I wondered what had hit me and in the end someone in the family had to go to my husband and say, 'I think you'd better pop in to see Maureen because she's in a right state.' He came and stayed with me for about six weeks to try and sort things out.

"A few weeks after the surgeon phoned me up and he said to me, 'Maureen, would you like to come out for lunch with me because I'd like to tell you about Paul.' He pulled up in this bloody great Mercedes, a rose in his lapel and we went to a place up the Old Kent Road. He said, 'I don't think you were fully aware on that day how close Paul was to death.' He said they'd had to bring him back twice on the operating table and that he'd only pulled through because of his fitness, because he'd been an athlete and he was so strong."

"At one point he was gone for two to three minutes," explains Lee. "He took it right to the limit. The surgeon actually took Paul's heart and squeezed it to get it pumping again. He was lucky. He was so close to dying.

"I'll tell you one thing that was funny about all this," chuckles Lee, "and that was his colostomy bag. The thing is, he couldn't control it and it made a big noise, not that he cared. Two or three months down the line we were in the pub talking to these two birds at the bar. All of a sudden there's this disgusting noise coming from Paul. They're like, 'What the f--k was that?!' So Paul, keeping a perfectly straight face, opens up his shirt and says, 'Look, it's only my bag!' They ran a mile!"

****

"It was rare to see old faces from Arsenal," Maureen reflects, "but a couple of the players came down to see him, to try to talk him off the drugs."

One of those was Alan Sunderland.

"I met Paul again at a testimonial. They'd wanted me to play but I was injured at the time but I still came down to watch the game. I met Paul afterwards in the players' lounge. He was down on his luck. He had this bag hanging out where he'd just been stabbed. He looked terrible, to be honest. He looked ill. I guess I felt a bit sorry for him but we picked up again, he gave me his number and I took to going down to see him. I went to dinner a few times down there with him and his mum. It was in a tower block, I think. It was a bit of a rough area to be honest. But I went down to see him, we'd go for a drink. We were good friends. He was a good young kid, a nice young lad. His career was finished before it had started."

****

Sunday Times journalist Rob Hughes was another who felt sympathetic to Paul's plight.

"December 1985 would have been when we got to know each other. I met him when he was back on his feet after the stabbing. To be blunt, it was the stabbing that attracted me. I had seen the header against Juventus and asked from time to time at the club how Paul was convalescing after his injury. The stabbing came as a shock and I contacted his mum."

Hughes wrote an article about Paul which appeared in the *Sunday Times* on 29th December 1985. Hughes concluded the piece by calling upon the football community to "begin to educate and prepare teenagers in its care for life in the outside world. It must…face up to the Paul Vaessens."

"I actually got quite a response to the article," Hughes reports. "Various readers offered help of a medical nature, including sports physicians and a surgeon, and then there was the offer from Clapton FC." Chairman Mike Fogg wrote to Hughes, "In your interesting article *The Giddy Fall from Highbury to Heroin*, in today's edition of the *Sunday Times*, you quote Paul Vaessen's

Mother as saying that Paul 'never cared for nothing more than football' and hoping that he will play again at what ever level he can. We would be very pleased to offer Paul the opportunity to train and, fitness permitting, play at Clapton. Whilst the Old Spotted Dog Ground is a far cry from Highbury, he would receive a warm welcome and have the opportunity to play in Vauxhall Opel League football."

"Clapton made the offer in writing and by phone," Hughes goes on. "I went to see them, told Paul and waited. I actually wrote him a long letter because he was ducking me."

8 January, 1986

Dear Paul,

First, I'm sorry we were unable to meet before the article in last week's Sunday Times. Time was short during Christmas week and, with no direct way of contacting you, I spoke to your Mum. I think she could tell my intentions were to write a fair and balanced piece, not to rake up further trouble for you.

The reaction I've had from Arsenal fans, and from people who had simply not thought about the consequences of injury, really do show there are people out there who want to know what happened to you, and want to help if they could.

I'm not trying to patronise. I was devastated when my own knee was wrecked before I was 18; I was lucky that people I'd never met pushed me towards a new profession; but if I regret anything now it is never allowing myself to even try to get back and use what ability I had at a level that demanded less punishing training.

The leap from Highbury to non-league may still haunt you, but if you still deep down have any urge for the game the two enclosed letters may be worth following up. Miracle cures might be fantasy, and the surgeon mentioned is far away in Middlesbrough, but I have contacts with specialists nearer to London if you feel ready to seek a second

191

opinion or perhaps intense physiotherapy to strengthen muscles around the knee. And who knows what healing nature might have done while you've been away?

Secondly, the offer from Clapton sounds to me too good to kick in the teeth. It's not, as Mike Fogg writes, Arsenal; but it is football. I'm damn sure you would be able to express your talent and rediscover the thrill of being able to outwit players again...

With best wishes,

Rob Hughes

"Paul responded in January," says Hughes. "He told me, 'Sorry. I've been getting myself together to write. You will be having a letter pretty soon. First things first, I'll go and see what the surgeon has to say. The article turned out pretty well for me.'

"From memory it was late February before I (almost) got him to Clapton. In fact I drove him there but never got him in. I never got him inside the ground. I drove him down and he took one look and he almost got out of the car and ran.

"I never saw him again despite the best efforts of Maureen and best intentions of Mike Fogg, the Clapton Chairman. I personally think it was tragic he never tried it. My view of Paul is that he'd tell you one thing – maybe it was drugs talking – but he'd talk to you and then go off and do the exact opposite to what he'd just told you."

Maureen's own suspicions are that Paul simply couldn't face going from Arsenal all the way down to amateur level.

"I was just trying to help him," states Hughes. "To me he was like a child. He always would try but he couldn't hold himself together. His mum was at her whit's end. I had her on the phone sometimes for hours and to be honest I couldn't tell her what to do. All I could do was try and fix this thing with Clapton.

"I don't think anything or anybody – only his mum – helped him after his stabbing. I remember one time his mum was on the phone to me. She told me how he was sitting there in front of her with scabs all over his arms and that he was telling her he wasn't on drugs and she could see that he was. And I can remember at one point me saying there's no point in me taking him to a football club

192

in that state because they won't let him across the threshold. And she would be saying to him, 'Paul, I've talked to your dad. You've got to come out of it.' And he would try.

"We spoke an awful lot on the phone – he cried, quite a lot, quite easily - and there was never a lack of will with him but what there was was a lack of will power. In other words, he couldn't get himself to kick it. And he was ashamed as well. He was all the things you get in somebody whose life is in despair like that. He was ashamed of what he was doing. At the same time he couldn't kick it and he couldn't break the cycle."

STUCK IN A MOMENT

12
Sympathy for the Devil

"We are each our own devil, and we make this world our hell."

Oscar Wilde

For the next seven years Paul was together with Debbie.

"I knew who he was years before he knew who I was. I've always liked football since I was tiny. I used to live in Lucey Way, dead opposite Paul. Years ago my mum and dad and his mum and dad used to go to lots and lots of parties together. They were all married very, very young, in their early twenties. My mum would obviously speak to me about Maureen and I found out that her son was playing football. I was thirteen, fourteen and I used to go and catch glimpses of him driving past in his little red sports car. I didn't know a lot about cars but I knew all about the footballers. I didn't see that much of him, just saw him coming and going. Then he didn't live there any more, he moved, he got married and I thought, 'Oh well'. Then all of a sudden he was back. Then he got stabbed. He actually got stabbed on my daughter's birthday. He nearly died. I met him just after that.

"It was *Live Aid* day, 13th July 1985. He came and knocked on my door, out of the blue. It was really strange. I'd got out of the bath, I had a towel wrapped around my head and there was a bang, bang, bang on the door. I went out on the balcony and I nearly fainted. I just looked over and thought, 'What do I do? What do I say?' I went, 'Hello. I can't really talk to you at the minute,' and he said, 'What are you doing later?' It was the first time I had actually spoken to him. He had the front of the devil! He came over about five o'clock and he never went home until early the next day. We just hit it off from the start. We sat there watching the concert and yakking away until five o'clock in the morning. We got on so, so well. There was just something there and it just went on from there.

"Within the first week of me knowing him I'd seen all his

195

scars, where he'd had the operations, the stab wounds and all that. He didn't actually go in to a lot of detail about the stabbing but I think it had scared him, the fact that he was that close to dying and not coming back.

"It was a few weeks later I first came across the drugs. I knew nothing at all about drugs. Nothing. Paul wasn't like the normal junkies you see walking the streets. He was so vain. His hair had to be just so, he was always in the bath. He went to a needle exchange, he wouldn't share anything. It was vanity, I suppose. He still had his self-respect. He couldn't bear to be seen talking to the junkies.

"Anyway, I saw him with a bit of foil. I didn't know what it was he was doing. He just said, 'It's okay, it's not anything for you to be that concerned about. I know what I'm doing but I don't ever want you near it.' I did ask him what it was and he said, 'It's a bit of smack but don't worry, I know what I'm doing. I'm not going to get back on it.'

"Of course we used to talk about football. He hated coming out of football. He would have rather died than come out of football. He would rather have not had his life at all. It was what he lived for. He had that opportunity to train out in Malta but he wasn't interested. He didn't want to go to Malta. He wanted what he couldn't have any more. He'd had a taste of the high life and that's what he wanted. He didn't want Fisher Athletic, the likes of the lower leagues, the likes of just anyone. He'd been up there and that was that. He wasn't coming back down from that. That's why he took the drugs. He couldn't cope with life. He couldn't cope with being someone then not being someone.

"Paul was a very, very complex person, extremely complex. He was very deep. We had lots of very deep discussions. Paul was very spiritual but in a dark way. He questioned religion and people's faith and everything because he couldn't believe people could be, as he would say, so pure when there were so many temptations. He believed in the devil. He was fascinated with the devil.

"He was convinced that there were powers out there influencing things, that it wasn't actually drugs or women or drink or whatever which was evil, it was the devil. He thought he had what he called an affiliation with the devil, like the devil was a friend of his. We used to have long, long conversations about it. I think he thought

196

he was going to actually meet the devil. I said to him, 'I think you need to face him, not go and meet him. I think you need to face him, face the fact that you don't want to live.' He didn't believe in God. He wasn't religious. Never. Never in a million years. He was very deep, complex. He was also so clever, something most people don't realize about him. He was very, very intelligent.

"What didn't help Paul was that he had a compulsive, addictive personality. When he didn't take drugs, he drank. Excessively. If it wasn't illegal drugs or drink then it would be prescription drugs. He knew how to get them and he'd take the whole lot in one go, enough to kill a normal person. Nothing could be done on a level. It was all or nothing, no half measures, not in any sense of his life. He was also suffering from manic depression. When he was up he was up but when he was down he was very quiet and withdrawn.

"We were inseparable for a good seven to eight months and then Paul realised he was getting too heavy with the drugs. He had started injecting so in 1986 he went to a rehab centre and he was away for a long while, nine months. He wanted to sort himself out. While he was away I made it my business to find out everything I could about drugs. I knew nothing about drugs. I was so naïve. I wanted to find out as much as I could because I wanted to know what I was dealing with because you can't fight something unless you know what you're dealing with.

"He came out and boy did he look well, he looked so well. And typical of Paul he came over, banged on the door, 'Guess who's back?!' And he laughed about it. He was back on track again.

"By Christmas 1987 I was pregnant with Jamie. Paul was absolutely over the moon. Everything seemed to be going fine. He was working as well, he was working on a construction site. He was doing really well and then I saw a couple of old faces from the past talking to him and I thought, 'No, no, not again. What's he doing?' And then I noticed his eyes because by now I knew what I was looking for. His pupils were tiny.

"By the time I was actually having Jamie, Paul was still at work. How the hell he kept a job down I don't know. Paul was fascinated with the birth. He loved a bit of blood and gore! He used to love telling me all the gory details about all his operations, to wind me up. But he was also fascinated with Jamie. He was really good

197

with him.

"He managed to sort himself out again for a little while but was soon back at it. But even when he was on it, we were still okay. We were happy, there wasn't a problem.

"We tried to get our own place but I couldn't get anything off of the council. Then we found out there was a flat going empty, the people had moved out. There was a window open and I thought, 'F--k it.' We got in, changed the locks. We made it lovely. It was great while we were there. We lived there for about seven months before we got caught and were evicted.

"I remember I went in one day and he was with this guy – I couldn't stand this guy – and they had stuff, drugs out in the kitchen. My eldest from a previous relationship was by now four and a half and I had Jamie in the pram, he was about six or seven months old. I came through the door and this guy legged it. I said to Paul, 'We're playing games again are we?' I picked it up and put it down the sink. I looked at him and he was itching to stop me but wouldn't. And I just whacked him one and he went, 'Well, I deserved that.' I said, 'You see this here? My Lisa? She would know there's something wrong. She's not a baby any more. You can't keep doing this whilst she's here.' As she got older she used to say to me, 'Mum, why does Paul keep going to sleep every time I try and talk to him.'

"By the time Jamie was coming up to two and a half, I was back at my mum's because we still couldn't get a flat. Paul was with his mum. Paul knew he needed to get away from the area. It didn't matter how many times he came off the drugs, a month or two later he was back with the old crowd. And he knew he needed to get away. It was like a sort of joint decision, it was cruel to be kind for both of us. He had to go away and move away. As much as I didn't want him to, I knew he had to and he didn't want to go but he knew he had to. We split up some time in 1991 and I didn't hear from him again for three years.

"He did ask me to marry him one day, in a shop, on his knees. I was pregnant with Jamie. I said, 'Paul, please get up. Don't do this to me. Get up or I'm walking out!' And he started walking on his knees. A nutcase he was.

"I made a lot of sacrifices for him but he wasn't a bad person. He never stole from me, he never took from me, he never did anything bad to me, he wasn't violent, he wasn't anything that most

198

people associate with junkies. Whether he was on it or not, he was a good person. There were a lot of things to like about Paul. The bad side of him was the drugs but other than that there was nothing that was bad about him. Personality-wise, he was a bit full of himself, you know? But considering who he was and what he had been, why shouldn't he be?"

****

"During the early nineties I worked at Bermondsey Employment Office (Job Centre)," says Anthony Jones, "and had the pleasure of meeting Paul on several occasions over the years. I interviewed him when he first signed on and once I realised who he was we became good acquaintances and he always asked for me when he signed on.

"Despite the problems he was clearly having with life, he was always a charming, friendly and reasonable guy, and very proud of his time at Arsenal.

"I remember him discussing two goals with me – his goal for Arsenal versus Tottenham and the famous goal against Juventus.

"The last time I saw him was when he came to say goodbye as he was moving away from Bermondsey. He had managed to kick his habit and was confident that he was on the road to recovery, and I wished him well."

STUCK IN A MOMENT

13
Better Man

"There is something magical about watching a man who has lost himself find his way back home."

Jon Landau on Elvis Presley (1968)

I go to sign out but there's a panic behind me. Branca has been checking the tools and instruments against the itinerary, which is done in order to catch anybody trying to slip something out, and there is a knife missing. Everybody stands still. Phone calls are made. Nurses arrive. Ten minutes of searching and interrogation later and it is found, in the pocket on the front of Branca's apron, which she is wearing.

I slip my coat on, sign out, say thanks. And so ends another session of occupational therapy at the Bethlem Royal Hospital in Beckenham in the London Borough of Bromley. It is December 2006 and I am on the road to recovery following a nervous breakdown. Coming in to work one day on the train, I got half the way there, got off at St.Albans, turned around and went back home, not to leave the house again for a year except to receive Cognitive Behavioural Therapy for Obsessive Compulsive Disorder and Major Depressive Disorder at The Priory and then Maudsley hospitals in London. As things didn't improve – indeed, the psychologist I saw at the Priory told me more or less to simply snap out of it – I requested that I be reassessed with a view to undertaking treatment as an inpatient. They agreed and so I was sent to 'Bedlam', one of the oldest and most renowned psychiatric hospitals in the world, for a three month stay.

And of all the characters I encountered during that time, the one that stands out is Don.

Don.

The Don.

The Guvnor.

The Kingpin.

The Big Cheese.
The Knowledge.
Our own R. P. McMurphy.
Our Grouty.
Our Tony Soprano.

When I arrived at the Bethlem, Don was one of the first people I met. He was there on the ward that first day and after only ten minutes it was clear that I was being taken under his wing, treated as some kind of pupil, apprentice. Taking care of induction, he told me what was what and what and who was where.

As time passes, it becomes apparent that Don is treated a little differently to the other patients. In fact, he seems to run the whole show. He's got everybody – the consultants, therapists, pharmacists, even the catering staff – at his beck and call, in his back pocket, on the pay roll. Most of them are simply scared of him. I must admit I found him a little intimidating at first but I grew to like him. That's the thing about being in a place like this. You can hit it off with people whose paths in normal circumstances you would never have crossed. For some reason, your past doesn't matter. You're all equal. Except for Don, of course.

The professionals are no doubt fascinated by him as he has been in and out of places like this – as well as custodial ones – for the best part of his life. He's a living, walking case study. He's had the lot. None of the patients really know what he's in for this time. And nobody asks. Fact is, he's been drugged up to his eyeballs most of his adult life. He's got an encyclopaedic knowledge of prescription medications which would make Elvis Presley jealous. And if you're after something, he can more than likely lay his hands on it, including *Viagra* which he keeps in the glove compartment of his little Mercedes.

Don has been so drugged up he's turned up in countries with no idea as to how he got there.

"Budapest?! I'd never even heard of f--king Budapest! How the f--k did I get here?!"

But get there he did and they looked at his passport, his papers, saw he was the Lord of Lambeth, made frantic phone calls and the next thing they're whisking him off in a limousine to an embassy or something and putting dancing on in his honour. I've seen the pictures. Because he *is* the Lord of Lambeth. He bought the title and the accompanying deeds to a square inch of land somewhere in Devon off of the internet.

Like most of us he is a bundle of contradictions. He shoplifts from Sainsbury's if he thinks things are too dear but would give you his last penny. He's been raided at dawn but is the first one in to church for Holy Communion. He helps old ladies across the street before kicking the living daylights out of men half his age at a local kick boxing club.

Don does look after himself. He obviously keeps himself fit, eats sensibly. He sits in the restaurant in the corner where his back is covered and he can see the door, see who's coming in and out. He dresses well too, looks after his hair and his skin. He's got pots and pots of E45 cream back in his room.

This is Don's home from home and during your induction you get a guided tour, Don pointing out all the departments and wards. I find out later he has spent time in almost all of them.

"You don't want to worry about any of that lot in there. They're f--king lunatics in there. They don't come out. They keep them jabbed up in there. You don't have to worry about that lot. They don't even get out of bed, except for the Christmas do."

Amongst his better known fellow patients are singer Lena Zavaroni, dating back to the time she was struggling with anorexia, and Caspar Fleming, son of the James Bond creator, Ian Fleming, who tragically died from a drugs overdose in October 1975.

One name he doesn't mention is Paul Vaessen.

Paul and Don were at the Bethlem at the same time in the early nineties. They may have met, I don't know. They certainly would have made a formidable duo.

"Paul spent three months in the Bethlem," says Lee, "as I did later on. He was in there for therapy but also for detox. I used to go and visit him there. We used to jump over the wall and go and have a few beers and a Chinese.

"He was in there with some right characters, I can tell you. There was Lawrence of Arabia, a bloke who went around with a sheet wrapped around him and over his head. There was another bloke who thought he was Napoleon. There was the Mad Axeman of Deptford who just walked into Paul's room one day, while Paul was sitting there, and unplugged Paul's telly and walked out with it. And then there was this woman who had a phobia about wood. She would go up to doors and confront them. She'd stand there and psych herself up and shout at the doors, 'I'm going to walk through you!!' She had to pick up sticks and hug trees as part of her therapy."

It wasn't the first time Paul had sought treatment and rehabilitation. Paul was in Featherstone Lodge, a detox centre run by the Phoenix House charity (patron Prince Charles) in a quiet side street in Forest Hill, South London, for eighteen months.

"They really tested him there," Lee continues. "While he was there, inside that environment, he was, as with all his stints in rehab, very positive, confident. He'd go in, do the treatment, talk the talk but when he used to get out he used to crumble straight away, within twenty four hours. A year and a half he was there at Featherstone Lodge, then he came out and bang, he was back on the gear. One problem was that when he was prescribed methadone as part of his therapy, he became addicted to that instead of the heroin.

"I used to ask him why he did it, why go through all that and go back to the gear and he'd say, 'I needed the break. Physically and mentally I needed the break.' He treated these places as a stop gap, a safe house, a retreat, even sometimes to escape from going to court."

According to Maureen's partner Ernie, "The trouble with the rehab up until then was that he came back to the same place. When he came out he was on top of his game. He was one hundred percent better at the time. If he'd moved to a different area or a different town or whatever but he came straight back to the same area. There was no way he was going to be able to avoid those people. He walked straight back into it."

But in 1993 Paul did things a little differently. In May of that year he entered a hospital detoxification unit in Bexleyheath.

"It was a desperate struggle for seven weeks." Paul would later reflect, "and I was tempted to leave many times."[45] But he saw it out and instead of settling back down in South Bermondsey, in September 1993 Paul made his way to Andover for rehab at *St. Vincent's*, owned by the *Coke Hole Trust*.

The trust started off life in the late sixties as little more than a place where Andover's 'unclubbables', its hell's angels and the like, could gather two evenings a week and just be themselves. Established in a church, the trust, run initially by a pair of committed Christians who gradually started taking in young homeless people, eventually grew to become one of Britain's first rehabilitation centres for former drug dependents.

Paul stayed there for eighteen months and underwent a transformation.

"Drugs have never really been a problem but a symptom of my problems," explains Paul on a short documentary about the trust. "Until I actually could take a step out of myself, to look at myself, to try and deal with the reasons why I do things, then nothing ever changed."

Seated rather ironically in front of a stain glass window, Satan's former right-hand man – "that's how I would describe myself" – continues. "I was completely selfish. I would have actually used or manipulated anyone at that particular time to get what I wanted which ultimately was drugs. When I came to the trust I realised it wasn't anything that this world could give me, there was nothing in this world that could fill that void inside of me. But it was something that Christ gave me, you know, which was unconditional love."

With his demons now apparently a thing of the past, life was taking on new purpose for Paul.

"I'm taking English, Maths, Psychology and Human Biology for a two year period and that's a short-term goal for me because ultimately my long-term goal is I want to train to become an occupational therapist which is kind of a big challenge for me. It's a big commitment in my life. It could be six years of my life I'll be doing that but I feel much more confident and able now to achieve my goals."

"One other idea we came upon," says Lee, "was for Paul to go round all the clubs, from fourth to first division, giving lectures to the kids to encourage them to make a life for themselves outside football, to have something to fall back on."

"Paul told me that in a letter he sent me," recalls Nicky Law. "I was just coming towards the end of my career. I was at Chesterfield at the time and we'd just won promotion in the play-off final against Bury at Wembley. It was a strange letter but he said he'd seen me on telly and he left me a phone number to ring him on. I was a bit apprehensive, you know. He was wanting to meet up but I had a young family and, having heard one or two things about him, I thought it probably wasn't a good idea. Anyway, I rung him a couple of times and he told me that he was on the mend and that he had this idea to go into clubs and do a bit of talking to the young lads, to pass on his experience."

In June 1994 Paul would give an exclusive interview to the *News of The World* in support of their war on drugs in football.

"There are a lot of young kids out there who are doing drugs and feel they have lost all hope. I know because I have lived through the same thing. I'm telling my story to show there is a way out."[46]

He was half way through his stay in the Andover rehab centre and said, "For the first time in years people (at *St. Vincents*) were being nice to me and didn't want anything in return. I now know I had been searching all my life for something that was missing. I had to reach the stage where I had no-one else to turn to before I turned to Christ.

"I'm starting to take responsibility for myself. There's no magic wand. I'm still going through the long process of recovery. But I have a meaning, purpose and hope in my life now and can face things without drugs."[47]

"He was looking for salvation," states Leon, "to get out of the shit he was in, to get over his problems."

"I've got his bibles and self-help books from the time he was down there in rehab," says Maureen. "He wrote in the columns about the state of mind he was in at the time and highlighted passages which I guess he felt were relevant to him. He had this book called *The Broken Body* which was sort of a philosophical book. He made all these notes in the margins by the passages which I suppose he felt spoke to him in some way:"

So they think they are worthless, just a nuisance –
maybe even evil.
And from this loneliness
arises anguish and confusion,
an inner brokenness,
no trust in themselves or in others.
This in turn leads to violence,
depression, disturbed behaviour,
and so they are put aside even more,
rejected.
They sense that they belong nowhere and to no one...

BETTER MAN

It seems better to escape
into a world of dreams and illusion or even madness
rather than live in this pain of isolation and despair.
The dream world is sometimes so much better
than the real world:
There one feels at least a sense of control,
a measure of consolation.[48]

Maureen saw a clear improvement in Paul.

"For the first six months he was in rehab in Andover we weren't allowed down there at all. Then we had a call to say we could go down to see him. He looked totally different. When he finished there he was about fifteen stone. He'd gone in there ten stone. He looked so well. He did very well there. He did come off of the drugs for quite a while. I thought he'd turned a corner."

Leon concurs.

"He managed to get himself on an even keel for quite a while after the rehab. We all wondered how long it would last."

****

It was early 1995 and there was a fresh start for two former addicts, one higher in profile than the other. Paul Merson returned to the Arsenal side after a three month absence for rehabilitation having gone public with his penchant for gambling, alcohol and drugs in November the previous year. At the same time a re-born Paul Vaessen, who was still at Arsenal in April 1982 when Merson signed schoolboy forms, left *St.Vincent's* in search of new beginnings.

"I met Paul when I was living in Andover," says Sally. "I'd gone to live in Andover because I went to a treatment centre there, the *Coke Hole Trust*. I'd already left and was going to college. I used to go to church every Sunday and Paul started attending as well. When he left the centre, that's when we started seeing each other. It was a Baptist church. He was already into religion. He got baptised in the summer after he left the treatment centre. It was a Christian rehab. You didn't have to take it up but it was shoved down your throat a bit. They were all very kind there, though. He was doing

207

very, very well during this period. He was clean.

"I'd never heard of him. I didn't believe it when he told me he'd played for Arsenal. I was never interested in football. It was only when my brother confirmed it for me. I said to my brother, 'There's this guy I've been seeing and he reckons he played for Arsenal.' I thought it was just a line, that he was just trying to chat me up but my brother said it was true.

"Paul was a bit of a charmer. Everybody liked him, everybody. He was very funny, hilarious. He could tell a joke, tell a story. He did get a lot of attention and he was always happy. But there was a side to him that nobody could ever get to, a side that was pretty dark and he never really let me see that very much.

"He used to talk a lot about Arsenal. There were a lot of funny stories he used to tell me. He had some good times there. He spoke about the feeling he had after he scored that goal against Juventus. He said he'd never ever experienced, up to that point, anything - drugs, whatever – anything that even came near to that feeling."

Neighbours who got to know Paul agreed. Tracey Claus told Kevin Mitchell and Jamie Jackson for their article, *The Terrible Death of a Forgotten Hero*, published in *The Observer* in March 2002, "When he was straight he was a really nice guy. He used to talk constantly about his time at Arsenal. He told the story of scoring the goal in the semi-final many a time. You could see it meant a lot to him."

Another neighbour, David Jones, also told Mitchell and Jackson, "His eyes used to light up when he talked about Arsenal."

"There were occasions," Sally continues, "when Arsenal asked him to come back and play charity matches but he wouldn't have anything to do with it. A little bit of it was down to shame because of the drugs but also he just felt hurt about the way he'd been treated.

"As far as playing football goes, he went back to the rehab when they had some sort of fun day or something and he played a match there. And later on my father's local club had some special Christmas game and Paul and his brother went and played in that. And he used to have a kick-about with the kids where we lived but apart from that he didn't go anywhere near football. He wasn't interested in it, he didn't follow it any more. As I said, I've never been one who's really been into football or understood it and I'd never heard of him before but I did feel the emotion, the passion he'd once felt for it and the hurt he felt. It was very sad.

"People used to badger him to talk about Arsenal, like in the pub. We never had to spend a penny in the pub. Everyone knew he'd played for Arsenal. Sometimes, though, it was the last thing he wanted to talk about. It really did depend on how he felt at the time, although I think sometimes he did like the bit of admiration he got.

"He realised he had so many fair weathered friends when he was a football player who were just there because of the fame and for nothing else really. Lots of people dropped him and let him down. He said he was left virtually on his own. He said it was a big fall going from someone who was admired to someone nobody wanted to touch. They seem to help them more nowadays. Look at Gazza and Merson. In Paul's day you didn't have that.

"I do remember I was round his flat, his bedsit when he got a phone call one day before Paul Merson did that press conference. He got a phone call from him, asking for his advice about what he should say knowing Paul had been in a similar position. God knows how he got his phone number.

"Anyway, we lived together in Andover for a while. Paul was at college because he hadn't done his 'O' levels or CSEs at school. He was trying to get them so he could go on to train to be a physio. That was his plan. But then I fell pregnant with Jack. I already had Abigail so Paul decided he needed to get a job, with the thought of maybe picking things up in the future. My dad found him some work where he was working as a paint sprayer. That was down in Farnborough so he moved in with my father. I used to go down and visit at weekends but moved down there not long before Jack was born. We had our own flat. Jack was born in January 1996. Paul loved Jack to bits, he really did. Jack could do no wrong in his eyes."

****

"Paul was thirty six when he had that last operation on his left knee," Maureen recalls. "He needed a complete new knee but they said he wasn't entitled to one because of his relatively young age. Apparently they last about ten years or so and you can only have it done twice so they suggested that because he was in so much pain – it kept giving way – he have it fused. He had a steel rod outside his leg going down over the knee so that he couldn't bend it whatsoever while it fused together."

"That was a really, really awful time," Sally continues. "At the time he was working, he had a car. He was no saint but life was alright, life was good but his knee was getting more and more and more painful. They said the only thing they could do to lessen the pain was to have it fused like that. On reflection, I think they could have done something else with his knee.

"I don't think either of us really anticipated what impact it was going to have on our lives. I had a new baby and Paul needed looking after, he needed pushing around in a wheelchair which he hated. It was tough, it was so tough for him. He was so, so depressed, incredibly depressed and to actually see a man, a big strong man reduced to that was very, very painful. His leg was fused straight. He did manage to walk without crutches in the end but he couldn't bend his leg at all so he sort of hobbled along. But it took a long time to get to that point. He was in a wheelchair for six months."

Paul had to give up work, his aspirations of becoming a physiotherapist having fallen by the wayside.

"Sitting in doors all day," says Sally, "he started drinking a lot more, mixing his alcohol with his painkillers and antidepressants. It was awful to see him like that. He changed. It was like he was a different person. It wasn't my Paul, it wasn't the Paul I'd met at all. He dabbled with drugs before the operation but all in all he was off drugs for quite a while. But the operation was the turning point. It started off with prescription drugs then escalated. And he wouldn't go back to those who had helped him at the *Coke Hole Trust*. Because he had relapsed, I think he felt shame and guilt about contacting them, that he'd let them down.

"He became very, very unpredictable. Like with the Asda business. That was so embarrassing. My mother worked there. He was on painkillers, sleeping tablets and he was mixing them with alcohol. I don't know what was in his head obviously but he stole a pair of tights! Now, why would a man steal a pair of tights?! He wasn't a cross-dresser! So it was obvious he didn't know what he was doing, he didn't know what he was doing at all. He hadn't gone

210

out to steal anything. He wasn't out trying to shoplift to get money
for drugs or anything like that. He'd just gone completely cuckoo. It
was embarrassing but I felt so bad for him."

Paul was found in the supermarket's toilet talking to himself.

"The police were called," Sally continues, "and he was
arrested. There was some sort of a tussle outside the store. Paul said
he was protesting about his leg and was pushed to the floor and into
the van. The police said Paul lashed out and kicked an officer."

Paul was sentenced to ninety days for assault but his
conviction and sentence were later quashed on appeal. Solicitor
Andrew Purkiss told the court, "This is a very tragic case. Twenty
years ago, my client was on top of the world with everything to look
forward to. But, at twenty one, he was told by doctors he would be
crippled if he played professional football again. His whole life was
turned upside down and he was totally desperate. In those days there
was no counselling or after-playing help and he was told by Arsenal,
'Goodbye and good luck.'"[49]

"He did start doing very, very strange things," says Sally.
"He was so unpredictable and that in the end is what split us up
because it started to affect the children. My parents were worried,
obviously. But I knew it wasn't Paul, it was the drugs and it all
started off with the operation."

Paul was eventually evicted by court order from the house
after a number of incidents.

"I know Paul wasn't exactly in his right mind," Maureen
reflects, "I know he was going off of his head so maybe Sally was
safeguarding the children against him. But he wouldn't have hurt
anybody. He wasn't very well and nobody seemed to give him a
chance."

With nowhere to go, Paul asked Lee if he could come and
live with him in Bristol. Lee agreed. It was something he'd live to
regret.

STUCK IN A MOMENT

14

He Ain't Heavy, He's My Brother

"The younger brother must help to pay for the pleasures of the elder."

Jane Austen, 'Mansfield Park' (1814)

When I visited Warwick Bean at *The Castle* pub restaurant in Outwood, Surrey which he owned at the time, I caught him in contemplative mood.

"You know, I think of me and I think of Paul Vaessen and I wonder whether it's better to have been like me and never to have known whether I would have made it in the top flight or not, or to be like Paul and have got there for that short time and had that magic moment."

It struck me as a compelling and crucial question: Would Paul have been better off without Turin?

It's a difficult one.

"I suppose realistically I would have loved to have had the magic moment," says Warwick, "because your place in history is there forever."

Most of us would probably say the same.

Most of us would opt for Paul's Turin moment.

But that is ignoring something.

It was a moment Paul would re-live in his mind countless times, which he would re-tell over and over in conversation with anybody willing to listen and which he would re-enact time and again with the kids in the local park. But throughout the remainder of his days that memory also served as a constant reminder of how high he once flew and, critically, how far he had fallen.

"It was a tragedy him scoring that goal," one eminent football writer told me.

213

The bottom line is that whatever way you look at it, blessing or curse, Paul was stuck in Turin, stuck in a moment.

Warwick Bean has, of course, lived happily on without his moment. So have thousands of others.

One of them is Paul's brother, Lee.

Lee too was once a footballer. With an ex-pro as a father and a local hero as a brother, you wouldn't have expected anything else.

"Basically, it was a footballing family," says Lee. "Now I'm not blowing my own trumpet but my old man used to say to me, 'You're twice the player your brother is but you're lazy.' Where I played as a kid, for Leeford FC who were a Sunday league side based in Eltham, they used to call me the 'Centre Circle Kid' because I never came out of the centre circle! They'd ask me to come back and help out the defence but I was a bit lippy at that age and would say, 'Why do you want me to track back? I've just set up three goals!' Because I could play the game. I could ping the ball thirty, forty yards and hit a bumble bee on the arse. My dad, who had some experience behind him, said I had the best left foot he'd seen in years.

"We were a top side at Leeford, top of the league but whilst I was there I was head-hunted by Kingfisher FC. They're still about today. They were a new club and were basically cherry-picking the best players from the league. I was only thirteen, fourteen and was playing with kids at least a year older than me. Physically, I wasn't as advanced as the others. That year or two makes a lot of difference when it comes down to physique. But the thing is because I had the ability and I could read the game, I could hold my own and got away with it.

"I remember whilst I was at Kingfisher we won the cup and Paul, who had come down to watch me, was pulled out of the crowd to present the cup and the medals. I also played for South East London Comprehensive where I went to school and for four years we were unbeaten, the nearest anyone got being a 2-2 draw.

"Then one Sunday this guy came up to me and introduced himself. He was a scout for West Ham and he asked me if I fancied going down to train with them. It was in Thamesmead. I trained with the youth team, sixteen year-olds. They wanted to put me in the side at fourteen.

"I was there about eighteen months. Dad used to take me down there every Wednesday in his Post Office van. Then when he couldn't do it any longer, I didn't have the money to get the buses and trains so it sort of faded away. Anyway, it was quite a trek across London but not as bad as the journey down to Southampton. My PE teacher took four of us – the cream of the crop, if you like – down there for a couple of training sessions but it was just too far to go.

"Paul also got me a trial at Arsenal. He said to them, 'You've got to see my brother play. He's got more talent in his big toe than I've got in my whole body.' So Paul drove me down to London Colney and when I got there, there were five games going on and about two hundred kids involved. I was put on the bench for my match. Half-time came and I wasn't brought on. Fifty minutes came and I was still on the bench, sixty minutes, seventy minutes. It got to eighty minutes and the coach finally turned around and said, 'Okay, young Vaessen. Get your boots on.' Well, I'd had enough by now so I told him to shove it up his arse. I said, 'How on earth can you tell what sort of player I am in ten minutes?' And that was that, except I made sure I got some expenses. Even though Paul drove me there, I told them I'd got a cab and they gave me £98 each way!

"By then I had seen what had happened to Paul, with the injury, and decided to back off from football a bit. I was already feeling twinges and things in my knees when I was fourteen and actually tore a ligament myself when I was fifteen and was warned off the football by the doctors. They said if I carried on I would end up like my dad and my brother. They said there was a weakness in the knees and that it was probably hereditary.

"I did play a bit later for Dogan Arif at Fisher. I played a few games there but that was it.

"I do look back and wonder what might have been but if it had gone the same way as my old man and Paul, I'm not sure that, emotionally, I would have been able to handle it. So I backed off. I lost my bottle because when you see your hero sitting on the sofa crying his eyes out because he can't play any more, it hits you. It hits you hard.

"You see, when I was growing up Paul was my idol. He was doing what I wanted to be doing. He was playing for one of the top clubs in the world, aged sixteen. I loved him. Of course I idolised him.

"And I tried to do whatever I could to help him out. When I left school I had various jobs, working as a labourer on a building site then in the post room of *Marathon Oil* in Marylebone. Then I became a sprinkler fitter and started to earn a good wage. It was about then that Paul really started to struggle."

"Paul used to fleece his brother," Maureen admits, "take all his wages from him, everything. He didn't steal it, my Lee gave it to him. We tried to tell him, 'Please don't give your brother any money.' He was ruining Lee's life as well as his."

"I was giving him money to stop him going out thieving," says Lee. "He wasn't any good at it and I didn't want to see my brother going out getting nicked.

"When I was working as a sprinkler fitter, before Paul got involved, I was earning good money. If I had a good week at work I could earn up to a grand but I'd be lucky if I saw £100 of it. I should have been well off, in my own house, in nice new clothes but I had nothing because I gave it all away to Paul. I was working seven days a week and had nothing to show for it. I was twenty years old, working my fingers to the bone and I had nothing.

"Friday was pay day and he used to be there sitting on the landing outside the front door on a Friday afternoon, waiting for me to come home.

"I used to give him £25 at the beginning of the day for quarter of a gram of gear. I used to say to him, 'Try and make it last the day.' But he'd ask for £50 and say he'd let it last him a couple of days but the following morning he'd be asking for more. Some weeks I probably gave him seven, eight hundred quid.

"It got to the point where I basically got fed up working my bollocks off for nothing, paying for everything. In the same week I split up with my girlfriend, I lost my job. I remember I came home and Mum was in the kitchen and Paul was sat in the living room with his feet up on the coffee table, out of his head. I went to tell Paul about losing my job. He said, 'Well, where am I going to get the money for my gear then?!' I said, 'Go out and get yourself a job.' He didn't seem that bothered, he seemed happy enough and I thought this stuff can't be that powerful. I was depressed and I just said to him, 'Give me a line of that f--king stuff. Show me some of that wonder drug. It can't be that good.' And instead of saying no, he gave

216

me some. It made me sick and I was out of my head the rest of the day. Like him, I didn't give a f--k about anything. I'm 99.9 per cent sure I wouldn't have gone anywhere near drugs if it hadn't have been for Paul. It was just there, you know, for the taking. But I'm not blaming Paul. It was my choice. He didn't force it on me."

The Vaessens now not only had one boy on drugs, but two. And they weren't averse to selling the family silver.

Beat officer Laraine Kempster recalls, "I was called out to Paul's mum's house on one occasion to report a burglary. She'd been cleared out. All the electricals, anything of value, all gone. I asked her if she had any idea who might have done it. She was in a right state, and from what she said to me, it was obviously one of her sons. She was just too distraught, though, to take it any further."

"I got home from work one night and sat down," Maureen recalls. "I was thinking to myself, 'Something's not right here. Something's missing. What's missing?' It was my telly!"

The boys were keeping some pretty suspect company.

"This time," recalls Lee, "Paul was at a spill in the middle of Peckham. They were called spills because they took the spill-over from the pubs. They were open until the early hours of the morning and this one was out the back of a kebab shop. There were some unsavoury characters there. They'd be all tooled up. That was the sort of company me and Paul were keeping in those days.

"Well, there was some kind of an argument, someone had a pop at Paul and he's hit them. They pulled out a Stanley Knife and ran the blade across his right hand, cutting all his tendons. Then they cut him from his ear to the corner of his mouth. As I say, that's the sort of people we were hanging around with. You lived by the sword and you died by the sword."

Like Paul, Lee went off the rails and was in and out of court. He also ended up doing time.

"Once Paul woke me up in the middle of the night to help him with a job. We had to lift this gear out of a warehouse so I got on the roof and all of a sudden loads of old bill appeared. Paul pointed up at me and shouted, 'He made me do it! My head's full of barbiturates!' He got sent to rehab. I got sent to prison."

In late 1994 Lee moved up to Bristol to undergo secondary rehabilitation. It was either that or prison.

"I was going down again," says Lee, "and I'd just had

enough."

He had been clean for six months when he met Ruth during the following summer and in April 1996 baby Olivia arrived.

Things went well for the next few years.

Until Paul arrived.

"Paul went to live with Lee in Bristol with his partner, Ruth and their daughter," recalls Maureen. "Paul had had to leave Farnborough and Lee couldn't bear to see his brother out on the street. Lee had been doing so well but apparently Paul caused havoc up there. Lee and Ruth found it very hard having him and in the end having Paul there split them up."

"I said to Paul," Lee continues, "'You can come down but please, whatever you do, don't use.' But he did and eventually, so did I. It was difficult for me. I'm an addict and every morning as I went out to work I could hear him chasing gear in the toilet. I couldn't handle it. After a while, I just said, 'F--k it, give me some of that.'

"I asked Ruth to leave with Olivia for their own good. I didn't want to drag Ruth down. She wanted to stay and help but I insisted she went.

"I lost everything, my job, my partner, my kid, my house. At the same time I'd done everything for Paul. I'd got him a flat, a job, a car, a telly, a video recorder. He didn't have to pay for anything. And I ended up living with Paul. I had lost it all."

****

Sally would still travel up to Bristol so he could see Jack. Paul would also get back to London occasionally to see family.

"The memory I've got of Paul," reveals cousin Jackie, "is when he came to see me this time. Paul and Lee came to my house one day in the late nineties. Now, my son, Charlie, was mesmerized by Paul because Charlie was football mad. He didn't like Arsenal! Manchester United and Arsenal don't like each other much do they?! But he was captivated as he sat there and looked at Paul and looked at this person in real life who actually ran on to a proper football pitch. Charlie was only about eight at the time. And Paul sat with Charlie and spoke to him, 'So, Charlie, tell me about your football.'

218

He was so engaging and Charlie was just mesmerized. And they really had a nice chat."

"Obviously, I was quite young when I met Paul," says Charlie. "Although I did know about his troubled past, that never really bothered me. All I was interested in was listening to him talk about his days at Arsenal. He turned up one day in the summer with Aunt Nel and his brother Lee. It was strange, I didn't know what to expect, but I was really excited about meeting him. I was skateboarding outside when they turned up and I saw him get out the car and he hobbled towards me - because of his shot knee, he couldn't straighten it - and introduced himself. I think for the next three hours we all just sat in the lounge talking about his Arsenal days and other family stuff. But my greatest memory of Paul is that despite his knee, he still came and played football with me in the garden. I was in goal and he was shooting pens at me and I remember thinking, 'Hold on a minute, this geezer used to play for Arsenal!' and I was in goal wearing my Man United top."

Jackie continues, "I was watching from an upstairs window and I was quite upset because Paul's legs were so bad. He actually looked quite disabled. I couldn't see how the same man could have scored that goal against Juventus which had gone down in history because, looking at him now in my small garden, he couldn't even barely manage to kick a ball."

"After playing football outside," Charlie recalls, "we spoke and I said how much I wanted to be a pro footballer. And he said to me, 'Listen, if you want something, really want something, you'll get it.'"

****

During the late nineties, Paul was beset by depression. And there were brushes with the law when he was fined £160 and banned from driving for three years for drink-driving in February 1999 and then fined £200 for theft nine months later. Still Paul evaded prison.

Paul went back to Farnborough to try and pick things up again with Sally and Jack but things didn't wotk out. Finally, on

219

the eve of the new millennium, 31st December 1999, there was one last row.

"That was the last time I saw him," says Sally. "We had an absolutely massive, massive, massive row and the police were called again because it ended quite violently. I never did it but the neighbours used to end up calling the police because they were worried about me and the children.

"And then he disappeared. He did try to contact me after that, quite a few times, but I felt that it was a bit pointless. I had really tried with him. It was so sad. When we were first together it was fun, it was really, really fun. It was a really good time. I loved him to bits, completely loved him to bits. That's why I found it so hard to leave him. It was only because it almost became a choice between him and the children that it had to be like that."

Paul moved back to Bristol where he came across an old associate.

"It was 2000 when I bumped into Paul in Bristol," says Adam Rutherwood, "having known him at the height of his footballing career and in stark contrast, converging on that path of self-destruction, we had quite a bit to catch up on.

"I lived on the Pepys Estate in Deptford where Sarah, who would become Paul's wife, lived. It was a lively place with some unforgettable characters. With the customary amount of crime and drugs for an inner city estate, it seemed to draw people in from all over. It wasn't far from Lucey Way where Paul lived which back then was seen as a much less unruly area.

"It was more at our end in Deptford where everyone came to get what they needed. The group I knocked about with were all good kids from good families – about ten of us – although you could see early on that we were going off the rails. It was quite unbelievable what we'd get up to in the name of entertainment. It wasn't unusual to see ten or so kids at 3am under the influence of high grade LSD on a 'walkabout', one or two risking life and limb for added amusement. Other activities included firing air pistols at one other and regularly swimming in the River Thames. Back then, even the fish wouldn't use it. Surviving your early teens became an achievement in itself.

"We used to see Paul now and again when he would come to visit Sarah. We would have been about fifteen then. A few years later, just after Turin, a few of us joined him on holiday to Malta. We

220

began to see more of him after his injury occurred. By that time, around '82, I think Paul had already hit the self-destruct button.

"I'd graduated on to Class As by that time. Most of us had. It was as if the whole estate started experimenting with whatever was available. There were no references, no generation before us that drugs had wreaked havoc on, we had no idea what was in store.

"Paul began to spend more time on the estate but it would be sporadic. The next time I saw him, in the mid-80s, he was in a bad way. I was shocked I guess. Remembering the holiday to Malta in 1980, with Paul physically at his peak and now almost emaciated, that's what really got me. Soon after I heard he had been stabbed. How tragic I remember thinking, though par for the course with this way of life.

"The last time I saw Paul was again in Bristol, late 2000. He looked well and he seemed genuinely happy. I saw him a few times over the next couple of months and then he disappeared. I heard he'd relapsed, which for a recovering addict is like getting back into the ring with Mike Tyson. You know you're going to get battered.

"Whatever Paul did, it was usually to the extreme, although when he came up to Bristol, I thought that was what he needed, to get away from everyone and everything but clearly, it wasn't enough. You know addiction is the only activity that the longer you practise it, the worse you get at it."

15
Last Christmas

"I'm too sensitive. I need to be slightly numb in order to regain the enthusiasm I had as a child."

Kurt Cobain (suicide note)

"Me and my mum, Nelly, went up to Bristol for the weekend to visit Paul," recalls Maureen. "We got up in the morning and found Paul slumped in his chair, obviously under the influence. My mum asked what was wrong with him and I just said that he was tired. When Paul woke up, somehow we got into a row about who I was going to leave my money to and who would be executor of my will. I think I upset him. I said things to him that I shouldn't have said. I was so mixed up myself. I just wanted to shock him out of what he was doing, to get himself straight. You see, we often bounced off each other, didn't see eye to eye. We were too similar and Paul was set in his ways. He had been since an early age. He had a mature head on young shoulders. Sometimes you just couldn't get through to Paul and we clashed and he said, 'Get out of my house,' so we did.

"We made up when Paul came to stay for Christmas 2000. We asked him to spend Christmas with us and he came down for two weeks and stayed at his nan's house because we didn't really have room for him.

"He wasn't in a good way. He wasn't in the best of health. I didn't realize how bad he was. His leg was terrible, it was all ulcerated but he wouldn't tell me why. He couldn't get his trainers on properly. He couldn't hardly walk.

"He was out of it most of the time. My mum's sister, Rose, came to stay as well. They didn't know too much about the drugs so I had to keep my eye on things. There were good days and bad days to be honest."

Paul took the opportunity to catch up with Debbie and his son, Jamie, while he was in London.

223

"I'd seen him earlier in the year," says Debbie, "and that's when I noticed his leg. His leg was really dry and his toes were black. He'd say, 'Nice colour!' when I asked him about them. That's all he would say about it but I knew. I knew he had gangrene in his toes and we both knew what that meant. He said to me, 'My dad's going to try and get me a place down here. I can't go hopping around Bristol, can I? If I'm stuck in a wheelchair I'm going to need someone to push me about,' trying to make a joke of it. That time Paul came down, everything went well. We had a bit of a fling and we left on such good terms.

"At Christmas, though, it was different. I knew he was up to something, that he was taking something and he got all defensive, saying I was getting on at him and he left. We spoke on the phone after that and he was very apologetic but I never saw him again."

"When he went home," Maureen continues, "he collapsed getting onto the coach back to Bristol and was taken to St. Thomas Hospital. I think that's when he had his first stroke because he seemed to lose the use of his left arm after that.

"I got a call and went to see him in hospital. I went to see him and he was a nasty piece of work, oh dear Lord. He made me feel about three feet tall in front of everybody at the hospital. He really showed me up. We had a big row and I left. It was the last time I saw him alive.

"We did speak again later, on the phone. We were at loggerheads again. We always clashed over his drug problems but we did always manage to make up and talk on the phone. Paul admitted how terribly lonely he was, staring at all four walls, but we made peace with each other. Paul would ring but sometimes he'd be out of it. I'd say, 'I'll speak to you when your head's right.'

"The last letter he wrote to me was in January 2001 – two days before Jack's birthday. He wanted to make sure Jack got a present and card from his daddy."

29/01/2001

Mum,

Please write in Jack's card that his Daddy loves him and misses him very much and hopes to see him soon. Please mum, this means an awful lot to me.

Please put the card stuck to the present so he knows it's from me and say this is your present from your Daddy who misses you very much and hopes to see you soon. Please do this for me as you are the only person I can count on. Please don't let me down.

Please make things alright for me and Jack as there is not a day that I don't think about him.

Thanks mum.

Lots of love.

Paul x

Paul's idea for a gift was a football strip, his first choice being England or West Ham. Not Arsenal.

"Now you tell me what sort of person comes across?" says Maureen. "I cried. I cry every time I read it. Paul was fighting to get access to Jack, to be able to see him, only if it was just once a month. I've got all the solicitors letters still today. He never got to see Jack again, only through photos from me.

"Leon stayed up in Bristol with Paul for two weeks," says Maureen. "Lee was back in London and went to him and told him that Paul was in a really bad way. Lee was concerned Paul was so down he was going to kill himself so Leon went up to Paul."

"I went up to Bristol to see him a few months before he died," confirms Leon. "He was okay. He showed me his new shower. He was pleased with that and they'd also put in some new carpet."

Maureen adds, "Because of his leg – it was rigid so he had a bad limp – he had one of those walk-in showers, like a wet room."

"I stayed a few days with him," Leon continues, "but I think he wanted me to stay longer. He was lonely, on his own and I think that irked him. But he couldn't come back down to London because he had to stay away from certain people, certain places for his own good."

Things were only to get worse for Paul.

"The last few months of his life," says Lee, "his mind was going."

"In his kitchen, on the wall by the cooker," says Maureen, "he had a noticeboard, a pinboard with various things on it but all around it, on the frame, was writing. It was all about his life, different stages in his life, things that were important to him like his kids, his family, his brother. It went all the way round the board."

"He had also taken to writing down scriptures in notebooks," Lee adds. "He was writing down mad things, things that didn't make sense."

"Why he'd written on the pinboard like that I don't know," Maureen reflects, "but I do know that towards the end of his life Paul was not right in his mind. My Paul was in a bad way those last eight months from Christmas to when he died. He was schizophrenic by now. His mind was going.

"One incident I was told about, he was walking up and down the road all day long. His neighbours were concerned and came out to see him. They asked him, 'Are you alright, Paul?' and he said, 'I'm trying to find my brother. He's only seven.' If Lee was seven years old, that would make Paul thirteen so he'd reverted back to thirteen years of age. They said, 'Are you sure, Paul?' and he's replied, 'Yeah. My nan and granddad are inside waiting for us. They sent me out to look for my brother but I've lost him.' Well his granddad had been dead some twenty years or so. So they called an ambulance and they took him away to hospital. His mind was all over the place."

"He had no clothes on as well," Lee adds. "He was sectioned and taken to a psychiatric hospital where he stayed for seven weeks. He had completely regressed. He had no idea about football. He had no idea that he'd once played for Arsenal. And he had no idea about drugs.

"Of course, he came out of the hospital clean and it wasn't until he bumped into somebody in the street who asked him if he was still selling his methadone and tablets, that it hit him. He went to the doctors and they gave him a month's worth of prescriptions, for methadone, valium, amitriptyline and temazepam. He was also mixing those tablets with drink again. He was drinking heavily, three two litre bottles of *White Ace* cider a night. It was all to escape. That's what it, the drugs, the drink, was all about, to escape from the reality that he couldn't play football any more. He was killing himself slowly."

226

16
A Sort of Homecoming

"Success is a public affair. Failure is a private funeral."

Rosalind Russell, 'Life is a Banquet' (1977)

Paul was on his own. He didn't, couldn't work because he had enough trouble standing and walking. He didn't go out that much, except for the occasional trip to the shops to stock up on strong cider, to the doctors to see his GP or to the chemist to pick up his prescriptions. Like most depressives, Paul slept a lot, to escape from his problems, his knee, the memory of the injury. The drugs helped him stay there that bit longer.

"I have absolutely no pleasure in the stimulants in which I sometimes so madly indulge. It has not been in the pursuit of pleasure that I have periled life and reputation and reason. It has been the desperate attempt to escape from torturing memories, from a sense of insupportable loneliness and a dread of some strange impending doom."[50]

Paul wanted to get back to that sunny afternoon in August 1977 when he wore the red and white colours of Arsenal for the first time at Hitchin Town. He wanted to feel again the driving rain of Leipzig in September the following year when he made his first team entrance. He wanted to relive his league debut at Stamford Bridge alongside Malcolm Macdonald in May 1979 and longed to hear again the cheers that cascaded down from the North Bank when he shared four goals with Frank Stapleton against Brighton six months later. No doubt he returned to Easter Monday 1980 and to White Hart Lane to head in to the goal at the Paxton Road end over and over again.

And, of course, there was Turin. Always Turin.

Paul dreamed his dreams on the sofa so he could hear

227

anybody who did happen to call. One visitor was Jason Murphy who Paul had known for a couple of months.

Jason knew Paul was a bit of a drinker and had also recently witnessed Paul smoking heroin.

"I got the impression he liked the effect of taking the drugs because he didn't have anything else in his life."

He did, of course, have other things in his life but circumstances prevented him from enjoying them. Jamie and Jack were miles away from Bristol but Paul was trying to get himself together so he could try and be a dad again.

"Towards the end," says Lee, "I thought things were starting to get back on track a bit. Paul had slowed down with the drugs. He was taking methadone. He had managed to re-connect with Jamie and was desperate to see Jack. But I had to come back to London for a year to sort myself out, go into detox. I feel guilty about it now. I think I left Paul isolated."

"At about 8.30am on Wednesday 8th August I called at his flat," Jason told Avon and Somerset Constabulary. "I knocked on the door and Paul opened the curtains of the living room. He let me in, and I stayed and chatted to him for between fifteen and thirty minutes. He seemed okay, but we didn't talk about anything in particular. He asked me why I hadn't gone in to work, and seemed normal. When I left, he asked me to get him some cigarettes while I was out. I took them back to his flat at, I think, about 11am. I put the cigarettes and his change on the fireplace and said I was going to go and try and see my girlfriend in Manor Farm.

"I returned to the flat at some time between 2pm and 3pm. The first thing I noticed was water coming out from under the front door. I saw the water was coming from the bathroom, so I opened the bathroom door. I saw Paul curled up on the floor."[51]

"He must have gone in for a shower," says Maureen, "and whatever's happened there, he's gone down like a ton of bricks. When he's gone down he must have tried to lever himself up because of that leg and he's pulled the radiator off of the wall and that's what flooded the bathroom. And then he's just gone down again. His mate's come back, pushed that door open and took one look at him and he knew, he knew."

Jason tried to rouse Paul but was unable to. He couldn't find Paul's mobile phone so, as there was no response from next door, he ran to the house across the road and borrowed the phone to call for help. Jason, and the ambulance service which arrived some five minutes later, tried to revive Paul for almost three quarters of an hour.

It was no good.

Paul was certified dead on arrival at Southmead Hospital, Bristol at half past three in the afternoon.

"The police came and just knocked on my door," Maureen recollects. "He died on the Wednesday and they didn't get to me until the Friday so he'd been dead two days and I was still carrying on as normal."

"They had to trace him," Ernie suggests. "I suppose they were looking round Bristol for some relatives."

"My partner Viv took the call," recalls Leon. "It was Maureen. I was asleep and Viv had to come and tell me.

"After about half an hour of crying I actually felt a little bit relieved, you know, that it was all over. It had been worrying me for a few years, about his health. It wasn't totally unexpected."

Maureen continues, "When the police came and told me what had happened to Paul, I had to go and tell Lee. He was down in London staying with my mum so we went over there to find him.

"When we got there we saw him walking across the green. When he saw us he started running. He thought Ernie was after him about something. He ran and I had to shout out, 'Lee, it's your brother.' He stopped in his tracks, turned round and said, 'He's dead, isn't he, Mum?' He knew. He knew as soon as I said it. He went down on his knees. He was broken."

"I have to say part of me thought, 'Thank f--k for that,'" Lee admits. "Then the guilt took over and it eventually led me back into drugs myself."

"I had to let Paul's doctor know he'd passed away," Maureen says, "and he said, 'Oh my God.' You see the funding had just come through for Paul to go away and start a two year rehabilitation programme the following month, starting on 25th September. He was on methadone because he was off of the heroin at the time. He was being programmed to go into therapy. His doctor said, 'Don't tell me this. He's been working on this for eighteen months to go away and get himself straight and now you're telling me that he's died.'"

229

****

Paul's passing attracted little attention. There was no mention in any of the national newspapers. It was only after the adjourned inquiry concluded in October that Paul made the free local paper, the *Bristol Observer*, on Friday 2nd November 2001, sandwiched in amongst the adverts. The reporter was obviously unaware of Paul's previous life as a top flight footballer. To them, to most he was merely another addict.

Bristol Observer, 2nd November 2001:

Drugs finally beat addict

Addict Paul Vaessen was found dead in his Henbury home by a friend after overdosing, an inquest heard.

(He) had been battling with a drug habit and was on methadone therapy, a substitute for heroin, when he died on August 8.

Mr Vaessen was found in his bathroom at Dorester Close by Jason Murphy, who called an ambulance upon discovering his friend.

A post mortem revealed high levels of drugs in Mr Vaessen's blood.

Coroner Paul Forrest recorded a verdict of accidental death.

As Kevin Mitchell and Jamie Jackson put it in their 17th March 2002 *Observer* article, *The Terrible Death of a Forgotten Hero*, "Vaessen in death was almost as anonymous as he had been in those moments before he ran on to the pitch in Turin."[52]

On Tuesday 21st August 2001 Paul came home to South London for good. He was cremated at the Lewisham Crematorium.

It was round to Maureen and Ernie's place after. The birds, Nelson and Eddie, kept everyone entertained. But they'd had to be kept quiet when the vicar came round to discuss the service a few days before.

"I was a bit worried about my parrots," recalls Maureen, "that they'd misbehave a bit and use bad language. So I covered them up to fool them it was night time and they only started talking when we were nearly done. But they behaved themselves, didn't use any swear words or anything like that!"

Music at the service was provided by the *Cocteau Twins*. Paul chose it. Debbie was over at Maureen's place helping to organize things and was looking at the *Heaven or Las Vegas* album from 1990 which Paul loved. When Debbie got down to track eight, *Wolf in the Breast*, the lamp in the room flickered off and on again.

"That was it!" says Debbie. "It was a sign from Paul from up above. Or down below. No doubt he would have preferred the latter."

> *Laughing on my bed, I've pretended I knew the way*
> *Especially when, I'll revenge, all I'll need's that day*
> *It's my body, puzzles the trick in me*
> *I lend it out to borrow, it might survive*
> *My baby's cries*
> *Laughing on my bed*
> *I've pretended I knew the way*
> *Especially when*
> *I'll revenge, all I'll need's that day*
> *I'll feel perpetual*
> *I feel perpetual*

"Lee gave a 25 minute eulogy," Maureen recounts. "He was on drugs at the time too. People didn't know how he found the strength to get up and do it. The truth is he had to have some drugs to get him through the day.

"In his eulogy he said, 'Look, we all know why Paul died. Paul, I idolised you, put you up on a pedestal. We'll meet up again, Bruv.'"

The strains of *Eternity* by Robbie Williams - *"I know you'll find your freedom/Eventually/For eternity"* – accompanied the mourners on the way out.

Childhood friend Paul Rulton was there.

"The last time I saw him was years ago on a bus. He didn't recognise me, he was spaced out.

"At the funeral I felt angry. It wasn't a great turn out. I told people around South Bermondsey what had happened to Paul. Some said, 'Good riddance.'

"He is still my best friend, though. He will always be my

231

best friend."

"Mark Richardson, who was my best pal at the time, told me," recalls Steve Gorham. "I can't honestly say I was shocked but I was very sad."

"It was at Paul's funeral that I was first told," reveals Maureen. "I was talking to one of his old school mates, wondering how on earth he first got into drugs, you know, and what a waste of a life it was. He said, 'Maureen, I'm going to tell you something now but don't get upset about it but Paul was taking tablets around thirteen, fourteen years of age.' That was the first time I knew."

Nobody came from Arsenal. They were probably busy. Arsenal were playing at home that day. For the record, they lost 2-1 to Leeds United but would go on to claim the title nine months later. They did, however, having found out about Paul from Debbie's daughter Lisa, send a wreath in the shape of a football, signed rather strangely, 'from directors, players and staff at Highbury Football Club.' They also put a note of condolence in the matchday programme:

Arsenal Football Club were greatly saddened to hear of the recent death of Paul Vaessen...

A striker, Paul represented Arsenal in the late 1970s and early '80s, scoring nine goals in 27 first team starts, after joining Arsenal as an apprentice at the age of 15...

The highlight of Paul's brief career was undoubtedly scoring the goal against Juventus that took Arsenal through to the Final of the European Cup Winners' Cup in 1980 as an 18-year-old substitute. Our thoughts are with Paul's family and friends.

Despite this, some of Paul's former colleagues were unaware of what had happened until I approached them about this project. 'How is he?' I was asked several times.

When Paul's former teammates did find out, there was, of course, shock and sadness.

"I actually didn't go to the funeral," says fellow South Londoner, Kenny Sansom. "I said to my wife, 'I don't really want to go. I'll find it too upsetting.'"

Sammy Nelson's response was typical. "Paul was a good kid, a really nice guy. I was really, really shocked when I heard the news."

"I never really spoke to Paul after he left the Arsenal," Brian McDermott reflects. "We never used to go out and socialise so I lost touch with him really after Arsenal. When I heard about Paul, it was a shock. Obviously it was a shock."

At the inquest the coroner recorded a verdict of accidental death. "He actually died of toxic poisoning," states Maureen. "He was being prescribed amitriptyline, methadone and temazepam but he abused the prescriptions. He'd take a whole strip of tablets instead of just one. So, yes, he had high levels of drugs in his body but it wasn't heroin or anything like that. It was medicated stuff, methadone and prescription drugs.

"Anyway, it went down as accidental death but I'm not quite so sure. I asked his doctor if he could tell me what state of mind Paul was in towards the end because I'd heard one or two things. He said that Paul had been diagnosed as schizophrenic and as having manic depression and I'm just thinking that with all these things wrong with him, he'd had enough. He had Hepatitis C, he was a cripple and on top of everything else his doctor told me that they'd had to tell Paul that because the state of his leg was so bad he would lose it within a year. His leg really was in a state. When he was stabbed he had his spleen taken out and as a result he had really bad circulation. And I'm just wondering whether, knowing all that, being on his own with the depression setting in, he's thought to himself – it has crossed my mind, I don't mind admitting it – that he's had enough. He didn't have much going for him, do you know what I mean? I knew my Paul could only take so much."

Paul's former neighbour and confidant at Lucey Way, Sue, agrees. "I think Paul knew what he was doing. He knew exactly what he was doing."

"He knew exactly how much to take," Maureen goes on. "He was an old hand at it. When he was found he had taken not one but two whole strips of amitriptyline. You take two of those tablets and you're out like a light. Two empty packets of that. Two packets of temazepam as well.

"Sometimes I think, at the back of my mind, I think he took his own life. He had had enough. His body was scarred to hell. He

233

knew there was a strong possibility of losing that leg. He knew he was hurting a lot of people and he didn't want the next twenty, twenty-five years, whatever he had left of his life, he didn't want it to be like how it was now. His body was broken.

"He'd seen more in his life than what a lot of youngsters have and he knew where he was heading and how bad he was. He said it to Debbie and he said it to his brother, 'I don't want to reach forty and be like how I am now.'

"He was thirty nine when he died."

Debbie concurs.

"Paul had this obsession about dying. He was convinced he wouldn't make forty. He told me within weeks of meeting him that he wouldn't live to the age of forty and he stood by that all the years I knew him. It really used to scare me.

"I personally think he had some insight into his death and I think he'd seen it happening. He used to have lots of nightmares, lots of dreams.

"He had this fascination. There was something in him which made him very inquisitive. He always wanted to know more than humans know. And you don't know anything until your spirit actually does go across. Paul wanted to know what the spirit would know. Paul spoke to me about suicide, what it would be like. He was curious to know what, who you'd see. He was fascinated with the film, *Flatliners*."

"Halloween morning. Rotting pumpkins. Burning leaves. Black cats mating like rats in the alley. It was as if...it was as if we felt no fear, as if we were already dead and had nothing to lose by dying."[53]

Paul had said similar things to Sally.

"My mum came round to tell me that Paul had died and it was quite weird because I sort of knew before she said it. I was expecting him to die because of the state he was in and the fact that he was living on his own. When we were together I'd actually been on a course that they ran at the local DDU – Drug Dependency Unit – to know how to resuscitate people who overdose and I did that specifically because Paul was my partner.

"And he always said, he always, always said he was going to die before he was forty. He always said. He said that loads of times,

'I will die before I'm forty'. And this was right from the beginning of our time together."

Paul had hinted at it when he told the *News of the World* in 1994, "You don't see many 60-year-old drug users wandering the streets."[54]

"I felt grief and guilt," Sally goes on, "because I'd left him and he'd died. He was in so much pain, emotionally. He was in a lot of pain. I've got letters from him and they don't really make sense. He wasn't Paul any more."

Sue provides another insight.

"If you couldn't convince Paul at the beginning when he first got his injuries that this was not going to be the end of the road, if you couldn't convince him then, what chance did you have when his mind was completely fuddled with heroin and whatever? You never stood a chance. And as much as we'd go over it, Paul and I, over and over and over it again, he'd always go back to the same thing, 'If I ever became terminally ill or something was bestowed upon me, I'll go out with a bang.'"

"I never doubted it was anything other than suicide," says Rob Hughes. "He'd spoken to me in the past about it."

"Paul rang me up at two, three or four o'clock in the morning," Lee confides, "and he was very low, he was so down. He was going on about things, about how bad his leg was, that they were going to take it away. He was talking about suicide but I'd heard it all before. I said, 'Look. I'm fed up with this. If you're going to do it, just do it.'

"I suppose I gave him permission to do it, the permission he was looking for."

"Sometimes I think he took his own life, then," Maureen tells me, "then other times…I don't know. I can't make my mind up. You know, his mind wasn't straight at the end. He may have forgotten he had taken his methadone and medication already that morning and taken it all again. I just don't know. There were also signs that he was fighting. It looks like he pulled the radiator off the wall trying to pull himself up again. I don't know, I really don't."

"We'll never really know what happened," Lee concedes. "Maybe he did take too many tablets, realised what he'd done and was going to have a shower to shake himself out of it."

For Maureen there is no rest.

"There's all these questions and no answers. I suppose I won't get answers until I see him again.

"What I do know is that he died a very terrible death and that he was very lonely. I do know that. That played on my mind. I had to go to counselling for that because it played on my mind so much, that I hadn't seen him for eight months. We spoke on the phone but you couldn't always get much sense out of him when he was out of it on the phone. The guilt, the guilt, the guilt. The guilt came over me tremendously because I hadn't seen him for eight months. That played on my mind. Could I have helped him more? He died on his own, none of his family around him, you know what I mean? To me, you know, nobody should die like that, completely on their own."

****

"My Dad's ashes are scattered down at Albins," says Laraine Kempster. "I was down there one day, on the way out, looked down and lo and behold, I saw Paul's grave. It's no use saying that it doesn't affect you because it does. I've known so many people in this area. I still drive past places, people's houses now and think, 'I haven't seen such and such for a while. I wonder what they're up to, if they've moved?' It seems each time I go down to Albins there's another one in there. It's so sad. And most of them are so young that you can only assume that their addiction got the better of them somewhere along the line, and that it ended tragically. I get very sad when I think about it, when I think about Paul. As I say, he was always a gentleman with me. Personally, I haven't got a bad word to say about him."

****

"It was closure for me when Paul Vaessen died," says Sue. "It was closure. There had to be more for him than what was on offer. It didn't matter how much he went into therapy, how many rehabs he went in. It didn't matter. You couldn't give Paul back what

236

he craved. And what he craved was taken away from him so cruelly and that was the end of it. He always used to say to me, 'I can never, ever, no matter what I do in my life, I can never have that back again.' And no matter what you said to him, no matter how you put it, that's how he felt. And then he'd talk about the past. Again. And how it was. And although he made the best of a bad thing - he used to try - it was never enough. Nothing was ever enough. Because he had it in his hands and he lost it and it wasn't his fault that that happened. And he couldn't live with that."

STUCK IN A MOMENT

Epilogue
The Legacy

"Take the world to a better place
Given them all just a little hope
Just think what a legacy
You now...will leave."
'The Legacy' by Iron Maiden (2006)

My wife says it's a man thing, this relentless quest to leave a marker that says 'I was here'. I doubt many people in this world would have heard of me even if this book does get published. And there are still many, many people, as the *Bristol Observer* showed, who have never heard of Paul Vaessen. To those who knew him in later life he was just a hopeless, lonely drug addict and, as we know, it is often the case that, "The last action stains the retina and informs the legacy."[55]

I only hope that Paul didn't die thinking he hadn't left one. Because he did. Paul left more markers behind than many of us get to. His legacy was threefold: Jamie, Jack and Turin.

Indeed, with regards to the latter, every time chance throws Arsenal and Juventus together in competition, such as in the Champions League in the 2001-02 and 2005-06 seasons, Paul's name crops up again. On 5th April 2006 when the Gunners played Juve in the quarter-final, second leg at Stadio Delle Alpi, the television cameras panned across to the travelling Arsenal fans and we caught sight of a banner paying tribute to Niccolo Galli, a promising youngster who starred in Arsenal's F.A. Youth Cup triumph in 2000, the 17-year-old having been killed in a road traffic accident in his native Italy in February 2001. Taking up the majority of the banner created by Emirates worker and well-known Gunners

239

fan Michael Farmer, were the words, 'PAUL VAESSEN ARSENAL.'

Not that *i bianconeri* needed reminding, as Rob Hughes imparts.

"I knew some of the Juventus players," says Hughes, "and they were in awe of Paul.

"It must have been ten years after that goal I was sitting at a conference and Bettega was there too. When he saw me he jumped up and the first name he mentioned was Paul Vaessen. He remembered that goal. He asked me, because he didn't know, how would he know, he asked me, 'What happened to Paul Vaessen?'

"It's going a bit over the top to say this maybe but Bettega mentioned Paul in the same breath as John Charles, because of Charles being so fantastic in the air. Bettega was remembering Paul in that light."

"It was a fantastic moment for a young man," Paul's former boss Terry Neill says of Paul's exploits against Juventus. "There aren't many people in their entire lives who get a glorious moment like that, that no one can take away."

What was taken away with that tackle at White Hart Lane at the end of January 1981 was Paul's future and Paul couldn't handle it.

"I think it's a real lesson," explains former teammate and current manager of Leeds United, Brian McDermott, "the Paul Vaessens of this world, people who have got those injuries, they really need to be looked after closely by their clubs, both emotionally and physically.

"But your problem with football is that you're in this little bubble. When you're a young fella you're really only looking at yourself whereas now I'm an older man I notice things. I look around at players now and I look to see if they've got things going on or problems. I know Paul had horrendous injuries and that's a really lonely time because it's so difficult to get yourself back to doing what you love. You know, I can understand now how difficult it is when you can't do what you love. And when you do finally get back you can't do what your body could do before.

"I think the thing is with football, you know, there's two things. If you get injured, you can't play, you're not the same, it does affect you massively, it affects your form. And also, when we finished playing the rewards for us weren't like they are now and you

240

know you've got nowhere to go. I mean, I was lucky. I stayed in football but a lot of kids wander around at my age thinking, 'What am I going to do now?'"

There is a need to prepare these football-obsessed youngsters for the possibility of failure, to prepare all professionals for the reality of life after football. As journalist Rob Hughes wrote in 1985 in a rare piece highlighting the problems faced by Paul and others in his position, "Football...must begin to educate and prepare the teenagers in its care for life in the outside world."[56] It's a sentiment which still rings true today.

You would like to think, then, that Paul left another legacy, that some of the recent improvements we have seen in terms of the availability of support, counselling and therapy to young sportspeople via, for example, Tony Adams's Sporting Chance Clinic and the Professional Footballers' Association, have come about partly because of what happened to Paul.

****

I am a long way from home, perhaps not so much geographically but economically, yes. I am in London's Belgravia, the exclusive Sloane Street, SW1, waiting rather tentatively outside the splendid Baku Restaurant, specialists in Azerbaijani cuisine.

I'd spent the morning in McDonald's.

I have adopted a new dress code for this occasion, linen blazer, crisp new shirt and tie, trimmed beard and barnet. I still can't help thinking, however, that I am sticking out like a sore thumb.

It's not a surprising venue for this meeting. My host has been in the employ of Azerbaijani Premier League side Gabala FC for the past three years. He joined the club as manager in May 2010 with the objective of taking this emerging outfit to the Champions League within thirty-six months. He left the club for family reasons in November the following year but, based back in the UK, now carries out an advisory and ambassadorial role for the club.

I spot him coming down the road towards me and suddenly find myself very nervous, finding it difficult to pretend I'm cool, calm and unfazed when inside I am behaving like a hysterical love-struck schoolgirl.

Meet Tony Adams.

MBE.

Doctor of defence.

Arsenal legend.

Champion.

Iconic leader.

Inspirational survivor.

Yes, survivor.

Bullying, public ridicule, prison, bed-wetting, alcoholism. Tony Adams has seen them all off.

With the pleasantries and gushing over with, we settle down in the lounge bar and get down to business. And our business is saving the life of Paul Vaessen.

Firstly, I want to know a bit more about Tony's recovery. I want to find out why he survived and Paul didn't. I want to find out whether, having saved himself, Tony Adams could have saved Paul Vaessen.

Tony starts off with a chilling disclosure which will sound only too familiar to those who were closest to Paul.

"I didn't think I was going to make thirty. I couldn't believe it. I sobered up at twenty nine. I just didn't think I'd make thirty the way I was living. I had no plans whatsoever for living after thirty.

"But, you know, you don't have to go to your grave. There is a way out.

"August 16th 1996 I threw the towel in. I wasn't happy with the life that I had. I had no wife, no kids, no house, nothing. I had nothing. I had got to the point where I didn't want to drink any more but I was still getting drunk and it scared the living daylights out of me. I had lost all control, all power over it. I just decided that I didn't want that life anymore and threw myself into AA. I went to ninety meetings in ninety days. I still go to AA meetings now because it's there waiting for you, doing press-ups outside your door.

"There was no help from Arsenal, not in those days. That's why I set the Sporting Chance charity up. I don't blame Arsenal. They didn't know about the illness of addiction. George Graham, he used to have a drink or two in his youth but he didn't know about the illness of addiction. They can have sympathy with you but they can't

242

really understand. They don't really know what you're going through. Arsene Wenger knew a little bit. He was brought up in a pub and he knew a bit about the illness. But there was nowhere to go. Luckily I fell into AA. Paul Merson got sober before me. He took me to one of my first meetings."

Having gone public, Tony started receiving calls for help from other players.

"Now, I'm not a therapist," Tony confesses. "Other people got me sober. I quickly realised that one-to-one I wasn't particularly good at it. So I got the guy who got me sober on board."

Originally the idea was to set up a foundation with a pool of money to put people through *The Priory* but there was something missing. Patients - athletes - needed to be able to train at the same time as undertaking therapy. Training would not only keep them from their addictions but would also ensure they were fit physically, as well as mentally, to return to their professions when treatment was over.

Sporting Chance was therefore born in September 2000.

Paul had just under a year to live.

If only Paul had known, had reached out for help.

"Because he would have had to have wanted it," says Tony. "You know, this illness runs so deep. The denial is huge. I'm amongst the minority who find recovery and deal with it on a daily basis. It's very cunning and some people take it to the grave like Paul did, like George Best did.

"The other thing Paul would have had to do if he had come to us was to go on an inner journey to try and find out what made him tick. When you come into recovery and you put down alcohol, gambling, drugs, what you're left with is you. I had to make that inner journey to find out why I escaped into alcohol, why I drank if I won, why I drank if I lost? What was my make-up, what was the thing that made me that little bit different, a little bit insecure? What it was, you know, was that as a kid my ears were too big, my nose was too big. People used to take the piss out of me and that kind of crippled me and I didn't know how to deal with it. What I did was play football. And later on I stayed sober playing football. If I focussed in on football, I didn't have to drink. But the minute the football stopped, I was left to my own devices and I'd start drinking. And I think increasingly part of this drinking myself into oblivion most of the time was trying to end it but not really wanting to. I didn't know how to live so to ease the pain away, I got out of my head. Paul was probably in that place. But the trick of it is to find out what makes you tick. Paul would have needed to have been willing to go on that journey.

"I know there were certain points in his life when Paul did throw up his hands in acknowledgement, certain periods, like when he found God, when he was clean. I would have liked to have had a crack at Paul. If we could have got him at that point then we would have laid out a lot of tools for him to pick up. And that's all you can do. All you can do is lay it all out in front of the guy. I think if he had come and lived with me for six months, I could have helped him. And then, if he had stayed sober and clean, I think we would have definitely been able to use Paul at my charity. He would have been an ideal candidate. We would have trained him up to be a therapist or a counsellor. He could have been involved with the lectures we give to the Premier League, Football League and Rugby Football League, sharing his experiences."

Just as Paul had planned for a while back in the mid-nineties.

"That's if he stayed clean and sober," Tony adds. "Unfortunately, some people do have to pursue it to the gates of Heaven."

I like to think that Tony Adams could have helped Paul. Indeed, I'd recommend an hour with Tony to anybody who is looking to change the course of their life. My hour was as good as any I ever spent at *The Priory* or the *Bethlem* and I came out of it refreshed and ready to take up the fight once more.

"If you're going through pain, you know, keep going," Tony said reassuringly as we parted, handing me a business card for his charity. "Just keep going."

****

Steve Gorham now lives in Sidcup, Kent but he still spends more time than not in Bermondsey where his business – he is a partner in an office supplies company – is based. He is also a season ticket holder at the New Den where he bumps, from time to time, into members of the old school gang, such as Paul Rulton. He also sees Paul sometimes on the sidelines watching the successful St. Joseph's Old Boys Football Club Veterans for whom John Morgan still plays. Steve, John and Gerry Avery meet up for a beer pretty regularly.

"I often think of the 'old days' as they were happy times, and at the time we were a close bunch. I tend to think of Paul when Arsenal play in big games and I remember Juventus and his interviews after always makes me smile.

"My abiding memory of Paul is the absolute belief that he was going to make it, totally unshakeable. He was the best footballer I ever played with, he had the lot.

"In my view Paul was always going to be a pro and when the dream was taken away somebody should have known he would need help to adjust. Perhaps even people like me should have offered help.

"I did see Paul a few times after he left school as he sometimes came out for a beer. I watched him play for Fisher a couple of times and had a chat, and even after things weren't going so well, I saw him a couple of times in Bermondsey but I think he has been largely forgotten.

"My main feeling when remembering Paul is one of sadness and of what could have been for him. I will be honest and say I enjoy saying I used to play with him, that he was my pal etc. I guess it is some form of reflected glory. A great legacy would be if his story helped any other youngsters who suffer the same kind of heartache."

****

During the 1980s, Adam Rutherwood had joined Paul on the unforgiving journey into addiction.

"I was one of just a few to escape the chaos and turn it around," says Adam. "It was early '92 when I left London to get into rehab in the West Country. It was a painful process, facing up to who you'd become and what you had done, like picking glass from a wound. You have to do it to start the recovery process. Things began to improve fairly quickly for me and I decided to stay in that part of the country. I would visit London on the weekend to see my family, who were the main driving force for my recovery.

"I spent the next couple of years gaining the qualifications I should have achieved whilst at school, although Scott Lidgett in Bermondsey wasn't somewhere most kids excelled. I worked several jobs in those early years and continued my education.

"It was shortly after Paul died that I knew I wanted to play a part in easing the devastation addiction had caused to so many people I had grown up with. I wanted to put my experiences to good use. It was put on hold whilst I studied business management. I wasn't sure what I would do, although it now began to feel like a calling.

"I was aware of the lack of safe accommodation for people leaving rehab. I already owned one property by now, a huge six bed Victorian house that was being let to students. I decided to put it to better use. The first wave of guys flourished, I soon had a waiting list and my vocation was clear."

Since its inception in 2004, Adam has added extensively to his property portfolio and the project has gone from strength to strength. After a UK-wide competitive tendering process in 2008, the project was awarded two government contracts.

"We have housed and supported over 500 recovering addicts since that time.

"It's called *The Junction*," Adam continues, "you know, at the end of the road there's a junction. Do you want to go the right way or the wrong way? You're at a junction, a crossroads. Your decision will ultimately determine your destiny, choose wisely."

The Project provides accommodation and support for men and women at all stages of addiction, including detox. The spaces are already funded so it's a bit like crisis intervention. If you really want help, you only need pick up the phone.

"You know, human beings will make a change for one of only two reasons; inspiration or desperation. Most will wait until their situation becomes desperate. Pain is a great motivator. We offer inspiration as well. You don't have to wait to hit rock bottom, you can jump off of that 'misery-go round' at any point.

"Addicts sometimes substitute one drug for another which is a bit like changing cabins on the Titanic. Cleaning up is never about capability, it's about motivation, desire and belief. If what you've tried hasn't worked, try again, try something else. Don't give up. Failure is simply the opportunity to begin again, this time more intelligently.

"I think that absolutely Paul was part of my motivation for the work I've done, he really was. It was for him and those like him who failed to escape their addiction. And, of course, for their families. They too suffer the desperation and devastation of addiction and their pain, unlike the addict, isn't medicated.

"I wanted to give something back. I'm helping people like Paul. Me and Paul, we kind of shared a path for a while and I suppose it's like that junction again, only we each took a different turning…"

****

"I went to a fortune teller a while ago," says cousin Jackie, "and I knew Paul was going to come through, I just knew he was. I was having trouble with my son at the time. He'd just started University and he didn't like it, he needed to go out to work to pay his rent and he couldn't get to grips with it all, you know? I was really worried about him. Anyway, this lady said, 'Who's Paul?' She said, 'He's got a bad leg' and I said, 'Oh, I know exactly who that is.' So she said, 'He just wants to reassure you that everything will be alright with Charlie and that you're not to worry about him.' And apparently he said, 'Don't worry, he won't turn out like me.'"

****

I caught Lee at the library. He was printing out an article from *Wikipedia* about Paul to show to one of his mates who didn't believe that his brother had once played for Arsenal. Here was the evidence. It wasn't the first time Lee's claims had been met with incredulity. On one occasion I was required to speak to another disbeliever in order to corroborate Lee's story.

Lee is Paul Vaessen's brother. It's a description he's not

always welcomed.

"Yes, I've lived a lot of my life in Paul's shadow," Lee reflects. "For most of my life I was known as Leon Vaessen's son and Paul Vaessen's brother. I didn't have my own identity.

"When I was a kid playing football, the crowd used to shout things like, 'Oh, you're not as good as your brother.' The way I used to deal with it was I used to beat a player and then, knowing that their dad was on the touchline watching, I'd go back ten yards and beat them again.

"That's not to say I'm not proud of Paul. Of course I'm proud of him. He achieved in life, in his professional career, what I'd wanted to achieve. And he had such passion for the game. He was the one running up and down the stands for that extra hour after training. He was the one in the gym for that extra hour. He played for one of the best sides in world football. Who wouldn't be proud of that?"

Lee's been clean now these past eighteen months. He's on a low dose of methadone and takes other medications to address his depression and aches and pains. He's just had both cartilages taken out of his right knee, the result of wear and tear from playing football as a youth, years of doing heavy laboring work and, of course, that hereditary weakness.

He lives alone these days, still in Bristol in a studio flat owned by a housing trust which provides lodgings for people who, in one way or another, need looking after. He's been there two years now. He survives on £100 per week, £20 of which goes to the Metropolitan Police for the damage he caused to a police car in an incident a year or so ago. When things get tough he knocks on John's door to ask for a teabag, some sugar, a few slices of bread.

John is Lee's only true friend in Bristol. Lee is lonely but he's always been a loner by nature. And it's his choice he's on his own. Four years ago he buried his partner, Kathy, who he nursed through cancer. He was working then but had to pack up when his back got too bad. It's ten or even eleven years since he's seen Olivia. She is seventeen now.

Lee doesn't watch football at all these days. He doesn't think Paul would like it much either.

"He'd hate it today, all the dancing and diving, the rolling over, the protection players, especially goalkeepers, get. Even the

248

ball is half the weight it used to be in my day. It's ridiculous. When me and Paul played you were told to go out and get stuck in, be fair, if it's a fifty-fifty ball, go for it. If you were knocked up in the air, you just got up, dusted yourself down and got on with it. And when you scored it was just a 'well done, mate' and a pat on the back. No one dived. It was an unwritten rule. I remember sitting in Covent Garden one day with Paul, Alan Sunderland, Brian Talbot and a few others and they were saying how they'd really laid into one of their team mates for throwing a dive during a game. That's how it was. It was a different game back then. Today it's too commercial. It's all about the money. Paul didn't care about the money. He cared about the game and he just loved playing.

"To be honest, he wasn't a good brother to me. He just saw me as a source of money. He took the piss out of me. I lost everything over him.

"The last time I saw him, we had a blazing row and he drove off in his transit van. I can still see his face looking at me through the window.

"But I miss him, of course I miss him. I woke up yesterday morning and put my glasses on and I thought, what with my grey hair as well, how Paul would take the piss if he could see me now. And, yes, I welled up. Every now and then I sit on my bed and shed a few tears. You know, for quite a few years we were inseparable. We did everything together. We were like the Ronnie and Reggie of South Bermondsey. We were alright together.

"But I've not really dealt with his death properly. I don't want to acknowledge it really. I did respect him and I did love him."

****

"You know, he made some mistakes," Leon reflects, "but he was my first born. I can go back to those mistakes and overlook them, push them to one side. I never knew the full truth about it all anyway.

"It's lovely when it's all going for you, like with the football. One minute you're scoring an historic goal against Juventus, the next you're getting abuse hurled at you. But that's how it goes. It didn't

249

just happen to Paul.

"Of course I think of him often. To be honest, though, I try to keep it towards the back of my mind but every now and then it comes out, sometimes when I'm alone, and you get to thinking. The way I look at it is you can't change history. You've just got to get on with what's in front of you."

****

Maureen and I clicked from the off. We have since become quite close friends. Maureen's been through her fair share of counselling. In April 2008 she undertook some more, accompanying me to Kenny Sansom's book launch at the glistening Emirates Stadium. It was an emotional evening for her, it being the first time she had returned to Arsenal (albeit not Highbury) since Paul left the club twenty five years before. It was awkward but she was glad she had accepted the invitation. She went for Paul and felt that in doing so - and in collaborating on this book - she'd brought him back to life for a while.

When I put to Maureen the idea of attending Kenny's event, like when I pitched the idea of the book to her right at the beginning, I was apprehensive. I thought that talking about Paul may be upsetting to her. I needn't have worried.

"People never used to talk about Paul and all I wanted to do was talk about him, to keep his memory alive."

Maureen remembers the good things, the silly things like the time Paul came home with that perm.

"I said, 'Oh my God! What's happened to your lovely hair!?' He said, 'Don't worry about it, mum. We've all got perms at the Arsenal!'"

She also remembers the bad and the ugly and the price the family had to pay.

"I wouldn't wish drugs on anybody because it's a killer for families, it destroys families, it destroys. I had a happy, loving family and it absolutely destroyed us."

Maureen had to learn what William S. Burroughs called the 'junk equation'.

EPILOGUE – THE LEGACY

"Junk is not, like alcohol or weed, a means to increased enjoyment of life. Junk is not a kick. It is a way of life."[5]

Junk – heroin – became a way of life not only for Paul but for Maureen, Leon and Lee, until it ended with Paul's death on 8th August 2001. But he died more than one death along the way. And in so doing, he caused a lot of people a lot of heartache and pain.

Some of that heartache and some of that pain will never go away.

"I sometimes wonder where I got the strength from. I didn't think I was a very strong person but it's come from somewhere, the strength has come from somewhere because I've had a lot to deal with but I have managed to get on with life, you know? I mean, I'll never forget him.

"I've been in conversations where people have been talking about drug addicts and I try and let it go over my head. But from time to time, you know, you can't help but say something. Somebody will say something like, 'Yeah, they're the scum of the earth aren't they?' I know I shouldn't but I say, 'Pardon? They're not *all* scum of the earth.' Then they realise what they've said, who I am and they say, 'Sorry. We know your boys aren't.' But I say, 'No. You meant what you said. You look at them like they're the scum of the earth. I don't. I look at this as an illness.' I do. Paul got in with the wrong crowd and ended up with an illness. That's how I see it.

"What I do know is that Paul never cared for nothing more than his football. He often went back to his past, how it used to be. I think he'd have liked to have gone back there again."

Maureen was pleased to see Kenny, who'd been the source of such fun at Paul's twenty first birthday bash. It brought back fond memories. Also there was Terry Venables. Maureen was, I think, flattered that Terry remembered her Paul. He, like so many I've met on this journey, was genuinely shocked to hear that Paul was no longer with us.

We part at Arsenal tube station.

"I don't think I'll ever really come to terms with it," Maureen admits. "I'm only just beginning to accept that he's gone. There are so many things I wish I'd said to him. They just go round and round in my head. I wonder whether I did everything I could for him, whether there was anything more I could have done. I ask

251

myself was I a good mother? Was I a nasty mother? Did I do this right? Could I have done that better?

"One thing that does play on my mind is the fact that we were hardly talking those last few months. There was just that one conversation on the phone and that one letter from Paul about Jack. We were at loggerheads. I just couldn't get my head round why he chose the path he did, the drugs and everything.

"He wasn't a bad boy. He took a knock in life – his early retirement - and he couldn't get over it. I wish we'd talked about it more at the time but he wouldn't open up to me. When I think about it, I started losing him around thirteen, fourteen. That's when he really got a mind of his own and started doing what he wanted."

There are so many ifs.

"I go and see him and talk to him. I talk to him every night. When he came home that last Christmas he turned up with this silly hat on. He said, 'D'you like my hat, Mum?' I said, 'It looks silly but I suppose if it keeps your head warm…' I keep that hat on my bed-post. I hold it every night. I can still smell his hair. I tell him I love him, that I miss him. I say, 'You silly bastard, Paul. You silly bastard.'"

****

And if the night runs over
And if the day won't last
And if your way should falter
Along this stony pass
It's just a moment
This time will pass[58]

252

Appendix 1
Don't You
(Forget About Me)

"To live in hearts we leave behind is not to die."

Thomas Campbell

Ken Friar (Arsenal Director):

"Arsenal Football Club were deeply saddened when they learned of the death of Paul Vaessen.

"For many football fans, Paul's name will always be synonymous with his winning goal in the European Cup-Winners' Cup Semi-Final against the mighty Juventus, earning the Gunners a place in the Final. But his time at Arsenal was about more than one stellar teenage moment. He was 'one of ours', by that I mean a player who had joined us when just a boy – 15 years-old when he started as an apprentice – and he became educated in the ways of Arsenal, both on the pitch and within the Club as a whole, where he became aware of the traditions and ethos of 'the Arsenal way'.

"Paul was very popular within the Club and he was an instant hit with fans even before his heroics in Turin, as the 18 year-old had already scored in a 2-1 win at White Hart Lane that season and it was desperately sad that so much early promise was never fulfilled as injuries destroyed his fledgling career. It was a very sad day for everyone when it became apparent Paul couldn't play on and it must have been devastating for the young striker.

"Paul's life ended tragically at an age when he should have been in the prime of his life and everyone at Arsenal Football Club would like to offer their sincere condolences to his family for whom his death must still be desperately difficult to contemplate."

253

Sammy Nelson (former Arsenal player):

"The Juventus match was really a fantastic game and for Paul, for him to be at the back post to head it in, it was absolutely fantastic. To score the goal he did was an event. But to score against Juventus in Turin and beat them on their own pitch was unheard of. Paul was a folk hero. Me and all at Arsenal are really thankful for what he did on that night in Turin because he made history. He made history and you know he was a lovely guy."

Kevin Foord (Arsenal fan):

"Brady to Rix and then a deep cross for Vaessen to nod home. Fantastic. Only yesterday I was telling my 16-year-old about the goal. I was fourteen and a fanatical Gooner. I can remember being gutted after the 1-1 first leg result and taking loads of flak from my plastic Manc schoolmates (in Tunbridge Wells!). I was convinced that we were going to win the Cup-Winners' Cup that year but we were foiled by the Valencia keeper, Carlos Pereira, who was on the six yard line when he saved Rix's penalty.

"Thinking of Paul's name brings all the memories flooding back: Brady leaving; losing to West Ham in the F.A. Cup Final that year; O'Leary and Young with Mario Kempes and Rainer Bonhof in their pockets in the Cup-Winners' Cup Final and how proud I still am of my team after all these years!

"PV was part of that rich tapestry and I hope that he is at peace…wherever he is!"

Fred Street (former Arsenal pysiotherapist):

"I was the Arsenal physiotherapist/trainer when we played Juventus in the European Cup-Winner's Semi-Final in Italy. For Paul Vaessen it was amazing. His finest hour."

Emilio Zorlakki (Arsenal fan):

"It was a terrible shame about Paul's injury problems. I remember Paul as a player with good technique for a striker and he scored some spectacular goals with both head and shots from outside the area. Unfortunately, he was a bit slow but in his defence it was difficult to tell if his knee problems and not playing regularly hampered any chance he might have had.

"What a terrible tragedy how Paul's life deteriorated and ended so early.

"For many Arsenal fans of that generation he will not be forgotten and Paul Vaessen's goal in Turin was one of the most famous goals ever scored by Arsenal. For that alone he will never be forgotten."

Kenny Sansom (former Arsenal player):

"He was just a really nice kid, a lovely kid. He was a good personality, he was bubbly, he was lively just like I was when I was a young kid at Palace. I just liked him. He came from the same manor as I did, so you're almost like friends before you meet.

"Obviously something went wrong and he paid the highest price. He chose the life he wanted, what he felt he had to do. You know, if I hadn't been a footballer I might have been a gangster.

"I'd never judge him, never. But I think what you've got to do is you've got to try and understand why he went there. Paul, Juventus 0 Arsenal 1. There's only one Paul Vaessen."

Sally (former partner):

"He was a lovely, lovely man and I know that the bad things he did were the illness, not him."

Barnaby Phillips (Arsenal fan):

"I don't know what demons haunted him but I do wonder whether he received all the help he needed from Arsenal and from us, the supporters. I'd like to think that he would have been better treated today."

Charlie Rogers (cousin):

"All I can tell you about Paul from my single meeting with

him is that he was just such a nice genuine guy and it's such a shame that things panned out the way they did for him."

Liam Brady (former Arsenal player):

"I left Arsenal to join Juventus in 1980 and I did not really have the chance to get to know Paul well. At that time Paul was a fine young man with a very exciting future ahead of him. Unfortunately injury took away that future and the disappointment led him into a life that too many young people are subjected to. His passing was a sad loss to everyone who knew him but must have been devastating to his family and loved ones. He will always be remembered by me."

Brian Talbot (former Arsenal player):

"I knew Paul as a young player coming through the system at Arsenal. I joined Arsenal when he was a young lad, he was coming through the system and he'd broken into the first team. Unfortunately, he never really got to be an established first team player because life didn't deal him good fortune, really.

"People remember him because of the goal he scored against Juventus which took us into the final and, don't get me wrong, he scored other goals and he had, if you like, some happy years at Arsenal.

"Obviously his life was tragic at the finish but I think as an Arsenal player people remember him in the way Geoff Hurst is remembered for his hat-trick in the World Cup final. People thought he'd got a good future in the game but unfortunately fate didn't play its part."

John Devine (former Arsenal player):

"My memories of Paul are of a very bubbly and fun person but a very good footballer who, if not for injuries, had a very exciting future in the game. What a sad loss. I remember fun times in the dressing rooms of Highbury as young lads and was shocked to hear of his passing. I wish his family my deepest sympathy and prayers for their loss. He was a great lad and I always remember his cheeky

256

smile and will miss him as we spent our youth together at Arsenal."

Vic Wright (fan):

"Paul Vaessen? He scored a cracker at Tottenham. In my eyes he's a god!"

Tom O'Brien (Arsenal fan):

"The brightest lights burn the briefest and it should never be forgotten how one man being in the right place at the very right time should create a still magical piece of Arsenal history.

"Rest in peace, Paul. You have your place in history."

STUCK IN A MOMENT

Appendix 2
Numbers

"And we all wonder, what they mean,
The highs, the lows, the in betweens,
Most of them mean absolutely nothing,
But some of them mean everything."

'Numbers' by Jason Michael Carroll (2011)

Format: Games started + appearances as substitute (goals scored)

	Youth					Reserves	
	South East Counties League	South East Counties League Cup	F.A. Youth Cup	Southern Junior Floodlit Cup	President's Cup	Football Comb-ination	Youth & Reserve Team Friendlies
1977-78	13(3)	1	0+1	0+2(1)	–	3+5(1)	4
1978-79	6(2)	–	1	1(1)	–	30(7)	6+1
1979-80	1	3(1)	2(1)	2(1)	–	26(12)	4(3)
1980-81	–	–	–	–	1(1)	13(6)	8(4)
1981-82	–	–	–	–	–	17(2)	5(3)
1982-83	–	–	–	–	–	0+1	2+1
TOTALS	**20(5)**	**4(1)**	**3+1(1)**	**3+2(3)**	**1(1)**	**89+6(28)**	**29+2(10)**

	First Team					
	Football League Division One	F.A. Cup	Football League Cup	U.E.F.A Cup	European Cup-Winners' Cup	First Team Friendlies
1977-78	–	–	–	–	–	–
1978-79	1	–	–	0+2	–	0+1
1979-80	8+6(2)	–	1(2)	–	1+2(1)	1+2(1)
1980-81	5+2(2)	–	–	–	–	0+1
1981-82	9+1(2)	–	0+1	2	–	0+1
1982-83	–	–	–	–	–	–
TOTALS	**23+9(6)**	**–**	**1+1(2)**	**2+2**	**1+2(1)**	**1+5(1)**

Notes

1 *Tie Stirs Memory of Very Different Heroes* by Ian Hawkey, *Sunday Times*, Sports Supplement, 26th March 2006, pg. 9.

2 Kenny Sansom in *To Cap It All: My Story* by Kenny Sansom with Rita Wright (2008), pg. 266.

3 *Junk* by Melvin Burgess (1996).

4 *Daily Express*, 9th April 1980, pg. 39.

5 *Gunners' Glory* by Graham Weaver (1998), pg. 102.

6 *Arsenal Hero's Drugs Hell* by David Barnes, *News of the World*, 5th June 1994, pg. 52.

7 *Arsenal Hero's Drugs Hell* by David Barnes, *News of the World*, 5th June 1994, pg. 52.

8 *Arsenal Hero's Drugs Hell* by David Barnes, *News of the World*, 5th June 1994, pg. 52.

9 *Hampstead & Highgate Express*, 25th April 1980, pg. 71.

10 *Arsenal Hero's Drugs Hell* by David Barnes, *News of the World*, 5th June 1994, pg. 52.

11 *Daily Telegraph*, 24th April 1980, back page.

12 *London Evening Standard*, 29th April 1980, pg. 1.

13 *Sunday Times*, 4th May 1980, pg. 31.

14 *Sunday Times*, 4th May 1980, pg. 31.

15 *Sunday Times*, 4th May 1980, pg. 31.

16 *Sunday Mirror*, 11th May 1980, pg. 47.

17 *Arsenal Football Club Official Annual 1981*, pg. 23.

18   *Islington Gazette*, 13th June 1980, pg. 52.

19   *Islington Gazette*, 13th June 1980, pg. 50.

20   *Arsenal Football Club Official Handbook 1980-81*, pg. 8.

21   *Revelations of a Football Manager* by Terry Neill with Brian Scovell and Harry Harris (1985), pgs. 100-101.

22   *To Cap It All: My Story* by Kenny Sansom with Rita Wright (2008), pgs. 80-81.

23   *Highbury: The Story of Arsenal in N5* by Jon Spurling (2006), pg. 176.

24   *Islington Gazette*, 4th September 1981, pg. 35.

25   *Daily Mirror*, 16th September 1981, pg. 31.

26   *Islington Gazette*, 25th September 1981, pg. 44.

27   *Highbury: The Story of Arsenal in N5* by Jon Spurling (2006), pg. 179.

28   *London Evening Standard*, 4th November 1981, pg. 44.

29   *Highbury: The Story of Arsenal in N5* by Jon Spurling (2006), pgs. 178-179.

30   *Highbury: The Story of Arsenal in N5* by Jon Spurling (2006), pg. 179.

31   *Highbury: The Story of Arsenal in N5* by Jon Spurling (2006), pg. 178.

32   *Highbury: The Story of Arsenal in N5* by Jon Spurling (2006), pg. 179.

33   *Hampstead & Highgate Express*, 5th February 1982, pg. 71.

34   *Hampstead & Highgate Express*, 12th February 1982, pg. 71.

35   *Hampstead & Highgate Express*, 5th March 1982, pg. 71.

NOTES

36   *Rebels for the Cause: The Alternative History of Arsenal Football Club* by Jon Spurling (2003), pg. 117.37

37   *David O'Leary: My Story* by David O'Leary with Harry Miller (1988), pg. 171.

38   *David O'Leary: My Story* by David O'Leary with Harry Miller (1988) pg. 172.

39   *Arsenal Hero's Drugs Hell* by David Barnes, *News of the World*, 5th June 1994, pg. 52.

40   *Arsenal Hero's Drugs Hell* by David Barnes, *News of the World*, 5th June 1994, pg. 53.

41   *Arsenal Hero's Drugs Hell* by David Barnes, *News of the World*, 5th June 1994, pg. 53.

42   *Arsenal Hero's Drugs Hell* by David Barnes, *News of the World*, 5th June 1994, pg. 52.

43   *Arsenal Hero's Drugs Hell* by David Barnes, *News of the World*, 5th June 1994, pg. 52.

44   *Arsenal Hero's Drugs Hell* by David Barnes, *News of the World*, 5th June 1994, pg. 53.

45   *Arsenal Hero's Drugs Hell* by David Barnes, *News of the World*, 5th June 1994, pg. 53.

46   *Arsenal Hero's Drugs Hell* by David Barnes, *News of the World*, 5th June 1994, pg. 52.

47   *Arsenal Hero's Drugs Hell* by David Barnes, *News of the World*, 5th June 1994, pg. 53.

48   *The Broken Body: Journey to Wholeness* by Jean Vanier (1988).

49   *The Terrible Death of A Forgotten Hero* by Kevin Mitchell and Jamie Jackson, *Observer*, Sports Section, 17th March 2002, pg. 9.

263

50   Edgar Allan Poe.

51   Jason Murphy's statement to Avon and Somerset Constabulary, 9th
      August 2001.

52   *The Terrible Death of a Forgotten Hero* by Kevin Mitchell and
      Jamie Jackson, Observer, Sports Section, 17th March 2002, pg. 8.

53   Oliver Platt as Randy Steckle in *Flatliners* (1990).

54   *Arsenal Hero's Drugs Hell* by David Barnes, *News of the World*, 5th
      June 1994, pg. 53.

55   Russell Brand, *Guardian*, Sports Section, 24th May 2008, pg. 16.

56   *The Giddy Fall From Highbury To Heroin* by Rob Hughes, *Sunday
      Times*, 29th December 1985.

57   *Junky* by William S. Burroughs (1953), pg. xxviii.

58   *Stuck In A Moment You Can't Get Out Of* by U2 (2000).

Sporting Chance

Sporting Chance delivers therapeutic services to professional and amateur sports people. The charity was initially established by Tony Adams to provide services for individuals suffering with issues relating to addictive disorders. He held three beliefs as core to its principles, firstly that the problem did and does exist within sport, secondly that there is a solution to the problem that can be tailored to meet the specific needs of sports people and finally that any person that is or has been involved in sport should have access to this confidential and professional service. These values have guided the charity to our current structure. However, it would also be true to say that our evolution has also been informed by over a decade of experience, one of the obvious changes being the need to develop services and relationships that serve a wider range of emotionally related issues.

The charity offers:

Residential Clinic: Sporting Chance runs the only sport-specific residential clinic for addictive disorders, we believe, in the world. The clinic delivers a twenty six day therapeutic intervention using a model of treatment recognised to address not only the exhibiting behaviours but underlying core issues. The charity employs a highly qualified team of therapists to deliver this element of the treatment programme. Alongside the therapeutic regime the facility offers an environment to enhance, maintain or promote physical wellbeing to the levels required in top level sport. This includes gym facilities, physiotherapists and nutritionists. We are also happy to work alongside clubs and individuals to tailor episodes of treatment to complement their physical objectives. All treatment episodes include support and access to aftercare on players' return to their daily lives. This service is designed for individuals with addictive disorders. They may express this

267

through their use of alcohol, drugs (be it illegal or prescribed) or gambling.

One-to-One Therapy and Counselling: Sporting Chance has created a network of therapists and counsellors across England, a service which has evolved out of the need of some individuals who have presented to the charity with issues other than an addictive disorder. We have worked with individuals with specific presentations such as depression or bereavement or at times of career change through injury or retirement. This service can be used by individuals with substance misuse issues including alcohol and gambling, and has been used when there has been good reason why residential treatment is not possible.

The Charity is predominantly supported by the Professional Footballers' Association (PFA) and works closely with them to ensure support for current and retired players.

Sporting Chance Clinic can be contacted either by:

e-mail at: info@sportingchanceclinic.com; or,

by telephone on: 0870 220 0714.

The Professional Footballers' Association (PFA)

PFA members - some four thousand current and fifty thousand former - are not only famous footballers in a celebrity spotlight but are also human beings and as such are subject to the same frailties and problems as everyone else.

The PFA has, since its formation in 1907, provided its members both current and former with support in a wide range of services through its three main funds - the Education Fund, Benevolent Fund and Accident Fund.

The Education Fund provides education and re-training programmes for players to enable them to make the transition from full-time professional football.

The Benevolent Fund is a hardship fund which provides assistance to former members experiencing financial difficulties and has provided loans to clubs in financial difficulties in order to ensure their survival and that members' wages are paid on time.

The Accident Fund provides assistance to former members who are suffering from injuries as a consequence of their playing careers and also for members who require rehabilitation. The PFA rehabilitation provision has been in place for almost twenty years, initially through Lilleshall National Centre and more recently at the National Football Centre, St. George's Park.

In the nineties the PFA became aware of more of its members experiencing problems with regards to emotional wellbeing and addictive issues and one such high profile member, Tony Adams, approached the Union in 2000 to discuss the Sporting Chance charity he had established. This charity would provide a more sports-related rehabilitation programme looking after not only addictive and emotional issues but also physical wellbeing to enable current members to maintain a high level of fitness and former members to go back into an environment which was familiar to them to aid them with their recovery. The PFA has been the major sponsor of the charity since 2001 and has had a close working relationship with Peter Kay, the then Chief Executive, himself a recovering addict who recently passed away, who was instrumental in developing the Sporting Chance Clinic to provide assessment, rehabilitation and also educational seminars to scholars and also senior players. PFA funding and support enabled Peter Kay and Sporting Chance to have a positive impact on the lives of hundreds of PFA members and their families to enable them to get their lives back on track and provides much needed support to members at all levels of the professional game.

The support of PFA members facing emotional issues has continued to develop and Michael Bennett, a former player with Charlton Athletic and Brighton and a qualified counsellor, has joined the PFA as Head of Player Welfare and has been instrumental in the establishment of a nationwide network of counsellors, many of whom are former players, to provide support to current and former members.

Gordon Taylor OBE
Chief Executive
PFA
20 Oxford Court
Bishopsgate
Manchester
M2 3WQ

0161 236 0575

Twenty four hour support line: 07500 000 777

www.thepfa.com